Mountain Bike AMERICA™

GREATER PHILADELPHIA

D1414534

Contact

Dear Readers:

Every effort was made to make this the most accurate, informative, and easy-to-use guide-book on the planet. Any comments, suggestions, and/or corrections regarding this guide are welcome and should be sent to:

Outside America™
c/o Editorial Dept.
300 West Main St., Ste. A
Charlottesville, VA 22903
editorial@outside-america.com
www.outside-america.com

We'd love to hear from you so we can make future editions and future guides even better.

Thanks and happy trails!

Mountain Bike AMERICA™

GREATER PHILADELPHIA

An Atlas of the Delaware Valley's
Greatest Off-Road Bicycle Rides

by Bob D'Antonio

The Globe Pequot Press

Guilford, Connecticut

Published by
The Globe Pequot Press
P.O. Box 480
Guilford, CT 06437
www.globe-pequot.com

Produced by
Beachway Press Publishing, Inc.
300 West Main St., Ste A
Charlottesville, VA 22903
www.beachway.com

Production Assistance given by Katie Salsbury

Rides 43 and 44 were researched and written by John Boyle. **Photographs:** John Boyle

Cover Design   Beachway Press

Photographer   Bob D'Antonio

Maps designed and produced by Beachway Press

Find Outside America™ at **www.outside-america.com**

Cover Photo: An autumn ride through French Creek

Library of Congress Cataloging-in-Publication Data is available.

ISBN 0-7627-0698-8

Manufactured in the United States of America
First Edition/First Printing

Acknowledgments

A book of this scope would not be possible without the encouragement and help of many people. First, I would like to thank my best friend and wife of 25 years, Laurel. Without her support and understanding of my love for the outdoors none of my books would have come to fruition. I would like to thank my son Jeremy and daughter Rachael for their support on this book. To my son Adam, thanks for the miles we've shared on the trails and the special time we've spent working together on this project. I will always cherish the wonderful experiences that we shared together, riding.

To all the wonderful folks at the bike shops who I hounded for information, thank you. Bill at Mount Gretna Bike Tours, your information on the trails in the Lebanon area was invaluable. Tom at Blue Mountain Sports in Jim Thorpe, your knowledge of the trails in the Jim Thorpe area made this a better book.

I should take a moment and encourage you to support your local bike shops. They are at the heart of mountain biking and are trying hard to protect the sport we love so much. Almost every shop that I visited, supported the idea of a quality mountain bike guide to the Philadelphia area, I hope I came through for all of you.

I would like to thank Scott at Beachway Press for being there and seeing this project through. Without the support of you and your staff this book would never turn out to be a book we all can be proud of. I would also like to thank Ryan at Beachway Press for your constant attention to details. Without your editing skills a lot of information would have fallen through the cracks.

I would like to thank all the public agencies that allow us to pursue the sport we call mountain biking. The Fairmount Park Commission, the Pennsylvania Game Commission, Pennsylvania State Parks, and New Jersey State Parks. I know it's not easy trying to please all the people who use public lands for recreation, but you're doing a fantastic job as caretakers of these wonderful lands.

Bob D'Antonio

Table Of

Contents

Southern Philadelphia Area

Western Philadelphia

Jim Thorpe

Northern Philadelphia

Appendix

Index

Meet the Author

Preface

TRAIL OBSTACLES:

Rocks, Roots, Trees and...Politics?

Mountain Bike America: Greater Philadelphia will help you find new trails. Other books on bicycling (and a lot of trial and error) will help you to develop the skills to ride those new trails. Still other books will show you how to fix your bike when you get a flat tire on those trails. But what do you do when your favorite trails get closed to bikes? Well, there's no book to remedy that, really. It all depends on you.

Well, not quite. You see—it depended on you. When trails close and bikes are banned, chances are the "problem" had already existed for a while. Maybe a few cyclists had been rolling carelessly past hikers on the trail, frightening them. Or maybe a few cyclists had been riding muddy trails, damaging them. Or maybe the "problem" was that a vocal opponent of mountain bikes had been bending the park management's ear for the past year, worrying them. And finally, because management hadn't heard from bikers, management just gave in.

You see, if some people have their way, mountain bikes will be restricted to pavement, private property, rail trails, and ski resorts in the off-season. Such people often get their understanding of our pastime from sensational television ads or magazine depictions of fearless teenagers engaged in death-defying feats. Sometimes, though, these people form their opinions based on a dangerous experience or a negative encounter on a trail. Fear motivates people. Scare someone today, even by accident, and your trail gets closed tomorrow.

Keeping Trails Open

Trail etiquette is a big part of the answer—the preventive solution. Just ask the International Mountain Bicycling Association (IMBA). Sure, the official IMBA "Rules of the Trail" are important. But simple courtesy, basic caution, and a little empathy for other trail users are the real requirements. In the long haul, they are more important than your bike gear, than your bike clothes—more important even than your bike. After all, a mountain bike isn't very useful if there isn't any place to ride it.

The second simple step to keep trails open is to join together with other cyclists. Join your local mountain bike club or association so your head gets counted and your voice gets heard. Besides, it's often a great way to meet other riders and learn about trails before they're published in a book or a magazine. A year's membership rarely costs more than twenty dollars, the cost of a bike tire. You'll find it's well worth it.

MORE

In Pennsylvania, Maryland, Virginia, and Washington, DC, one of the principal mountain bike groups is MORE—the Mid-Atlantic Off-Road Enthusiasts. Around since 1992, MORE is known for keeping trails open. For leading great rides. For building new trails and maintaining old ones. For raising money for parks. For educating riders. And, well—for giving mountain bikers a good name. Find out more about MORE by calling (703) 502-0359 or see their web page at www.more-mtb.org. Or write them at MORE, PO Box 2662, Fairfax, VA 22031.

Better than Lincoln Logs

And if you think breaking a sweat in the woods on your bike is fun, then working on trails might be more fun than you think. Who needs Erector Sets, Lincoln Logs or Legos, when you can build or maintain a real trail? Constructing a new treadway—or fixing an old one—will leave you with a sense of satisfaction that you can't buy in a bike shop. Skeptical? Call MORE and try it once. It's that simple. And it's fun.

IMBA

Speaking of simple, how much did your bike cost? And your helmet? And the bike rack for the car? Add it up, and think about it. Then consider writing out a check for the relatively paltry sum of twenty dollars to the International Mountain Bicycling Association (IMBA). IMBA is the national voice for mountain bikers, and twenty dollars gets you membership for a year—and helps support their effort to keep trails and land open to mountain bikers across the nation.

20-20-20

Twenty dollars to your local mountain bike group, twenty dollars to IMBA, and twenty hours a year as a trail volunteer. That's the recipe for access. That's the formula for keeping trails open and healthy. That's the ticket for preserving your fun. You've got the book and the bike. Time to do the rest.

This fine guide not only reveals some of the best shared-use trails around, but makes clear one crucial fact: cyclists' continued access to trails depends upon their courtesy toward hikers and equestrians and their willingness to help maintain those trails. The information in this book, and that message, is the key to some great riding!

Andy Carruthers

Andy Carruthers is one of the region's core mountain bike advocates, working diligently and successfully to keep local trails accessible to cyclists. Many thanks should go to him and all the volunteers who work to keep our trails open and healthy.

A note from the folks behind this endeavor...

We at Outside America look at guidebook publishing a little differently. There's just no reason that a guidebook has to look like it was published out of your Uncle Ernie's woodshed. We feel that guidebooks need to be both easy to use and nice to look at, and that takes an innovative approach to design. You see, we want you to spend less time fumbling through your guidebook and more time enjoying the adventure at hand. At any rate, we hope you like what you see and enjoy the places we lead you. And most of all, we'd like to thank you for taking an adventure with us.

Happy Trails!

Welcome to the new generation of bicycling! Indeed, the sport has evolved dramatically from the thin-tired, featherweight-frame days of old. The sleek geometry and lightweight frames of racing bicycles, still the heart and soul of bicycling worldwide, have lost much ground in recent years, unpaving the way for the mountain bike, which now accounts for the majority of all bicycle sales in the U.S. And with this change comes a new breed of cyclist, less concerned with smooth roads and long rides, who thrives in places once inaccessible to the mortal road bike.

The mountain bike, with its knobby tread and reinforced frame, takes cyclists to places once unheard of—down rugged mountain trails, through streams of rushing water and thick mud, across the frozen Alaskan tundra, and even to work in the city. There seem to be few limits on what this fat-tired beast can do and where it can take us. Few obstacles stand in its way, few boundaries slow its progress. Except for one— its own success. If trail closure means little to you now, read on and discover how a trail can be here today and gone tomorrow. With so many new off-road cyclists taking to the trails each year, it's no wonder trail access hinges precariously between universal acceptance and complete termination. But a little work on your part can go a long way to preserving trail access for future use. Nothing is more crucial to the survival of mountain biking itself than to read the examples set forth in the following pages and practice their message. Then turn to the maps, pick out your favorite ride, and hit the dirt!

WHAT THIS BOOK IS ABOUT

Within these pages you will find everything you need to know about off-road bicycling in the Greater Philadelphia area. This guidebook begins by exploring the fascinating history of the mountain bike itself, then goes on to discuss everything from the health benefits of off-road cycling to tips and techniques for bicycling over logs and up hills. Also included are the types of clothing to keep you comfortable and in style, essential equipment ideas to keep your rides smooth and trouble-free, and descriptions of off-road terrain to prepare you for the kinds of bumps and bounces you can expect to encounter. The major provisions of this book, though, are its unique perspectives on each ride, it detailed maps, and its relentless dedication to trail preservation.

Without open trails, the maps in this book are virtually useless. Cyclists must learn to be responsible for the trails they use and to share these trails with others. This guidebook addresses such issues as why trail use has become so controversial, what can be done to improve the image of mountain biking, how to have fun and ride responsibly, on-the-spot trail repair techniques, trail maintenance hotlines for each trail, and the worldwide-standard Rules of the Trail.

Each of the 44 rides is complete with maps, photos, trail descriptions and directions, local history, and a quick-reference ride information guide including such items as trail-maintenance hotlines, park schedules, costs, local bike stores, dining, lodging, entertainment, and alternative maps.

It's important to note that mountain bike rides tend to take longer than road rides because the average speed is often much slower. Average speeds can vary from a climbing pace of three to four miles per hour to 12 to 13 miles per hour on flatter roads and trails. Keep this in mind when planning your trip.

MOUNTAIN BIKE BEGINNINGS

It seems the mountain bike, originally designed for lunatic adventurists bored with straight lines, clean clothes, and smooth tires, has become globally popular in as short a time as it would take to race down a mountain trail.

Like many things of a revolutionary nature, the mountain bike was born on the west coast. But unlike Rollerblades, purple hair, and the peace sign, the concept of the off-road bike cannot be credited solely to the imaginative Californians—they were just the first to make waves.

The design of the first off-road specific bike was based on the geometry of the old Schwinn Excelsior, a one-speed, camel-back cruiser with balloon tires. Joe Breeze was the creator behind it, and in 1977 he built 10 of these "Breezers" for himself and his Marin County, California, friends at $750 apiece—a bargain.

Breeze was a serious competitor in bicycle racing, placing 13th in the 1977 U.S. Road Racing National Championships. After races, he and friends would scour local bike shops hoping to find old bikes they could then restore.

It was the 1941 Schwinn Excelsior, for which Breeze paid just five dollars, that began to shape and change bicycling history forever. After taking the bike home, removing the fenders, oiling the chain, and pumping up the tires, Breeze hit the dirt. He loved it.

His inspiration, while forerunning, was not altogether unique. On the opposite end of the country, nearly 2,500 miles from Marin County, east coast bike bums were also growing restless. More and more old, beat-up clunkers were being restored and modified. These behemoths often weighed as much as 80 pounds and were so reinforced they seemed virtually indestructible. But rides that take just 40 minutes on today's 25-pound featherweights took the steel-toed-boot- and-blue-jean-clad bikers of the late 1970s and early 1980s nearly four hours to complete.

Not until 1981 was it possible to purchase a production mountain bike, but local retailers found these ungainly bicycles difficult to sell and rarely kept them in stock. By 1983, however, mountain bikes were no longer such a fringe item, and large bike manufacturers quickly jumped into the action, producing their own versions of the off-road bike. By the 1990s, the mountain bike had firmly established its place with bicyclists of nearly all ages and abilities, and now command nearly 90 percent of the U.S. bike market.

There are many reasons for the mountain bike's success in becoming the hottest two-wheeled vehicle in the nation. They are much friendlier to the cyclist than traditional road bikes because of their comfortable upright position and shock-absorbing fat tires. And because of the health-conscious, environmentalist movement of the late 1980s and 1990s, people are more activity minded and seek nature on a closer front than paved roads can allow. The mountain bike gives you these things and takes you far away from the daily grind—even if you're only minutes from the city.

MOUNTAIN BIKING INTO SHAPE

If your objective is to get in shape and lose weight, then you're on the right track, because mountain biking is one of the best ways to get started.

One way many of us have lost weight in this sport is the crash-and-burn-it-off method. Picture this: you're speeding uncontrollably down a vertical drop that you realize you shouldn't be on—only after it is too late. Your front wheel lodges into a rut and launches you through endless weeds, trees, and pointy rocks before coming to an abrupt halt in a puddle of thick mud. Surveying the damage, you discover, with the layers of skin, body parts, and lost confidence littering the trail above, that those unwanted pounds have been shed-permanently. Instant weight loss.

There is, of course, a more conventional (and quite a bit less painful) approach to losing weight and gaining fitness on a mountain bike. It's called the workout, and bicycles provide an ideal way to get physical. Take a look at some of the benefits associated with cycling.

Cycling helps you shed pounds without gimmicky diet fads or weight-loss programs. You can explore the countryside and burn nearly 10 to 16 calories per minute or close to 600 to 1,000 calories per hour. Moreover, it's a great way to spend an afternoon.

No less significant than the external and cosmetic changes of your body from riding are the internal changes taking place. Over time, cycling regularly will strengthen your heart as your body grows vast networks of new capillaries to carry blood to all those working muscles. This will, in turn, give your skin a healthier glow. The capacity of your lungs may increase up to 20 percent, and your resting heart rate will drop significantly. The Stanford University School of Medicine reports to the American Heart Association that people can reduce their risk of heart attack by nearly 64 percent if they can burn up to 2,000 calories per week. This is only two to three hours of bike riding!

Recommended for insomnia, hypertension, indigestion, anxiety, and even for recuperation from major heart attacks, bicycling can be an excellent cure-all as well as a great preventive. Cycling just a few hours per week can improve your figure and sleeping habits, give you greater resistance to illness, increase your energy levels, and provide feelings of accomplishment and heightened self-esteem.

BE SAFE—KNOW THE LAW

Occasionally, even the hard-core off-road cyclists will find they have no choice but to ride the pavement. When you are forced to hit the road, it's important for you to know and understand the rules.

Outlined below are a few of the common laws found in Philadelphia's Vehicle Code book.

- *Bicycles are legally classified as vehicles in the Greater Philadelphia area.* This means that as a bicyclist, you are responsible for obeying the same rules of the road as a driver of a motor vehicle.
- *Bicyclists must ride with the traffic—NOT AGAINST IT!* Because bicycles are considered vehicles, you must ride your bicycle just as you would drive a car—with traffic. Only pedestrians should travel against the flow of traffic.

- *You must obey all traffic signs.* This includes stop signs and stoplights.
- *Always signal your turns.* Most drivers aren't expecting bicyclists to be on the roads, and many drivers would prefer that cyclists stay off the roads altogether. It's important, therefore, to clearly signal your intentions to motorists both in front and behind you.
- *Bicyclists are entitled to the same roads as cars (except controlled-access highways).* Unfortunately, cyclists are rarely given this consideration.
- *Be a responsible cyclist.* Do not abuse your rights to ride on open roads. Follow the rules and set a good example for all of us as you roll along.

THE MOUNTAIN BIKE CONTROVERSY

Are Off-Road Bicyclists Environmental Outlaws?
Do We have the Right to Use Public Trails?

Mountain bikers have long endured the animosity of folks in the backcountry who complain about the consequences of off-road bicycling. Many people believe that the fat tires and knobby tread do unacceptable environmental damage and that our uncontrollable riding habits are a danger to animals and to other trail users. To the contrary, mountain bikes have no more environmental impact than hiking boots or horseshoes. This does not mean, however, that mountain bikes leave no imprint at all. Wherever man treads, there is an impact. By riding responsibly, though, it is possible to leave only a minimum impact—something we all must take care to achieve.

Unfortunately, it is often people of great influence who view the mountain bike as the environment's worst enemy. Consequently, we as mountain bike riders and environmentally concerned citizens must be educators, impressing upon others that we also deserve the right to use these trails. Our responsibilities as bicyclists are no more and no less than any other trail user. We must all take the soft-cycling approach and show that mountain bicyclists are not environmental outlaws.

ETIQUETTE OF MOUNTAIN BIKING

When discussing mountain biking etiquette, we are in essence discussing the soft-cycling approach. This term, as mentioned previously, describes the art of minimum-impact bicycling and should apply to both the physical and social dimensions of the sport. But make no mistake—it is possible to ride fast and furiously while maintaining the balance of soft-cycling. Here first are a few ways to minimize the physical impact of mountain bike riding.

- *Stay on the trail.* Don't ride around fallen trees or mud holes that block your path. Stop and cross over them. When you come to a vista overlooking a deep valley, don't ride off the trail for a better vantage point. Instead, leave the bike and walk to see the view. Riding off the trail may seem inconsequential when done only once, but soon someone else will follow, then others, and the cumulative results can be catastrophic. Each time you wander from the trail you begin creating a new path, adding one more scar to the earth's surface.

- *Do not disturb the soil.* Follow a line within the trail that will not disturb or damage the soil.
- *Do not ride over soft or wet trails.* After a rain shower or during the thawing season, trails will often resemble muddy, oozing swampland. The best thing to do is stay off the trails altogether. Realistically, however, we're all going to come across some muddy trails we cannot anticipate. Instead of blasting through each section of mud, which may seem both easier and more fun, lift the bike and walk past. Each time a cyclist rides through a soft or muddy section of trail, that part of the trail is permanently damaged. Regardless of the trail's conditions, though, remember always to go over the obstacles across the path, not around them. Stay on the trail.
- *Avoid trails that, for all but God, are considered impassable and impossible.* Don't take a leap of faith down a kamikaze descent on which you will be forced to lock your brakes and skid to the bottom, ripping the ground apart as you go.

Soft-cycling should apply to the social dimensions of the sport as well, since mountain bikers are not the only folks who use the trails. Hikers, equestrians, cross-country skiers, and other outdoors people use many of the same trails and can be easily spooked by a marauding mountain biker tearing through the trees. Be friendly in the forest and give ample warning of your approach.

- *Take out what you bring in.* Don't leave broken bike pieces and banana peels scattered along the trail.
- *Be aware of your surroundings.* Don't use popular hiking trails for race training.
- *Slow down!* Rocketing around blind corners is a sure way to ruin an unsuspecting hiker's day. Consider this—If you fly down a quick singletrack descent at 20 mph, then hit the brakes and slow down to only six mph to pass someone, you're still moving twice as fast as they are!

Like the trails we ride on, the social dimension of mountain biking is very fragile and must be cared for responsibly. We should not want to destroy another person's enjoyment of the outdoors. By riding in the backcountry with caution, control, and responsibility, our presence should be felt positively by other trail users. By adhering to these rules, trail riding—a privilege that can quickly be taken away—will continue to be ours to share.

TRAIL MAINTENANCE

Unfortunately, despite all of the preventive measures taken to avoid trail damage, we're still going to run into many trails requiring attention. Simply put, a lot of hikers, equestrians, and cyclists alike use the same trails—some wear and tear is unavoidable. But like your bike, if you want to use these trails for a long time to come, you must also maintain them.

Trail maintenance and restoration can be accomplished in a variety of ways. One way is for mountain bike clubs to combine efforts with other trail users (i.e. hikers and equestrians) and work closely with land managers to cut new trails or repair existing ones. This not only reinforces to others the commitment cyclists have in caring for and maintaining the land, but also breaks the ice that often separates cyclists from their fellow trailmates. Another good way to help out is to show up on a Saturday morning with a few riding buddies at your favorite off-road domain ready to work. With a good attitude, thick gloves, and the local land manager's supervision, trail repair is fun and very rewarding. It's important, of course, that you arrange a trail-repair outing with the local land manager before you start pounding shovels into the dirt. They can lead you to the most needy sections of trail and instruct you on what repairs should be done and how best to accomplish the task. Perhaps the most effective means of trail maintenance, though, can be done by yourself and while you're riding. Read on.

ON–THE–SPOT QUICK FIX

Most of us, when we're riding, have at one time or another come upon muddy trails or fallen trees blocking our path. We notice that over time the mud gets deeper and the trail gets wider as people go through or around the obstacles. We worry that the problem will become so severe and repairs too difficult that the trail's access may be threatened. We also know that our ambition to do anything about it is greatest at that moment, not after a hot shower and a plate of spaghetti. Here are a few on-the-spot quick fixes you can do that will hopefully correct a problem before it gets out of hand and get you back on your bike within minutes.

• **MUDDY TRAILS.** What do you do when trails develop huge mud holes destined for the EPA's Superfund status? The technique is called corduroying, and it works much like building a pontoon over the mud to support bikes, horses, or hikers as they cross. Corduroy (not the pants) is the term for roads made of logs laid down crosswise. Use small-and medium-sized sticks and lay them side by side across the trail until they cover the length of the muddy section (break the sticks to fit the width of the trail). Press them into the mud with your feet, then lay more on top if needed. Keep adding sticks until the trail is firm. Not only will you stay clean as you cross, but the sticks may soak up some of the water and help the puddle dry. This quick fix may last as long as one month before needing to be redone. And as time goes on, with new layers added to the trail, the soil will grow stronger, thicker, and more resistant to erosion. This whole process may take fewer than five minutes, and you can be on your way, knowing the trail behind you is in good repair.

• **LEAVING THE TRAIL.** What do you do to keep cyclists from cutting corners and leaving the designated trail? The solution is much simpler than you may think. (No, don't hire an off-road police force.) Notice where people are leaving the trail and throw a pile of thick branches or brush along the path, or place logs across the opening to block the way through. There are probably dozens of subtle tricks like these that will manipulate people into staying on the designated trail. If executed well, no one will even notice that the thick branches scattered along the ground in the woods weren't always there. And most folks would probably rather take a moment to hop a log in the trail than get tangled in a web of branches.

- **OBSTACLES IN THE WAY.** If there are large obstacles blocking the trail, try
  and remove them or push them aside. If you cannot do this by yourself, call the
  trail maintenance hotline to speak with the land manager of that particular trail
  and see what can be done.

We must be willing to *sweat for* our trails in order to *sweat on* them. Police yourself and point out to others the significance of trail maintenance. "Sweat Equity," the
rewards of continued land use won with a fair share of sweat, pays off when the trail
is "up for review" by the land manager and he or she remembers the efforts made by
trail-conscious mountain bikers.

RULES OF THE TRAIL

The International Mountain Bicycling Association (IMBA) has developed these
guidelines to trail riding. These "Rules of the Trail" are accepted worldwide and
will go a long way in keeping trails open. Please respect and follow these rules
for everyone's sake.

1. *Ride only on open trails.* Respect trail and road closures (if you're
   not sure, ask a park or state official first), do not trespass on private property, and obtain permits or authorization if required.
   Federal and state wilderness areas are off-limits to cycling. Parks
   and state forests may also have certain trails closed to cycling.
2. *Leave no trace.* Be sensitive to the dirt beneath you. Even on
   open trails, you should not ride under conditions by which you
   will leave evidence of your passing, such as on certain soils or
   shortly after a rainfall. Be sure to observe the different types of
   soils and trails you're riding on, practicing minimum-impact
   cycling. Never ride off the trail, don't skid your tires, and be sure
   to bring out at least as much as you bring in.
3. *Control your bicycle!* Inattention for even one second can cause disaster for yourself or for others. Excessive speed frightens and can injure
   people, gives mountain biking a bad name, and can result in trail closures.
4. *Always yield.* Let others know you're coming well in advance (a friendly
   greeting is always good and often appreciated). Show your respect when passing
   others by slowing to walking speed or stopping altogether, especially in the presence of horses. Horses can be unpredictable, so be very careful. Anticipate that
   other trail users may be around corners or in blind spots.
5. *Never spook animals.* All animals are spooked by sudden movements, unan-
   nounced approaches, or loud noises. Give the animals extra room and time so
   they can adjust to you. Move slowly or dismount around animals. Running cattle
   and disturbing wild animals are serious offenses. Leave gates as you find them, or
   as marked.
6. *Plan ahead.* Know your equipment, your ability, and the area in which you are
   riding, and plan your trip accordingly. Be self-sufficient at all times, keep your bike
   in good repair, and carry necessary supplies for changes in weather or other conditions. You can help keep trails open by setting an example of responsible, courteous, and controlled mountain bike riding.

7. *Always wear a helmet when you ride.* For your own safety and protection, a helmet should be worn whenever you are riding your bike. You never know when a tree root or small rock will throw you the wrong way and send you tumbling.

Thousands of miles of dirt trails have been closed to mountain bicycling because of the irresponsible riding habits of just a few riders. Don't follow the example of these offending riders. Don't take away trail privileges from thousands of others who work hard each year to keep the backcountry avenues open to us all.

THE NECESSITIES OF CYCLING

When discussing the most important items to have on a bike ride, cyclists generally agree on the following four items.

- **HELMET.** The reasons to wear a helmet should be obvious. Helmets are discussed in more detail in the Be Safe—Wear Your Armor section.
  - **WATER.** Without it, cyclists may face dehydration, which may result in dizziness and fatigue. On a warm day, cyclists should drink at least one full bottle during every hour of riding. Remember, it's always good to drink before you feel thirsty—otherwise, it may be too late.
    - **CYCLING SHORTS.** These are necessary if you plan to ride your bike more than 20 to 30 minutes. Padded cycling shorts may be the only thing preventing your derriere from serious saddle soreness by ride's end. There are two types of cycling shorts you can buy. Touring shorts are good for people who don't want to look like they're wearing anatomically correct cellophane. These look like regular athletic shorts with pockets, but have built-in padding in the crotch area for protection from chafing and saddle sores. The more popular, traditional cycling shorts are made of skin-tight material, also with a padded crotch. Whichever style you find most comfortable, cycling shorts are a necessity for long rides.
    - **FOOD.** This essential item will keep you rolling. Cycling burns up a lot of calories and is among the few sports in which no one is safe from the "Bonk." Bonking feels like it sounds. Without food in your system, your blood sugar level collapses, and there is no longer any energy in your body. This instantly results in total fatigue and light-headedness. So when you're filling your water bottle, remember to bring along some food. Fruit, energy bars, or some other forms of high-energy food are highly recommended. Candy bars are not, however, because they will deliver a sudden burst of high energy, then let you down soon after, causing you to feel worse than before. Energy bars are available at most bike stores and are similar to candy bars, but provide complex carbohydrate energy and high nutrition rather than fast-burning simple sugars.

BE PREPARED OR DIE

Essential equipment that will keep you from dying alone in the woods:

- SPARE TUBE
- TIRE IRONS—See the Appendix for instructions on fixing flat tires.
- PATCH KIT
- PUMP

- MONEY—Spare change for emergency calls.
- SPOKE WRENCH
- SPARE SPOKES—To fit your wheel. Tape these to the chain stay.
- CHAIN TOOL
- ALLEN KEYS—Bring appropriate sizes to fit your bike.
- COMPASS
- FIRST-AID KIT
- MATCHES
- GUIDEBOOK—In case all else fails and you must start a fire to survive, this guidebook will serve as excellent fire starter!

To carry these items, you may need a bike bag. A bag mounted in front of the handlebars provides quick access to your belongings, whereas a saddle bag fitted underneath the saddle keeps things out of your way. If you're carrying lots of equipment, you may want to consider a set of panniers. These are much larger and mount on either side of each wheel on a rack. Many cyclists, though, prefer not to use a bag at all. They just slip all they need into their jersey pockets, and off they go.

BE SAFE—WEAR YOUR ARMOR

While on the subject of jerseys, it's crucial to discuss the clothing you must wear to be safe, practical, and—if you prefer—stylish. The following is a list of items that will save you from disaster, outfit you comfortably, and most important, keep you looking cool.

- **HELMET.** A helmet is an absolute necessity because it protects your head from complete annihilation. It is the only thing that will not disintegrate into a million pieces after a wicked crash on a descent you shouldn't have been on in the first place. A helmet with a solid exterior shell will also protect your head from sharp or protruding objects. Of course, with a hard-shelled helmet, you can paste several stickers of your favorite bicycle manufacturers all over the outer shell, giving companies even more free advertising for your dollar.
- **SHORTS.** Let's just say Lycra cycling shorts are considered a major safety item if you plan to ride for more than 20 or 30 minutes at a time. As mentioned in The Necessities of Cycling section, cycling shorts are well regarded as the leading cureall for chafing and saddle sores. The most preventive cycling shorts have padded "chamois" (most chamois is synthetic nowadays) in the crotch area. Of course, if you choose to wear these traditional cycling shorts, it's imperative that they look as if someone spray painted them onto your body.
- **GLOVES.** You may find well-padded cycling gloves invaluable when traveling over rocky trails and gravelly roads for hours on end. Long-fingered gloves may also be useful, as branches, trees, assorted hard objects, and, occasionally, small animals will reach out and whack your knuckles.
- **GLASSES.** Not only do sunglasses give you an imposing presence and make you look cool (both are extremely important), they also protect your eyes from harm-

ful ultraviolet rays, invisible branches, creepy bugs, dirt, and may prevent you from being caught sneaking glances at riders of the opposite sex also wearing skintight, revealing Lycra.

- **SHOES.** Mountain bike shoes should have stiff soles to help make pedaling easier and provide better traction when walking your bike up a trail becomes necessary. Virtually any kind of good outdoor hiking footwear will work, but specific mountain bike shoes (especially those with inset cleats) are best. It is vital that these shoes look as ugly as humanly possible. Those closest in style to bowling shoes are, of course, the most popular.
- **JERSEY or SHIRT.** Bicycling jerseys are popular because of their snug fit and back pockets. When purchasing a jersey, look for ones that are loaded with bright, blinding, neon logos and manufacturers' names. These loudly decorated billboards are also good for drawing unnecessary attention to yourself just before taking a mean spill while trying to hop a curb. A cotton T-shirt is a good alternative in warm weather, but when the weather turns cold, cotton becomes a chilling substitute for the jersey. Cotton retains moisture and sweat against your body, which may cause you to get the chills and ills on those cold-weather rides.

OH, THOSE COLD PHILADELPHIA DAYS

If the weather chooses not to cooperate on the day you've set aside for a bike ride, it's helpful to be prepared.

- *Tights or leg warmers.* These are best in temperatures below 55 degrees. Knees are sensitive and can develop all kinds of problems if they get cold. Common problems include tendinitis, bursitis, and arthritis.
- *Plenty of layers on your upper body.* When the air has a nip in it, layers of clothing will keep the chill away from your chest and help prevent the development of bronchitis. If the air is cool, a polypropylene long-sleeved shirt is best to wear against the skin beneath other layers of clothing. Polypropylene, like wool, wicks away moisture from your skin to keep your body dry. Try to avoid wearing cotton or baggy clothing when the temperature falls. Cotton, as mentioned before, holds moisture like a sponge, and baggy clothing catches cold air and swirls it around your body. Good cold-weather clothing should fit snugly against your body, but not be restrictive.
- *Wool socks.* Don't pack too many layers under those shoes, though. You may stand the chance of restricting circulation, and your feet will get real cold, real fast.
- *Thinsulate or Gortex gloves.* We may all agree that there is nothing worse than frozen feet—unless your hands are frozen. A good pair of Thinsulate or Gortex gloves should keep your hands toasty and warm.
- *Hat or helmet on cold days?* Sometimes, when the weather gets really cold and you still want to hit the trails, it's tough to stay warm. We all know that 130 percent of the body's heat escapes through the head (overactive brains, I imagine), so it's important to keep the cranium warm. Ventilated helmets are designed to keep heads cool in the summer heat, but they do little to help keep heads warm during rides in sub-zero temperatures. Cyclists should consider wearing a hat on

extremely cold days. Polypropylene skullcaps are great head and ear warmers that snugly fit over your head beneath the helmet. Head protection is not lost. Another option is a helmet cover that covers those ventilating gaps and helps keep the body heat in. These do not, however, keep your ears warm. Some cyclists will opt for a simple knit cycling cap sans the helmet, but these have never been shown to be very good cranium protectors.

All of this clothing can be found at your local bike store, where the staff should be happy to help fit you into the seasons of the year.

TO HAVE OR NOT TO HAVE...

(Other Very Useful Items)

Though mountain biking is relatively new to the cycling scene, there is no shortage of items for you and your bike to make riding better, safer, and easier. We have rummaged through the unending lists and separated the gadgets from the good stuff, coming up with what we believe are items certain to make mountain bike riding easier and more enjoyable.

- **TIRES.** Buying yourself a good pair of knobby tires is the quickest way to enhance the off-road handling capabilities of your bike. There are many types of mountain bike tires on the market. Some are made exclusively for very rugged off-road terrain. These big-knobbed, soft rubber tires virtually stick to the ground with unforgiving traction, but tend to deteriorate quickly on pavement. There are other tires made exclusively for the road. These are called "slicks" and have no tread at all. For the average cyclist, though, a good tire somewhere in the middle of these two extremes should do the trick.
- **TOE CLIPS or CLIPLESS PEDALS.** With these, you will ride with more power. Toe clips attach to your pedals and strap your feet firmly in place, allowing you to exert pressure on the pedals on both the downstroke and the upstroke. They will increase your pedaling efficiency by 30 percent to 50 percent. Clipless pedals, which liberate your feet from the traditional straps and clips, have made toe clips virtually obsolete. Like ski bindings, they attach your shoe directly to the pedal. They are, however, much more expensive than toe clips.
- **BAR ENDS.** These great clamp-on additions to your original straight bar will provide more leverage, an excellent grip for climbing, and a more natural position for your hands. Be aware, however, of the bar end's propensity for hooking trees on fast descents, sending you, the cyclist, airborne.
- **FANNY PACK.** These bags are ideal for carrying keys, extra food, guidebooks, tools, spare tubes, and a cellular phone, in case you need to call for help.
- **SUSPENSION FORKS.** For the more serious off-roaders who want nothing to impede their speed on the trails, investing in a pair of suspension forks is a good idea. Like tires, there are plenty of brands to choose from, and they all do the same thing—absorb the brutal beatings of a rough trail. The cost of these forks, however, is sometimes more brutal than the trail itself.

- **BIKE COMPUTERS.** These are fun gadgets to own and are much less expensive than in years past. They have such features as trip distance, speedometer, odometer, time of day, altitude, alarm, average speed, maximum speed, heart rate, global satellite positioning, etc. Bike computers will come in handy when following these maps or to know just how far you've ridden in the wrong direction.

TYPES OF OFF-ROAD TERRAIN

Before roughing it off road, we may first have to ride the pavement to get to our destination. Please, don't be dismayed. Some of the country's best rides are on the road. Once we get past these smooth-surfaced pathways, though, adventures in dirt await us.

- **RAILS-TO-TRAILS.** Abandoned rail lines are converted into usable public resources for exercising, commuting, or just enjoying nature. Old rails and ties are torn up and a trail, paved or unpaved, is laid along the existing corridor. This completes the cycle from ancient Indian trading routes to railroad corridors and back again to hiking and cycling trails.
  - **UNPAVED ROADS.** These are typically found in rural areas and are most often public roads. Be careful when exploring, though, not to ride on someone's unpaved private drive.
  - **FOREST ROADS.** These dirt and gravel roads are used primarily as access to forest land and are kept in good condition. They are almost always open to public use.
  - **SINGLETRACK.** Singletrack can be the most fun on a mountain bike. These trails, with only one track to follow, are often narrow, challenging pathways through the woods. Remember to make sure these trails are open before zipping into the woods. (At the time of this printing, all trails and roads in this guidebook were open to mountain bikes.)
  - **OPEN LAND.** Unless there is a marked trail through a field or open space, you should not plan to ride here. Once one person cuts his or her wheels through a field or meadow, many more are sure to follow, causing irreparable damage to the landscape.

TECHNIQUES TO SHARPEN YOUR SKILLS

Many of us see ourselves as pure athletes—blessed with power, strength, and endless endurance. However, it may be those with finesse, balance, agility, and grace that get around most quickly on a mountain bike. Although power, strength, and endurance do have their places in mountain biking, these elements don't necessarily form the framework for a champion mountain biker.

The bike should become an extension of your body. Slight shifts in your hips or knees can have remarkable results. Experienced bike handlers seem to flash down technical descents, dashing over obstacles in a smooth and graceful effort as if pirouetting in Swan Lake. Here are some tips and techniques to help you connect with your bike and float gracefully over the dirt.

Braking

Using your brakes requires using your head, especially when descending. This doesn't mean using your head as a stopping block, but rather to think intelligently. Use your best judgment in terms of how much or how little to squeeze those brake levers.

The more weight a tire is carrying, the more braking power it has. When you're going downhill, your front wheel carries more weight than the rear. Braking with the front brake will help keep you in control without going into a skid. Be careful, though, not to overdo it with the front brakes and accidentally toss yourself over the handlebars. And don't neglect your rear brake! When descending, shift your weight back over the rear wheel, thus increasing your rear braking power as well. This will balance the power of both brakes and give you maximum control.

Good riders learn just how much of their weight to shift over each wheel and how to apply just enough braking power to each brake, so not to "endo" over the handlebars or skid down a trail.

GOING UPHILL—Climbing Those Treacherous Hills

- **Shift into a low gear** (push the thumb shifter away from you). Before shifting, be sure to ease up on your pedaling so there is not too much pressure on the chain. Find the gear best for you that matches the terrain and steepness of each climb.
- **Stay seated.** Standing out of the saddle is often helpful when climbing steep hills with a road bike, but you may find that on dirt, standing may cause your rear tire to lose its grip and spin out. Climbing requires traction. Stay seated as long as you can, and keep the rear tire digging into the ground. Ascending skyward may prove to be much easier in the saddle.
- **Lean forward.** On very steep hills, the front end may feel unweighted and suddenly pop up. Slide forward on the saddle and lean over the handlebars. This will add more weight to the front wheel and should keep you grounded.
- **Keep pedaling.** On rocky climbs, be sure to keep the pressure on, and don't let up on those pedals! The slower you go through rough trail sections, the harder you will work.

GOING DOWNHILL—
The Real Reason We Get Up in the Morning

- **Shift into the big chainring.** Shifting into the big ring before a bumpy descent will help keep the chain from bouncing off. And should you crash or disengage your leg from the pedal, the chain will cover the teeth of the big ring so they don't bite into your leg.
- **Relax.** Stay loose on the bike, and don't lock your elbows or clench your grip. Your elbows need to bend with the bumps and absorb the shock, while your hands should have a firm but controlled grip on the bars to keep things steady. Steer with your body, allowing your shoulders to guide you through each turn and around each obstacle.

- *Don't oversteer or lose control.* Mountain biking is much like downhill skiing, since you must shift your weight from side to side down narrow, bumpy descents. Your bike will have the tendency to track in the direction you look and follow the slight shifts and leans of your body. You should not think so much about steering, but rather in what direction you wish to go.
- *Rise above the saddle.* When racing down bumpy, technical descents, you should not be sitting on the saddle, but standing on the pedals, allowing your legs and knees to absorb the rocky trail instead of your rear.
- *Drop your saddle.* For steep, technical descents, you may want to drop your saddle three or four inches. This lowers your center of gravity, giving you much more room to bounce around.
- *Keep your pedals parallel to the ground.* The front pedal should be slightly higher so that it doesn't catch on small rocks or logs.
  - *Stay focused.* Many descents require your utmost concentration and focus just to reach the bottom. You must notice every groove, every root, every rock, every hole, every bump. You, the bike, and the trail should all become one as you seek singletrack nirvana on your way down the mountain. But if your thoughts wander, however, then so may your bike, and you may instead become one with the trees!

WATCH OUT!
Back-road Obstacles

- **LOGS.** When you want to hop a log, throw your body back, yank up on the handlebars, and pedal forward in one swift motion. This clears the front end of the bike. Then quickly scoot forward and pedal the rear wheel up and over. Keep the forward momentum until you've cleared the log, and by all means, don't hit the brakes, or you may do some interesting acrobatic maneuvers!
- **ROCKS.** Worse than highway potholes! Stay relaxed, let your elbows and knees absorb the shock, and always continue applying power to your pedals. Staying seated will keep the rear wheel weighted to prevent slipping, and a light front end will help you to respond quickly to each new obstacle. The slower you go, the more time your tires will have to get caught between the grooves.
- **WATER.** Before crossing a stream or puddle, be sure to first check the depth and bottom surface. There may be an unseen hole or large rock hidden under the water that could wash you up if you're not careful. After you're sure all is safe, hit the water at a good speed, pedal steadily, and allow the bike to steer you through. Once you're across, tap the breaks to squeegee the water off the rims.
- **LEAVES.** Be careful of wet leaves. These may look pretty, but a trail covered with leaves may cause your wheels to slip out from under you. Leaves are not nearly as unpredictable and dangerous as ice, but they do warrant your attention on a rainy day.
- **MUD.** If you must ride through mud, hit it head on and keep pedaling. You want to part the ooze with your front wheel and get across before it swallows you up. Above all, don't leave the trail to go around the mud. This just widens the path even more and leads to increased trail erosion.

Urban Obstacles

- **CURBS** are fun to jump, but like with logs, be careful.
- **CURBSIDE DRAINS** are typically not a problem for bikes. Just be careful not to get a wheel caught in the grate.
- **DOGS** make great pets, but seem to have it in for bicyclists. If you think you can't outrun a dog that's chasing you, stop and walk your bike out of its territory. A loud yell to Get! or Go home! often works, as does a sharp squirt from your water bottle right between the eyes.
- **CARS** are tremendously convenient when we're in them, but dodging irate motorists in big automobiles becomes a real hazard when riding a bike. As a cyclist, you must realize most drivers aren't expecting you to be there and often wish you weren't. Stay alert and ride carefully, clearly signaling all of your intentions.
- **POTHOLES,** like grates and back-road canyons, should be avoided. Just because you're on an all-terrain bicycle doesn't mean you're indestructible. Potholes regularly damage rims, pop tires, and sometimes lift unsuspecting cyclists into a spectacular swan dive over the handlebars.

LAST-MINUTE CHECKOVER

Before a ride, it's a good idea to give your bike a once-over to make sure everything is in working order. Begin by checking the air pressure in your tires before each ride to make sure they are properly inflated. Mountain bikes require about 45 to 55 pounds per square inch of air pressure. If your tires are underinflated, there is greater likelihood that the tubes may get pinched on a bump or rock, causing the tire to flat.

Looking over your bike to make sure everything is secure and in its place is the next step. Go through the following checklist before each ride.

- *Pinch the tires to feel for proper inflation.* They should give just a little on the sides, but feel very hard on the treads. If you have a pressure gauge, use that.
- *Check your brakes.* Squeeze the rear brake and roll your bike forward. The rear tire should skid. Next, squeeze the front brake and roll your bike forward. The rear wheel should lift into the air. If this doesn't happen, then your brakes are too loose. Make sure the brake levers don't touch the handlebars when squeezed with full force.
- *Check all quick releases on your bike.* Make sure they are all securely tightened.
- *Lube up.* If your chain squeaks, apply some lubricant.
- *Check your nuts and bolts.* Check the handlebars, saddle, cranks, and pedals to make sure that each is tight and securely fastened to your bike.
- *Check your wheels.* Spin each wheel to see that they spin through the frame and between brake pads freely.
- *Have you got everything?* Make sure you have your spare tube, tire irons patch kit, frame pump, tools, food, water, and guidebook.

Liability Disclaimer

Neither the publisher, the producer, nor the authors of this guide assumes any liability for cyclists traveling along any of the suggested routes in this book. At the time of publication, all routes shown on the following maps were open to bicycles. They were chosen for their safety, aesthetics, and pleasure, and are deemed acceptable and accommodating to bicyclists. Safety upon these routes, however, cannot be guaranteed. Cyclists must assume their own responsibility when riding these routes and understand that with an activity such as mountain bike riding, there may be unforeseen risks and dangers.

Area Locator Map

This thumbnail relief map at the beginning of each ride shows you where the ride is within the state. The ride area is indicated with a star.

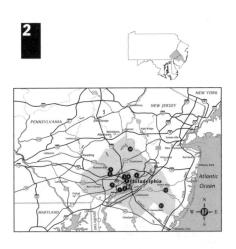

Regional Location Map

This map helps you find your way to the start of each ride from the nearest sizeable town or city. Coupled with the detailed directions at the beginning of the cue, this map should visually lead you to where you need to be for each ride.

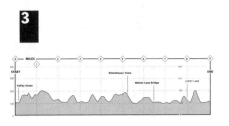

Profile Map

This helpful profile gives you a cross-sectional look at the ride's ups and downs. Elevation is labeled on the left, mileage is indicated on the top. Road and trail names are shown along the route with towns and points of interest labeled in bold.

MOUNTAIN BIKE GREATER PHILADELPHIA

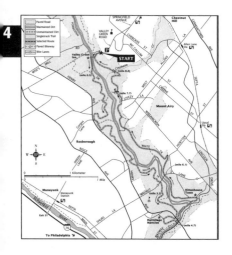

4 Route Map

This is your primary guide to each ride. It shows all of the accessible roads and trails, points of interest, water, towns, landmarks, and geographical features. It also distinguishes trails from roads, and paved roads from unpaved roads. The selected route is highlighted, and directional arrows point the way. Shaded topographic relief in the background gives you an accurate representation of the terrain and landscape in the ride area.

Ride Information (Included in each ride section)

📞 Trail Contacts:

This is the direct number for the local land managers in charge of all the trails within the selected ride. Use this hotline to call ahead for trail access information, or after your visit if you see problems with trail erosion, damage, or misuse.

🕐 Schedule:

This tells you at what times trails open and close, if on private or park land.

💲 Fees/Permits:

What money, if any, you may need to carry with you for park entrance fees or tolls.

🅝 Maps:

This is a list of other maps to supplement the maps in this book. They are listed in order from most detailed to most general.

Any other important or useful information will also be listed here such as local attractions, bike shops, nearby accommodations, etc.

e don't want anyone, by any means, to feel restricted to just the roads and trails that are mapped here. We hope you will have an adventurous spirit and use this guide as a platform to dive into Washington's backcountry and discover new routes for yourself. One of the simplest ways to begin this is to just turn the map upside down and ride the course in reverse. The change in perspective is fantastic and the ride should feel quite different. With this in mind, it will be like getting two distinctly different rides on each map.

For your own purposes, you may wish to copy the directions for the course onto a small sheet to help you while riding, or photocopy the map and cue sheet to take with you. These pages can be folded into a bike bag, stuffed into a jersey pocket, or better still, used with the **BarMap** or **BarMapOTG** (see www.cycoactive.com for more info). Just remember to slow or even stop when you want to read the map.

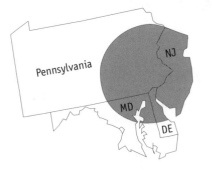

MOUNTAIN BIKE GREATER PHILADELPHIA

The Rides

1. John Heinz Ntn Wildlife Refuge/Lagoon Loop
2. Impoundment Loop
3. Fairmont Park Forbidden Drive
4. Wissahickon South
5. Wissahickon Gorge North Loop
6. Pennypack Park
7. Ridley Creek State Park
8. Valley Forge National Historical Park
9. Schuylkill River Trail
10. Tohickon Creek
11. Wharton State Forest
12. Lebanon State Forest
13. Brandywine Creek State Park
14. Middle Run Natural Area
15. Iron Hill Park
16. Fair Hill Natural Resource Mgnt Area
17. Nottingham Park
18. French Creek State Park/Red & White Loop

19. French Creek State Park/Turtle Loop
20. Blue Marsh Lake
21. Pumping Station
22. Walnut Run
23. Horseshoe Trail
24. Furnace Hills
25. Mount Gretna
26. Weiser State Forest
27. The Pinnacle
28. Lehigh Gorge State Park
29. Drake's Creek
30. Scrub Mountain
31. Broad Mountain Loop
32. Broad Mountain Connector
33. The Deer Path
34. The Pine Tar Trail

35. The American Standard
36. Flagstaff Mountain
37. Switchback Trail
38. Twin Peaks
39. Mauch Chunk Ridge
40. Jacobsburg State Park
41. Pohopoco Tract/Delaware State Forest
42. Round Valley Recreation Area
43. Delaware & Raritan Canal
44. Navesink Highlands

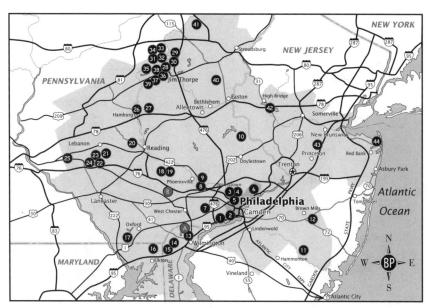

21

COURSES AT A GLANCE

1. John Heinz Ntn Wildlife Refuge/Lagoon Loop

Length: 8.9-mile loop
Nearby: Philadelphia, PA
Time: 1-3 hours
Difficulty: Easy

2. Impoundment Loop

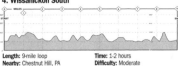

Length: 3.5-mile loop
Nearby: Philadelphia, PA
Time: 1 hour
Difficulty: Easy

3. Fairmont Park Forbidden Drive

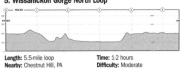

Length: 10-mile out-and-back
Nearby: Chestnut Hill, PA
Time: 1-2 hours
Difficulty: Easy

4. Wissahickon South

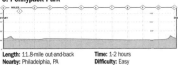

Length: 9-mile loop
Nearby: Chestnut Hill, PA
Time: 1-2 hours
Difficulty: Moderate

5. Wissahickon Gorge North Loop

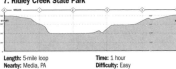

Length: 5.5-mile loop
Nearby: Chestnut Hill, PA
Time: 1-2 hours
Difficulty: Moderate

6. Pennypack Park

Length: 11.8-mile out-and-back
Nearby: Philadelphia, PA
Time: 1-2 hours
Difficulty: Easy

7. Ridley Creek State Park

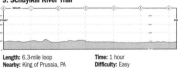

Length: 5-mile loop
Nearby: Media, PA
Time: 1 hour
Difficulty: Easy

8. Valley Forge National Historical Park

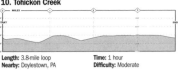

Length: 6.7-mile loop
Nearby: King of Prussia, PA
Time: 1 hour
Difficulty: Easy

9. Schuylkill River Trail

Length: 6.3-mile loop
Nearby: King of Prussia, PA
Time: 1 hour
Difficulty: Easy

10. Tohickon Creek

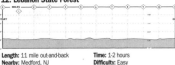

Length: 3.8-mile loop
Nearby: Doylestown, PA
Time: 1 hour
Difficulty: Moderate

11. Wharton State Forest

Length: 11.9-mile loop
Nearby: Hammonton, NJ
Time: 1-2 hours
Difficulty: Easy

12. Lebanon State Forest

Length: 11 mile out-and-back
Nearby: Medford, NJ
Time: 1-2 hours
Difficulty: Easy

13. Brandywine Creek State Park

Multiple Route Options

Length: 14-miles of trails
Nearby: Wilmington, DE
Time: Rider's discretion
Difficulty: Moderate

14. Middle Run Natural Area

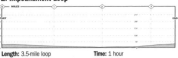

Length: 7.1-mile loop
Nearby: Newark, DE
Time: 1 hour
Difficulty: Moderate

15. Iron Hill Park

Multiple Route Options

Length: Over 15 miles of trails
Nearby: Newark, DE
Time: Rider's discretion
Difficulty: Moderate

16. Fair Hill Natural Resource Mgnt Area

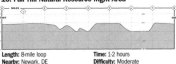

Length: 8-mile loop
Nearby: Newark, DE
Time: 1-2 hours
Difficulty: Moderate

Ride Profiles

17. Nottingham Park

Length: 6.1-mile loop
Nearby: Nottingham, PA
Time: 1 hour
Difficulty: Easy

18. French Creek State Park/Red & White Loop

Length: 6.2-mile loop
Nearby: Birdsboro, PA
Time: 1-2 hours
Difficulty: Moderate

19. French Creek State Park/Turtle Loop

Length: 10.9-mile loop
Nearby: Birdsboro, PA
Time: 1-2 hours
Difficulty: Moderate

20. Blue Marsh Lake

Length: 20.8-mile loop
Nearby: Reading, PA
Time: 2-4 hours
Difficulty: Difficult

21. Pumping Station

Length: 5.6-mile loop
Nearby: Lebanon, PA
Time: 1-2 hours
Difficulty: Moderate to Difficult

22. Walnut Run

Length: 10.1-mile loop
Nearby: Lebanon, PA
Time: 1-2 hours
Difficulty: Moderate

23. Horseshoe Trail

Length: 7.6-mile loop
Nearby: Lebanon, PA
Time: 1-2 hours
Difficulty: Moderate

24. Furnace Hills

Length: 8.1-mile loop
Nearby: Lebanon, PA
Time: 1-2 hours
Difficulty: Moderate to Difficult

25. Mount Gretna

Length: 7.6-mile loop
Nearby: Lebanon, PA
Time: 1-2 hours
Difficulty: Moderate

26. Weiser State Forest

Length: 10.8-mile out-and-back
Nearby: Port Clinton, PA
Time: 1-2 hours
Difficulty: Difficult

27. The Pinnacle

Length: 8.2-mile out-and-back
Nearby: Hamburg, PA
Time: 1-2 hours
Difficulty: Moderate

28. Lehigh Gorge State Park

Length: 21.3-mile point-to-point
Nearby: Jim Thorpe, PA
Time: 1-2 hours
Difficulty: Easy

29. Drake's Creek

Length: 14.6-mile loop
Nearby: Jim Thorpe, PA
Time: 3+ hours
Difficulty: Moderate

30. Scrub Mountain

Length: 8.9-mile loop
Nearby: Jim Thorpe, PA
Time: 1-2 hours
Difficulty: Moderate to Difficult

31. Broad Mountain Loop

Length: 10.4-mile loop
Nearby: Jim Thorpe, PA
Time: 1-2 hours
Difficulty: Easy

32. Broad Mountain Connector

Length: 12.3-mile loop
Nearby: Jim Thorpe, PA
Time: 1-2 hours
Difficulty: Moderate

COURSES AT A GLANCE

Ride Profiles

33. The Deer Path

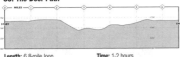

Length: 6.8-mile loop
Nearby: Jim Thorpe, PA
Time: 1-2 hours
Difficulty: Moderate

34. The Pine Tar Trail

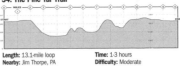

Length: 13.1-mile loop
Nearby: Jim Thorpe, PA
Time: 1-3 hours
Difficulty: Moderate

35. The American Standard

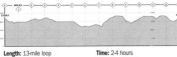

Length: 13-mile loop
Nearby: Jim Thorpe, PA
Time: 2-4 hours
Difficulty: Difficult

36. Flagstaff Mountain

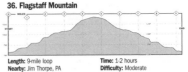

Length: 9-mile loop
Nearby: Jim Thorpe, PA
Time: 1-2 hours
Difficulty: Moderate

37. Switchback Trail

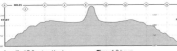

Length: 17.2 out-and-back
Nearby: Jim Thorpe, PA
Time: 1-2 hours
Difficulty: Easy

38. Twin Peaks

Length: 20.3-miles loop
Nearby: Jim Thorpe, PA
Time: 1-2 hours
Difficulty: Moderate

39. Mauch Chunk Ridge

Length: 10-mile out-and-back
Nearby: Jim Thorpe, PA
Time: 1-2 hours
Difficulty: Moderate

40. Jacobsburg State Park

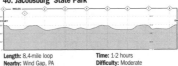

Length: 8.4-mile loop
Nearby: Wind Gap, PA
Time: 1-2 hours
Difficulty: Moderate

41. Pohopoco Tract/Delaware State Forest

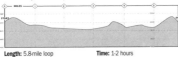

Length: 5.8-mile loop
Nearby: Blakeslee, PA
Time: 1-2 hours
Difficulty: Easy

42. Round Valley Recreation Area

Length: 10.4-mile loop
Nearby: Clinton, NJ
Time: 2-3 hours
Difficulty: Difficult

43. Delaware & Raritan Canal

Length: 30-mile point-to-point
Nearby: Princeton, NJ
Time: 3-4 hours
Difficulty: Easy to Moderate

44. Navesink Highlands

Length: 11.4-mile loop
Nearby: Highlands, NJ
Time: 2-3 hours
Difficulty: Moderate

The Rides

Philadelphia

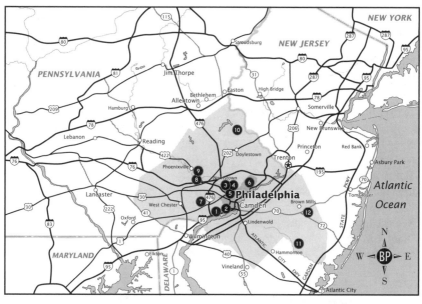

Area

John Heinz National Wildlife Refuge/ Lagoon Loop

Ride Specs

Start: From the parking area near the John Heinz Visitor Contact Station

Length: 8.9 miles

Approximate Riding Time: 1½ hours

Difficulty Rating: Easy, with no hills and no technical difficulties

Terrain: Tight singletrack trails, wide doubletrack trails, and gravel roads that travel through densely wooded areas and tidal marshes

Elevation Gain: 72 feet

Land Status: Department of the Interior/ National Wildlife Refuge

Nearest Town: Philadelphia, PA

Other Trail Users: Hikers, joggers, and birdwatchers.

Getting There

From Philadelphia, PA: Travel south on I-95 to the Bartram Avenue exit. Follow Bartram Avenue west to 84th Street. Go right on 84th Street to Lindbergh Boulevard. Turn left on Lindbergh Boulevard and follow the signs to the John Heinz Visitor Contact Station. Park in the lot just beyond the visitor center. *DeLorme: Pennsylvania Atlas & Gazetteer:* Page 96 A-1

Train: From Market East Station take the SEPTA R1 Airport Line to Eastwick Station. From the station turn left on 84th St and follow the driving directions to the Visitor Contact Station.

Tinicum Marsh is the largest remaining freshwater tidal wetland in Pennsylvania. Once over 5,200 acres, Tinicum Marsh was reduced to a mere 200 acres–yet another victim of urbanization. Thanks to the hard work of public and private agencies, the park has recovered over 1,200 acres. This unique ecosystem is located, surprisingly, just miles from downtown Philadelphia. Situated along the Atlantic Flyway, Tinicum is home to over 80 bird species. Nesting boxes have been placed throughout the refuge to attract migratory birds. Over 280 types of migratory birds have been recorded visiting the refuge. Ducks, Canadian geese, great blue herons, and various other migratory birds use Tinicum as a resting/feeding spot during their flights north and south. The refuge is also home to deer, turtles, frogs, and many other small wildlife.

There are over 50 species of wildflowers, as well as trees such as willows, locusts, maples, oak, and alders. Native plants such as cattails, rushes, and sedges are also visible and provide excellent food and cover for wildlife. Purple loosestrife and other non-native plants also thrive here. Steps are being taken, however, to limit the spread of these invasive plants. Once dismissed as a useless swamp, Tinicum Marsh has been recognized as a vital link in the health of the surrounding area. Thanks to the hard work of many volunteers and the United States Fish and Wildlife Service, the wetland is slowly recovering.

Your ride starts at the John Heinz Visitor Contact Station and goes southwest past a gate on a wide dirt and gravel road. Darby Creek is on your right, with the main impoundment on your left. At the 0.2-mile mark you pass a wooden bridge spanning the main impoundment. Continue straight to the observation tower. The observation tower is a great place to stop and enjoy the views and look for wildlife. The ride continues straight and at the 1.3-mile mark goes past a bird blind on the right. At mile 1.4 the ride goes left on a wide dirt road and heads past stands of cattails and mulberry trees as it leads toward Interstate 95. At mile 1.9 you go right. Here, not more than 100 feet away, are train tracks and Interstate 95—beyond that is the Philadelphia International Airport.

At the 2.5-mile mark the ride goes right and follows a tight singletrack trail on a 15-foot wide berm. The trail passes over bridges, through thick stands of cattails, and past several marshes. The marshes, which at one time were used as landfills, are being restored to their original state. Here you are riding on tight singletrack through a dense section of tall cattails between two tidal marshes. This section provides some of the most unusual riding in the area. Go right over a bridge and continue straight to a fenceline at Pennsylvania 420. From here, go left on a wide gravel road, with Interstate 95 on your right. Go left as the trail heads back into the marshes. Retrace your route back to a trail junction at the original 1.9-mile mark. From here go right and follow a beautiful grass-covered doubletrack trail along the edge of the main impoundment. There are benches along the trail to stop and view wildlife. At mile 8.1 the trail veers left and heads back to the parking area.

MilesDirections

0.0 START from the parking area just beyond the visitor center. Follow the wide dirt to the Observation Tower.

0.2 Pass a wooden bridge on left. Continue straight on wide tread and head to observation tower.

0.7 The observation tower is on the left. Continue straight. This is a great place to stop and view wildlife.

1.3 A spurs trail leads to a viewing blind; continue straight.

1.4 Come to a trail junction. Go left on a wide dirt road.

1.9 The trail forks here. Go right onto a wide gravel road.

2.1 Pass a spur road on right.

2.5 The road curves left and leads to gate. Pedal right to a singletrack trail at a sign marked R-12. Follow the Tidal Trail on tight singletrack and pass a viewing blind on your way to a bridge.

3.0 Cross over a bridge and weave along tight singletrack to second bridge crossing.

3.9 Cross over the wooden bridge, and then bear right onto a road which leads to trail junction at bridge.

4.0 Pedal right over the bridge and follow a tight singletrack trail across two more bridge crossings. Continue straight to wide gravel road.

4.5 Go left onto a gravel road. The road parallels I-95 and then rolls left to a trail junction.

5.0 Reach the trail junction. Continue straight and retrace the route back to a trail junction at the original 1.9-mile mark.

7.3 Reach the trail junction. Go right and then make a sudden left onto a wide dirt road. Continue straight to trail junction.

7.9 Continue straight. (A spur trail goes left. No bikes are allowed on this trail.)

8.1 The trail bears left onto wide dirt road.

8.9 Arrive at the parking area and your car.

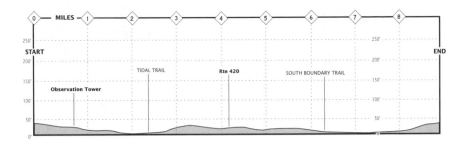

30

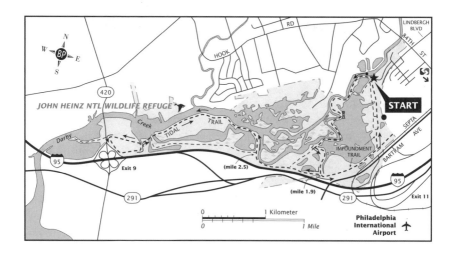

Ride Information

📞 Trail Contacts:
John Heinz Visitor Contact Station, 86th and Lindbergh, Tinicum, PA (215) 365-3118, *open 9:00 A.M. to 4:30 P.M.* • **Cycle Fit**, 320 South Chester Road, Wallingford, PA (610) 876-9450, *they offer local group rides*

🕐 Schedule:
Sunrise to sunset

❓ Local Information:
The Philadelphia Convention & Visitors Bureau, 1515 Market St., Philadelphia, PA; 1-800-537-7676 *www.libertynet.org/phila-visitor/*

❓ Local Events/Attractions:
Independence Mall, located between 4th and 8th streets, Philadelphia, PA home to the Liberty Bell, Independence Hall, Congress Hall, and other points of interest • **Italian Market**, 9th St. and Passyunk Ave, Philadelphia, PA • **South Street**, between 3rd and 8th Street, Philadelphia, PA • **Valley Forge National Park**, King of Prussia, PA (610) 783-1077

👥 Organizations:
Delaware Valley Bicycle Club (DVBC) – contact Cycle Fit for more information at (610) 876-9450

Ⓝ Maps:
John Heinz National Wildlife Refuge maps – *available at the contact station*

Impoundment Loop

Ride Specs

Start: From the parking area near the John Heinz Visitor Contact Station

Length: 3.5-mile loop

Approximate Riding Time: 20 min.–1 hour

Difficulty Rating: Easy due to being flat

Terrain: The ride follows a wide, flat dirt and gravel road around the main impoundment area

Elevation Gain: 28 feet

Land Status: Department of the Interior/ National Wildlife Refuge

Nearest Town: Philadelphia, PA

Other Trail Users: Hikers, joggers, and birdwatchers.

Getting There

From Philadelphia, PA: Travel south on I-95 to the Bartram Avenue exit. Follow Bartram Avenue west to 84th Street. Go right on 84th Street to Lindbergh Boulevard. Turn left on Lindbergh Boulevard and follow the signs to the John Heinz Visitor Contact Station. Park in the lot just beyond the visitor center.

DeLorme: Pennsylvania Atlas & Gazetteer: Page 96 A-1

Train: From Market East Station take the SEPTA R1 Airport Line to Eastwick Station. From the station turn left on 84th St and follow the driving directions to the Visitor Contact Station.

ant a ride where you can take the family? Want a ride where you can get a workout and spend time in a beautiful area full of migratory birds and rich plant life? Well, here's the ride for you. Located near the Philadelphia and Delaware county borders, the John Heinz Wildlife Refuge at Tinicum spreads out over 1,200 acres, safeguarding Pennsylvania's largest remaining freshwater tidal wetland. The main activities at the refuge are hiking, walking, jogging, fishing, cycling, bird watching, and canoeing. While the area may feel remote, it's actually close to both the Philadelphia International Airport and Interstate 95. At certain times of the day while you are riding along the trails, the music from the songbirds will replace the noise from the encircling areas. Take the time on your ride to stop and enjoy the serenity of this peaceful and diverse eco-system.

Your ride starts at the John Heinz Visitor Contact Station. Follow the Impoundment Trail along Darby Creek. The creek's water level is control by tides of the Delaware River. Notice the footbridge spanning the impoundment—no bikes are allowed, but feel free to walk this section. Next on the Impoundment Trail is the main observation tower, a two-tier tower with great views overlooking the main impoundment. At the 1.3-mile mark, a trail goes right to an observation blind. To make your trip more interesting, pick up a bird list at the visitor contact station and see how many different birds you can spot on your ride. Past the blind, the main trail goes left toward Interstate 95 and the eastern part of the refuge. Be on the lookout for rabbits, turtles, and other wildlife as you cruise along on the beautiful doubletrack trail. Several benches are located along this section. If you have the kids, these benches provide a great place to stop for a break. From here the ride goes under a thick canopy of deciduous trees and heads back to the parking area and your car. Want a longer ride? Check out the Lagoon Loop (Ride 1) in this book.

Ride Information

🟢 Trail Contacts:
John Heinz Visitor Contact Station, 86th and Lindbergh, Tinicum, PA (215) 365-3118, *open 9:00 A.M. to 4:30 P.M.* • **Cycle Fit**, 320 South Chester Road, Wallingford, PA (610) 876-9450, *they offer local group rides*

🕐 Schedule:
Sunrise to sunset

❓ Local Information:
The Philadelphia Convention & Visitors Bureau, 1515 Market St., Philadelphia, PA; 1-800-537-7676 *www.libertynet.org/phila-visitor/*

🟠 Local Events/Attractions:
Independence Mall, located between 4th and 8th streets, Philadelphia, PA

home to the Liberty Bell, Independence Hall, Congress Hall, and other points of interest • **Italian Market,** 9th St. and Passyunk Ave, Philadelphia, PA • **South Street,** between 3rd and 8th Street, Philadelphia, PA • **Valley Forge National Park,** King of Prussia, PA (610) 783-1077

🏢 Organizations:
Delaware Valley Bicycle Club (DVBC) – contact Cycle Fit for more information at (610) 876-9450

🔵 Maps:
John Heinz National Wildlife Refuge maps – *available at the contact station*

MilesDirections

0.0 START from the parking area. Follow the Impoundment Trail as it leads to the observation tower.

0.2 Pass a wooden footbridge on the left. Continue straight to the observation tower.

0.7 Arrive at the observation tower. This is a great place to stop and view wildlife.

1.3 Continue straight. (A spur trail leads to a viewing blind.)

1.4 Go left at a trail junction, still following the Impoundment Trail.

1.9 The ride goes left.

2.5 The ride bears left onto a wide doubletrack trail. Follow the fast, flat trail back to the parking area.

3.5 Arrive at the parking area.

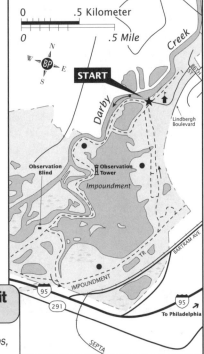

SEPTA - Greater Philadelphia Transit
www.septa.org

Destinations: *Philadelphia Metro Area , PA Suburbs, Trenton (NJ Transit), Wilmington: (215) 580–7800*
Fare: *Up to $5 one way.*
*[**Note: Regional Rail:** Bikes are permitted on off-peak trains only (reverse peak okay). No limits on maximum number of bikes depending on passenger loads. Groups call ahead during business hours for reserved space. **Subway and Route 100:** Bikes are allowed Monday–Friday after 6 P.M. and 9 A.M.-3 P.M. There are no weekend restrictions on the system.]*

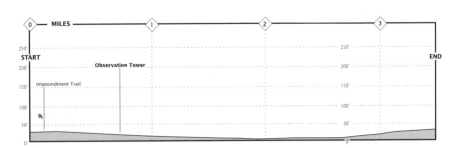

Ode to the Pennsylvania State Park System

ennsylvania is blessed with large tracts of public open space land. The health and well being of public land in Pennsylvania is at an all-time high and we can thank the public agencies that managed the lands for it. The ride you are about to do is located on land that is managed and maintained by the Pennsylvania State Game Lands Commission. The Game Commission is responsible for over 1,380,400 acres of public lands spread throughout the state. Each time a hunter buys a hunting license, the money he or she spends goes toward the purchase and maintenance of hunting lands. The Game Commission has an open policy and shares these lands with the general public. In fact, only 35 percent of the users are hunters, the remaining 65 percent are non-hunters that use the land for recreational purposes. Recreation such as hiking, bird watching, fishing, boating, mountain biking and nature study are popular and encouraged activities. Hats off to the Game Commission for the hard work and programs that benefit all citizens of Pennsylvania.

Pennsylvania also has one of the largest systems of state parks and state forests in the country. Over 2.4 million acres of public lands are open for citizens to pursue their outdoor activities. The state parks and state forest provide access to natural wonders, recreational opportunities, natural treasures and the opportunity to experience the beauty and solitude of open lands. There are over 2,000 miles of hiking trails that

weave through the state forests and state parks. Hikers and backpackers have access to trails in rugged, mountainous areas such as Ricketts Glen State Park or mellow, flat trails along the Delaware River in Delaware Canal State Park. Boating, fishing, swimming, picnicking, snowmobiling, hunting and biking are all activities that are popular in Pennsylvania State parks and forests. Camping is very popular in the state parks and forests. There are over 7,000 campsites that are available in 55 state parks. Eleven state parks provide lodging in rustic cabins with fireplaces, 14 other parks have modern cabins for year-round use. For the mountain cyclists there are literally thousands of miles of trail and roads that are open to cyclists in the state forest. From backcountry roads to bone crushing, rocky singletrack trails there enough trails in the state forest to satisfy the most extreme cyclists. So get outside and enjoy all the wonderful outdoor opportunities that exist in the great state of Pennsylvania.

3

Fairmount Park Forbidden Drive

Ride Specs

Start: From the Bells Mills Road parking area

Length: 10-mile out-and-back

Approximate Riding Time: 1–2 hours

Difficulty Rating: Easy, with no technical difficulties

Terrain: An easy gravel path that follows Forbidden Drive along Wissahickon Creek

Elevation Gain: 537 feet

Land Status: Fairmount Park Commission/ Philadelphia City Parks

Nearest Town: Chestnut Hill, PA

Other Trail Users: Hikers, joggers, sightseers, and horseback riders

Getting There

From Philadelphia, PA: Follow I-76 west to I-476 north. Go north on I-476 to exit 7 at Conshohocken. Go east on Ridge Avenue for 3.7 miles to Bells Mill Road. Turn left on Bells Mills Road and go for 0.9 miles. The parking area is on the right. ***DeLorme: Pennsylvania Atlas & Gazetteer:*** Page 82 D-2

✆ **Train:** From Market East Station take the SEPTA R8 Chestnut Hill West line to Chestnut Hill Station. From the station turn left on Germantown Avenue and then turn left on Bells Mill Road. Turn left on Bells Mills Road and go for 0.9 miles to the parking area.

T his is a great beginner ride that's suitable for the entire family. Your ride starts from the parking area on Bells Mills Road and takes the gentile gravel road down to Lincoln Drive and back. There are numerous sights and many places to stop along Wissahickon Creek, so pack a lunch, bring the family, and enjoy one of Philadelphia's most beautiful areas.

From the parking area, your ride goes south along Wissahickon Creek. At mile 0.6 you pass the Thomas Mill Covered Bridge on the left. Originally built in 1737, the bridge was restored in 1939 with funds provided by the Friends of the Wissahickon. Continue straight to the Valley Green Bridge and the Valley Green Inn. The Valley Green Inn is just one of many inns that operated near the Wissahickon. Today, it's the only one still in operation. Many mills and quarries also operated in the valley after the Revolutionary War, but by the 1850s their importance began to wane. Today none are in operation.

Your ride passes through old-growth forests of American beech, black walnut, hickory, and sycamore. The latest inventory of plants lists over 653 different plant species in the park. Along the creek and hillsides you'll see many small rocks and outcroppings. The bedrock in the area, conveniently called "Wissahickon formation," consists of schist, quartzite, gneiss, and pegmatite. It's the predominant rock in the Philadelphia area and can be seen in many old houses and bridges in the Germantown area.

At the 3.1-mile mark the ride drops down a small hill and goes under the Walnut Lane Bridge. Continue straight, crossing the Blue Stone Bridge. Built in 1896, the Blue Stone is a classic example of bridge construction from the turn of the century. Your ride turns around at Lincoln Drive and returns back to the parking area. Feel free to explore the area on your own as there are many sights to see in the park.

A good place to stop before or after the ride is the Andorra Natural Area, located on the site of the old Andorra Nursery. The center offers year-round programs on the social and natural history of the Wissahickon Valley. The Tree House Visitors Center offers exhibits, as well as detailed maps of over five miles of hiking trails throughout the center. Sorry, but the trails in the center are not open to bikes.

Ride Information

🕐 Trail Contacts:
Fairmount Park Rangers, Philadelphia, PA; (215) 685-2172 • **Fairmount Park Commission Visitors Center**, JFK Blvd. and N. 16th St., Philadelphia, PA; (215) 685-2176 • **Wissahickon Cyclery**, 7837 Germantown Ave., Chestnut Hill, PA; (215) 248-2829 – they offer group rides

🕐 Schedule:
Sunrise to sunset

💲 Fees/Permits:
Free, but permits are required. Call the park rangers at (215) 685-0052 for an application. Expect at least two weeks for processing. Best time to apply is in December for the upcoming year.

❓ Local Information:
The Philadelphia Convention & Visitors Bureau, 1515 Market St., Philadelphia, PA; 1-800-537-7676 or *www.libertynet.org/phila-visitor/*

💡 Local Events/Attractions:
Andorra Natural Area/Tree House Visitor Center, Andorra Rd., Philadelphia, PA; (215) 685-9285 • **Morris Arboretum**, 100 Northwestern Ave., Chestnut Hill, PA; (215) 247-5777 or *www.upenn.edu/Morris/* • **Woodmere Art Museum**, 9201 Germantown Ave., Philadelphia, PA; (215) 247-0476 • **The Cliveden Estate**, 6401 Germantown Ave., Germantown, PA; (215) 848-1777 or www.cliveden.org

🍴 Restaurants:
Valley Green Inn, Springfield and Forbidden Dr., Philadelphia, PA; (215) 247-1730 or *www.valleygreeninn.com* – *serves excellent fresh American style dishes in three quaint antique-filled dining rooms*

👥 Organizations:
Friends of the Wissahickon, 8708 Germantown Ave., Philadelphia, PA; (215) 247-0417 or *www.fow.org*

🅝 Maps:
USGS maps: Germantown, PA • **Fairmount Park Commission/ Wissahickon Trail System map**—general map *available from the park office for $2; more detailed map available at Valley Green Inn for $5*

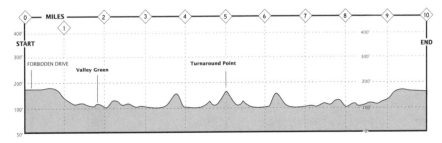

MilesDirections

0.0 START from the parking area. Cross over Bell Mills Road to Forbidden Drive. Go left onto Forbidden Drive.

0.4 Pass the old covered bridge on the left.

1.8 A spur trail goes right. Continue straight along Wissahickon Creek.

2.0 The Valley Green Bridge goes up and left. Continue straight along Wissahickon Creek.

2.1 The Valley Green Inn is on the right. This is a great place to stop and have brunch on a Sunday morning.

3.1 Come to a three-way trail junction. Continue straight down a small hill.

4.3 Cross over a small bridge and cruise down a short hill to Lincoln Drive.

5.0 At Lincoln Drive, stop for a short rest and then turn around and retrace your route back to Bells Mills Road.

10.0 Reach Bells Mills Road, the parking area, and your car.

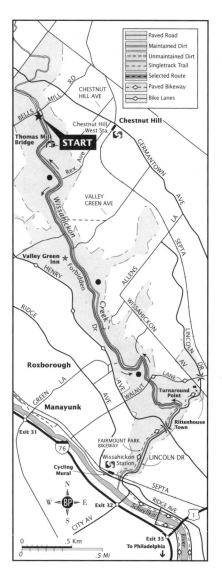

Wissahickon South

Ride Specs

Start: From the Upper Valley Green parking area

Length: 9-mile loop

Approximate Riding Time: 1–2 hours

Difficulty Rating: Moderate, with a few strenuous sections

Terrain: Singletrack, doubletrack, dirt and paved roads. The hills are short and steep with lots of rocks and roots for the expert rider to test his or her skills.

Elevation Gain: 791 feet

Land Status: Fairmount Park Commission/ Philadelphia City Parks

Nearest Town: Chestnut Hill, PA

Other Trail Users: Hikers, joggers, sightseers, and horseback riders

Getting There

From Philadelphia, PA: Follow I-76 west to I-476 north. Go north on I-476 to the Germantown Ave. exit. Go east on Germantown Ave. for 6.1 miles to Springfield Ave. Go right on Springfield Ave. and travel for 0.7 miles. Bear right on Valley Green Rd. and travel for 0.4 miles to a parking area on the right.

DeLorme: Pennsylvania Atlas & Gazetteer: Page 82 D-2

Train: From Market East Station take the SEPTA R8 Chestnut Hill West line to St Martin's Station. From the station exit turn left on St Martin's Lane and then turn right on Springfield Avenue and follow the driving directions to the Valley Green Inn.

Valley Green Inn.

The scenic Wissahickon Gorge, part of Philadelphia's Fairmount Park system, is a natural open oasis surrounded by an ever-swelling urban sprawl. First inhabited by Lenni-Lenape Indians, then Quakers and German immigrants, the park has a history as colorful as Philadelphia itself. It's hard to travel more than a mile in the park without seeing remnants of Philadelphia and America's past. After your ride, take the time to enjoy the sights and sounds of this wonderful natural area. Trout fishing, bird watching, flora and fauna identification, and hiking are some of the activies you can pursue before or after your ride.

Your ride starts at the Upper Valley Green parking area. From the parking area, go down to and over the bridge to the Valley Green Inn. Built in 1850, the inn still operates on a daily basis with all of the proceeds going to the Friends of the Wissahickon to maintain and protect the natural state of the area. Just past the

inn, your ride goes right and heads up a short, steep, loose rocky hill. At the top, go left and follow some great singletrack. Shoot down a nice downhill section to a bridge. Cross over the bridge and climb steeply to level tread. From here the ride drops down a steep hill to Forbidden Drive. Cruise along Forbidden Drive for a short distance and then make a right turn at mile 3.0 and go up a steep, rocky hill.

At the top of the hill, go left and cruise down to and past the public golf course. Make a right turn just past a small bridge and head through some very rocky tread which leads to Walnut Lane Bridge. Follow the trail past a gravel road and then drop down some tight singletrack to Wissahickon Creek. Go left on the bike path along the Wissahickon Creek.

Eventually you pass the historical Rittenhouse Townsite. This was the site of North America's first paper mill and the birthplace of David Rittenhouse (for whom Rittenhouse Square is named). The Townsite was established in 1690 and is just one of many historic sites in the area. Occasionally special events are held at the site. For more information call the Rittenhouse Townsite Historical Society.

Past the site, the trail turns to singletrack and goes back under Walnut Lane Bridge. Following the well-marked bike trail, you pass through several technical sections as you head up to Livezey Lane. If you look down and to the left you'll see

Ride Information

⊙ Trail Contacts:
Fairmount Park Rangers, Philadelphia, PA; (215) 685-2172 • **Fairmount Park Commission Visitors Center**, JFK Blvd. and N. 16th St., Philadelphia, PA; (215) 685-2176 • **Wissahickon Cyclery**, 7837 Germantown Ave., Chestnut Hill, PA; (215) 248-2829 - they offer group rides

⊙ Schedule:
Sunrise to sunset

⊙ Fees/Permits:
Free, but permits are required. Call the park rangers at (215) 685-0052 for an application. Expect at least two weeks for processing. Best time to apply is in December for the upcoming year.

⊙ Local Information:
[see Ride 3: Fairmount Park/ Forbidden Drive]

⊙ Local Events/Attractions:
Rittenhouse Townsite Historical Society, Wisahickon Ave, between Lincoln Dr. and Walnut Lane, Philadelphia, PA; (215) 438-5711 • [see Ride 3: Fairmount Park/ Forbidden Drive]

⊙ Restaurants:
Valley Green Inn, Springfield and Forbidden Dr., Philadelphia, PA; (215) 247-1730 or www.valleygreeninn.com - serves excellent fresh American style dishes in three quaint antique-filled dining rooms

⊙ Organizations:
Friends of the Wissahickon, 8708 Germantown Ave., Philadelphia, PA; (215) 247-0417 or www.fow.org

⊙ Maps:
USGS maps: Germantown, PA • **Fairmount Park Commission/ Wissahickon Trail System map**–general map available from the park office for $2; more detailed map available at Valley Green Inn for $5

the popular Climber's Rock. The trail goes right, leads through a gate, and then drops down past waterbars to Cresheim Creek. Climb the steep tread up from the creek and then make a great downhill run back to Valley Green Drive. Go right and you're home free.

MilesDirections

0.0 START from the parking area and go down Valley Green Road.

0.2 Cross over the bridge and then follow Forbidden Drive to just past the Valley Green Inn.

0.3 Go right and head up a hideously steep, loose rocky hill to a trail junction.

0.5 Go left on sweet singletrack.

1.0 Continue straight on wonderful singletrack. Struggle through a short technical section and then cruise down to a concrete bridge.

1.6 Go right and head over bridge. Make a

sharp left and climb up a steep low-gear hill, past several waterbars.

1.8 The grade eases. Follow sweet, fast singletrack down to a road.

2.6 Pedal left and then right onto Forbidden Drive. Go to a spur trail on the right.

3.0 Crank right up a steep, loose, rocky hill to trail junction.

3.2 Roll left onto a singletrack trail. Weave past a golf course and then drop down to a spur trail on the right.

Wissahickon Creek.

MilesDirections *continued*

3.8 Go right over small bridge. Jam up steep, rocky tread to sweet singletrack.

4.1 A spur trail comes in on right. Continue straight on singletrack, past a reclaim area. Pedal under a bridge. Continue on single-track to a paved road.

4.5 Cross a paved road to singletrack trail. Weave down on tight singletrack and go left at trail junction. Continue straight and head down to paved bike path.

4.7 Go left on the bike path and head to Forbidden Drive.

5.2 Cross Forbidden Drive to a bike-path. Follow the path to trail junction.

5.4 Go left and head up to and past the Rittenhouse Townsite.

5.6 Roll left and then right on a well-marked trail. Follow the singletrack to a trail junction.

6.1 The trail goes left and heads down past a water pipe. Crank up rocky tread and go under Walnut Bridge.

6.4 Crank up a short, steep hill. Angle left at the top and then crank past rocky tread

down to a paved road.

6.9 Cross the road to a singletrack trail. Crank through a short technical section and continue on singletrack to a trail junction.

7.4 Go right to a doubletrack trail. Make a quick left back onto singletrack tread. Crank past a rocky section to a trail junction.

7.7 Pedal left up a singletrack trail. Make a great downhill run past some tight berms. Pedal up a short, rocky hill to a paved road (Livezey Lane) and a contemporary house.

8.0 Go left and head down Livezey Lane to a yellow gate.

8.1 Go right at the gate and follow the singletrack to a trail junction.

8.4 Drop left and head down past several waterbars to a bridge. Cross the bridge and then crank up a steep, rocky, low-gear hill. Roll down to the Valley Green Bridge.

8.8 Go right and head up to the parking area.

9.0 Arrive at the parking area.

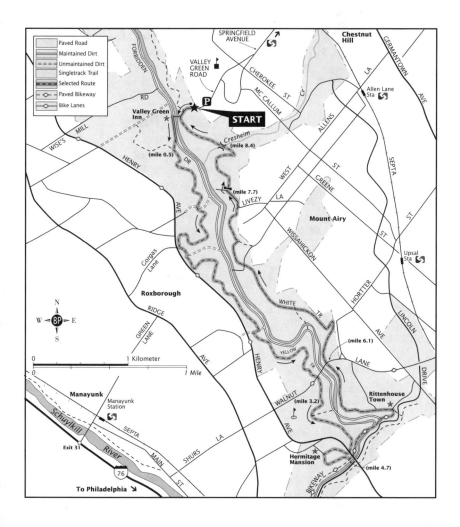

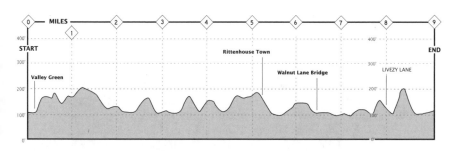

Wissahickon Gorge North Loop

Ride Specs

Start: From the Upper Valley Green parking area
Length: 5.5-mile loop
Approximate Riding Time: 1–1½ hours
Difficulty Rating: Moderate, with a few strenuous sections
Terrain: Singletrack, doubletrack, as well as dirt and paved roads
Elevation Gain: 365 feet
Land Status: Fairmount Park Commission/ Philadelpha City Parks
Nearest Town: Chestnut Hill, PA
Other Trail Users: Hikers, joggers, sightseers, and horseback riders

Getting There

From Philadelphia, PA: Follow I-76 west to I-476 north. Go north on I-476 to the Germantown Ave. exit. Go east on Germantown Ave. for 6.1 miles to Springfield Ave. Go right on Springfield Ave. and travel for 0.7 miles. Bear right on Valley Green Rd. and travel for 0.4 miles to a parking area on the right.
DeLorme: Pennsylvania Atlas & Gazetteer: Page 82 D-2

Train: From Market East Station take the SEPTA R8 Chestnut Hill West line to St Martin's Station. From the station exit turn left on St Martin's Lane and then turn right on Springfield Avenue and follow the driving directions to the Valley Green Inn.

Every mountain biker in the Philadelphia area should get involved with the Fairmount Park Commission to help keep access to the trails in the area secure for mountain bikers. This section of the park has some of the finest mountain biking trails in Eastern Pennsylvania. Cyclists should get involved with local groups like Friends of the Wissahickon to promote mountain biking in the park. With such a wide variety of trails, this is a wonderful place for riders of all abilities to pursue their sport.

Your ride starts at the Upper Valley Green parking area. Go down the gravel path to a trail junction. Go right and head up a short, steep hill. From the start, the ride is in your face with hard technical riding. At the 0.5-mile mark, your ride goes right. Follow the bike markers up a short hill. The ride then drops down past several waterbars. Patches of old growth can be seen throughout the park, with some trees more than 300 years old. At the 1.1-mile mark the trail becomes very rocky and you drop down to a dirt road.

Cross the road and climb up steep tread to the Indian statue. Mr. and Mrs. Charles W. Henry commissioned this statue as a tribute to the Lenni-Lenape Indians who inhabited the Wissahickon Gorge prior to its being settled by Europeans. The artist Massey Rhind carved the kneeling Lenape warrior in 1902. Though neither Rhind nor the Henrys chose the name, the statue is commonly called "Tedyuscung," after a famous Lenni-Lenape Chief.

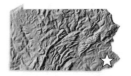

At the 2-mile mark the trail goes left and drops down to Wissahickon Creek. It then follows excellent singletrack along the creek to Bell Mills Road. Go left at Bell Mills Road and then left onto Forbidden Drive. Pedal to a wide, dirt, rocky trail on the right. Get ready to climb up the infamous Widowmaker Hill. The hill is very loose, rocky, and steep, so stay in low gear and hit it hard. The trail bolts left on good tread and at the 3.1-mile mark goes right up another short, steep hill. Veer left at the top of the hill and make a great downhill run to a bridge and Forbidden Drive. Turn right across the bridge and head up steep, smooth tread. Follow a wonderful singletrack trail up a short hill and then make a fast, rocky run down to Forbidden Drive. Bolt left at the bridge and cruise into the parking area.

Ride Information

🕔 Trail Contacts:
Fairmount Park Rangers, Philadelphia, PA; (215) 685-2172 • **Fairmount Park Commission Visitors Center,** JFK Blvd. and N. 16th St., Philadelphia, PA; (215) 685-2176 • **Wissahickon Cyclery**, 7837 Germantown Ave., Chestnut Hill, PA; (215) 248-2829 – they offer group rides

🕔 Schedule:
Sunrise to sunset

💲 Cost:
Free, but permits are required. Call the park rangers at (215) 685-0052 for an application. Expect at least two weeks for processing. Best time to apply is in December for the upcoming year.

❓ Local Information:
[See Ride 3 Fairmount Park/Forbidden Drive]

🔦 Local Attractions:
[See Ride 3 Fairmount Park/Forbidden Drive]

🍴 Restaurants:
[See Ride 3 Fairmount Park/Forbidden Drive]

👥 Organizations:
Friends of the Wissahickon, 8708 Germantown Ave., Philadelphia, PA (215) 247-0417 or www.fow.org

➖ Maps:
USGS maps: Germantown, PA • **Fairmount Park Commission/ Wissahickon Trail System map** - general map *available from the park office for $2; more detailed map available at Valley Green Inn for $5*

MilesDirections

0.0 START from the Upper Valley Green parking area. Pedal down to a trail at the end of the parking area. Continue straight to a trail junction.

0.2 Crank right and head up a short hill. Go down rocky tread and then up very steep, loose, and difficult rocky tread to a trail junction.

0.5 Go right on singletrack and head to a trail junction.

0.7 The trail drops down and travels past several waterbars.

1.1 The trail becomes very rocky.

1.3 Cross a road and then pedal up a steep hill to the Indian statue.

1.5 The Indian statue is on left. Continue straight on singletrack. Go past steep, rocky tread and drop down steep steps to a road.

1.9 Go right and pedal for a short distance to a trail on the left.

2.0 Drop left and head down excellent singletrack to Bell Mills Road.

2.6 Turn left and cross over a bridge to Forbidden Drive.

2.7 Go left and head to a second trail on the right—the Red, Yellow and Green Trail. Go right and head up a hideously steep, loose, rocky hill to a trail junction.

2.9 Go left and head down to trail junction.

3.1 Go right on singletrack and head to a trail junction.

3.5 Crank right and head up a steep hill to a trail junction.

3.7 Cruise left and head down tight singletrack to a trail junction.

4.1 Pedal right and head down fast singletrack to a bridge on the right.

4.2 Go right and ride across the bridge. Then, pedal up a steep hill on smooth tread to a trail junction.

4.6 Turn left and head down a fast singletrack run to Forbidden Drive.

5.0 Pedal straight to the Valley Green Bridge.

5.2 Turn left, go over the bridge, and head up to the parking area.

5.5 Hit the brakes. You're back at the parking area.

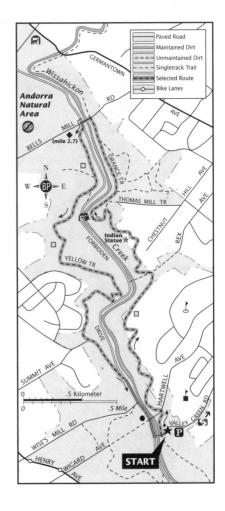

Cyclists passing under the "Climbers Rock."

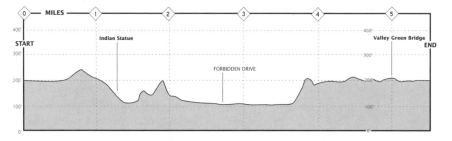

6

Pennypack Park

Ride Specs

Start: From the parking area at Pine Road
Length: 11.8 out-and-back
Approximate Riding Time: 1–2 hours
Difficulty Rating: Easy, with a few moderate hills
Terrain: Tight singletrack, doubletrack, gravel roads, and dirt roads. There are a number of short hills along the beautiful Pennypack Creek.
Elevation Gain: 86 feet
Land Status: Fairmount Park Commission/Philadelphia City Parks
Nearest Town: Philadelphia, PA
Other Trail Users: Hikers, joggers, sightseers, and equestrians

Getting There

From Philadelphia, PA: Go west on I-76 to the Roosevelt Blvd. exit. (U.S. 1) Go north on U.S. 1 to PA 232. Go north on PA 232 (Oxford Ave.) for 3.1 miles to Pine Road. Go right on Pine Road. Travel 1 mile to Pennypack Creek parking area on the right. *DeLorme: Pennsylvania Atlas & Gazetteer:* Page 82 D-3

⑨ **Train:** From Market East Station take the SEPTA R8 Fox Chase Line to Fox Chase Station. Exit the station and turn left on Rhawn Street then make a hard right to Pine Road at the intersection. Follow Pine Road for one mile to the Pennypack Creek parking area.

T his ride is another great outing within the city limits of Philadelphia. Popular with hikers, joggers, fisherman, equestrians, and cyclists, Pennypack Park is another jewel in the Fairmount Park Commission crown. The Pennypack Wilderness consists of aproximately 1,600 acres of woods, meadows, and wetlands, all of which are being restored and maintained by the Pennypack Watershed Association. The Pennypack Creek watershed contains over 55 square miles of forests, meadows, and wetlands. Winding its way past some of the more populated areas in Philadelphia, Pennypack Creek runs the length of the park and eventually drains into the Delaware River. Adjacent to the park and well worth a visit are the Pennypack Environmental Center on Verree Road and Fox Chase Farm on Pine Road.

Your ride starts at the parking area just off Pine Road. At the bathrooms, access the paved trail and then go left. Follow the Pennypack Trail (paved path) for a short distance. Go right and head over a bridge. Turn left at a trail junction and cruise on good tread to a trail junction at the 0.6-mile mark. Shoot left and head back down to the Pennypack Trail. Travel right under the bridge and pedal up to Shady Lane Road. Turn right and cross the bridge to a trail on the other side of Pennypack Creek. Go right and head down to a trail junction.

At the 1.0-mile mark, go right and follow the white blazes. For the next one-and-a-half miles the trail winds along Pennypack Creek on a beautiful, tight singletrack trail. At the 2.5-mile mark the ride goes right and heads down to Krewston Road. Turn right on Krewston Road and pedal to a trail on the left at the end of the bridge. Crank left up a short hill. At the top of the hill, turn left and follow a wide dirt trail back down to the Pennypack Trail. Turn right on the Pennypack Trail and go under the bridge. Make quick right just past the bridge onto a singletrack trail. The tread becomes rocky as you climb up a short, steep hill.

Ride Information

🕭 Trail Contacts:
Fairmount Park Rangers, Philadelphia, PA; (215) 685-2172 • **Fairmount Park Commission Visitors Center,** JFK Blvd. and N. 16th St., Philadelphia, PA; (215) 685-2176 • **Wissahickon Cyclery,** 7837 Germantown Ave., Chestnut Hill, PA; (215) 248-2829 – *they offer group rides*

🕔 Schedule:
Sunrise to sunset

❓ Local Information:
[see Ride 3: Fairmount Park/Forbidden Drive]

💡 Local Events/Attractions:
Pennypack Environmental Center, 8600 Verree Road, Philadelphia, PA;–*www.erols.com/hgabr/pec.html* • **Fox Chase Farm,** 8500 Pine Road, Philadelphia,PA; *www.erols.com /hgabr/farm.html – the last working farm in the Philadelphia, has been bringing in harvests and raising cattle for more than 300 years.*

The Franklin Institute Science Museum, Benjamin Franklin Parkway and 20th St. Philadelphia, PA; (215) 448-1200 or *www.fi.edu* • **Please Touch Museum,** 210 North 21st St., Philadelphia, PA; (215) 963-0666 or *www.libertynet.org/pleastch* • **The University of Pennsylvania Museum of Archaeology and Anthropology,** 33rd and Spruce Streets, Philadelphia, PA; (215) 898-4000 or *www.upenn.edu/museum* • **Afro-American Historical and Cultural Museum,** 701 Arch St., Philadelphia, PA; (215) 574-0380 or • *[see Ride 3: Fairmount Park/Forbidden Drive]*

🕼 Organizations:
Friends of Pennypack Park; (215) 934-PARK or *www.balford.com/fopp*

Ⓝ Maps:
USGS maps: Frankford, PA • **Fairmount Park Commission map –** general map *available from the park office for $2* • Pennypack Park map – *available at www.balford.com/fop*

Follow the trail down to a small stream crossing. Go left and follow the trail back to Pennypack Creek. Continue straight along Pennypack Creek to a concrete bridge going over Pennypack Creek at the 5.9-mile mark. Turn around here and retrace your route back to Krewstown Road.

At the 9.0-mile mark continue straight over Krewstown Road to a singletrack trail on the other side of the road. Drop back down to the Pennypack Trail. From here the ride goes left up a steep, rocky horse path. At the 9.8-mile mark you cross a small wooden bridge and follow the White Trail. Continue straight, following the White Trail and avoiding all side trails, to a horse path just past the Shady Lane Bridge. At the 11.1-mile mark go left up the Horse Trail and head back to the parking area.

MilesDirections

0.0 START from the parking area. Just behind the bathrooms is a paved bike path. Mileage starts here. Follow the bike path over the bridge to trail on the right.

0.2 Turn right and head up a short hill to a trail junction.

0.3 Turn left onto a wide dirt trail.

0.4 Continue straight and pass a spur trail.

0.6 The trail veers left down to the Pennypack Trail. Following the Pennypack Trail to the Shady Lane Bridge. Go west on Shady Lane Ave. to the other side of Pennypack Creek. Turn right and go down to a trail junction.

1.0 Turn right and follow a beautiful singletrack trail along Pennypack Creek.

1.7 The trail continues to follow along Pennypack Creek.

2.5 Go right and head down past a cut area to Krewston Road. Turn right on Krewston Road and ride to trail on the left just past the bridge.

2.8 Go left and then right up a steep, short hill to trail junction. Go left on a wide dirt trail.

3.1 Continue straight and pass a spur trail.

3.2 Continue straight down rocky tread to the Pennypack Trail. Go right on the paved Pennypack Trail and head to just beyond the bridge. The ride now turns right onto a singletrack trail and goes up a short, steep, rocky hill.

4.1 Go left on wide tread and head back toward Pennypack Creek.

4.2 Continue straight along the Pennypack Creek.

5.9 Arrive at a concrete bridge and go over Pennypack Creek. Turn around here and retrace your route back to the Krewston Bridge.

9.0 Go straight across Krewston Road to trail. Drop down to Pennypack Trail.

9.1 Go left on the horse path, up steep tread.

9.2 A spur trail goes left. Continue straight down to Pennypack Trail.

9.8 Cross over the Pennypack Trail. Continue following the White Trail.

10.3 Continue straight on the White Trail and go under the Shady Lane Bridge.

11.1 Go left and follow the singletrack trail.

11.5 Go right.

11.8 Arrive back at the parking area.

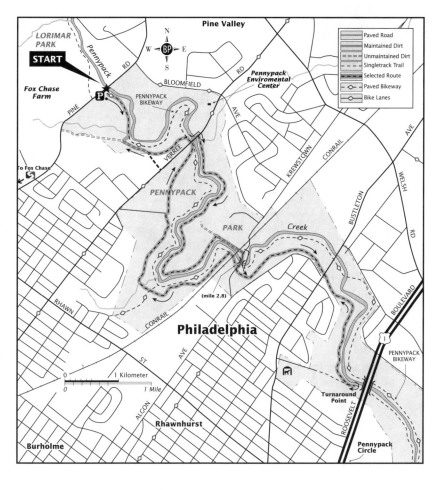

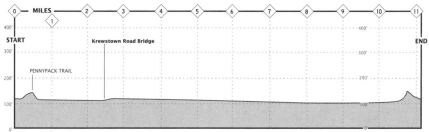

Ridley Creek State Park

Ride Specs

Start: From parking area # 15, near the park headquarters
Length: 5-mile loop
Approximate Riding Time: 45 min.–1 hour
Difficulty Rating: Easy, along a paved path with no technical difficulty
Terrain: Paved road and asphalt-paved trail
Elevation Gain: 245 feet
Land Status: Pennsylvania State Parks
Nearest Town: Media, PA
Other Trail Users: Hikers, joggers, and fishermen

Getting There

From Media, PA: Travel to U.S. 1 (Media Bypass) to PA 252. Travel north on PA 252 (Providence Road) for 2.4 miles. Turn left on Gradyville Road and drive for 1.1 miles. Bear left onto Sandy Flash. Drive for 1.5 miles and then turn right. Following signs to parking area #15.
DeLorme: Pennsylvania Atlas & Gazetteer: Page 95 A-7

T his is a great ride for all ability levels. Beginners will appreciate that the park is closed to motor vehicles and consists of paved roads and asphalt paths. Parents will be glad to see that there are a number of spots to stop and take a break with the kids. More advanced riders will probably benefit most from doing multiple loops. The expert riders have an opportunity to really push the big chain ring and get a great workout. For the majority of riders the tranquil setting along Ridley Creek is more than enough reason to visit. The only thing that bothers me is that bikes are not allowed on the parks numerous miles of dirt trails. With 2,607 acres in Ridley Creek State Park, that's a lot of park that you're missing. I jog these dirt trails all the time and rarely see other trail users. Mountain bikers in the area should try and get together with park officials and see if some kind of arrangement could be reached to allow even limited use of the many dirt trails.

This ride travels through some of the most beautiful terrain around Philadelphia. As always, be courteous to other trailusers and keep your speed in check when pedaling around hikers and joggers. From the parking lot you'll want to head to the asphalt trail west of the parking area. Go past a yellow gate, then turn left onto Forge Road. The Tyler Arboretum is on your right. Take note of the large stand of pines planted by the original owners as you pass by. On the left are some open fields which are gradually being reclaimed by trees. Drop down a steep hill to Ridley Creek, at the 1.3-mile mark. Go right here and head down to the old Sycamore Mills townsite.

Philadelphia Firsts

- *Oldest continuously occupied street in the Western Hemisphere: Elfreth's Alley, since 1728.*
- *First art school and art museum: the Museum of American Art of the Pennsylvania Academy of the Fine Arts, founded 1805.*
- *Oldest theater in continuous use in the English-speaking world: Walnut Street Theater, since 1809.*
- *The Philadelphia Orchestra was the first orchestra to appear in a motion picture (1937), on television (1948) and to tour China (1973).*
- *First city to guarantee religious freedom, beginning in 1682.*
- *First African-American church: Mother Bethel A.M.E. Church, established 1794.*
- *First zoo in America: Philadelphia Zoo, chartered in 1859 and opened in 1874.*
- *First July 4th event: 1776. Still a big celebration every year with the 12-day Sunoco Welcome America! festival.*
- *First Thanksgiving Day Parade: 1919.*
- *First botanical garden: Bartram's Garden, opened 1728.*
- *First stock exchange: Philadelphia Stock Exchange, 1790.*
- *First international-style skyscraper: PSFS Building, 1932. This was also the first totally air-conditioned building in America.*
- *First and oldest hospital: Pennsylvania Hospital, opened 1751.*
- *First World's Fair in America: Centennial International Exhibition, 1876.*

Sycamore Mills was once a thriving colonial village. The town's gristmill was built in 1718 and became the lifeblood of the village. Farmers from the area would bring grain to the mill to be process and sold to outlets in the Philadelphia area. The village, at one time, was home to a smithy, wheelwright shops, mill offices, and a library. Remnants of the mill and village can be seen on both sides of the creek. Continue straight down to a gate and a parking lot. From here, turn around and follow Sycamore Mills Road back along Ridley Creek.

At the 2.5-mile mark, those who like to fish may care to notice the small road that leads to Ridley Creek and a fishing platform, which is handicap accessible. At the 2.6-mile mark the road goes left away from the creek. Climb up a short hill through stands of old growth oaks, hickories, and walnut trees. Pass under a small bridge and then pass the park office on the right. At the 4.2-mile mark the ride goes left and heads up a paved path through a beautiful open meadow. Continue straight to Forge Road and the parking area, which is on the left, to complete your ride.

If you're looking to extend your stay at the park, check out the working colonial plantation in the northern part of the park. Here you have a chance to see how life was on a Quaker farm in the 1700s. The farm has period-dressed interpreters and an assortment of animals typically found on a Quaker farm. There's a small fee of $3.00 for adults and $1.50 for children and seniors. Also be sure to check out the before-mentioned Tyler Arboretum, which houses over 1,000 varieties of native and exotic trees and shrubs on 700 acres of former farmland. The arboretum's 20 miles of hiking-only trails crisscross through old farm sites, streams, and woodlands.

Ride Information

● Trail Contacts:
Ridley Creek State Park, Sycamore Mills Road, Media, PA; (610) 892-3900 • **Cycle Fit,** 320 South Chester Road, Wallingford, PA; (610) 876-9450 – *they offer local group rides*

● Schedule:
8:00 A.M. to sunset

● Local Information:
Delaware County Convention and Visitors Bureau, 200 E. State St., Ste. 100, Media, PA ; (610) 565-3983 or 1-800-343-3983 or *www.libertynet.org/delcocvb*

● Local Events/Attractions:
Colonial Pennsylvania Plantation, Ridley Creek State Park, Media; (610) 566-1725; *www.de.psu.edu/cpp/index.htm* • **Tyler Arboretum,** 515 Painter Road, Lima, PA; (610) 566-5431 or *www.vol.it/mirror/rhododendron/abouttyl.html*

● Maps:
Ridley Creek State Park/PA State Parks maps – *available from the park office*

MilesDirections

0.0 START from the parking area. Go left on Forge Road. Obey all signs for cyclists.
0.2 Tyler Arboretum is on the right. Continue straight.
1.3 Go right on Sycamore Mills Road.
1.6 Arrive at the old Sycamore Mills townsite. Turn around here and follow Sycamore Mills Road along Ridley Creek.

2.5 Continue straight. (A gravel road goes right to a handicapped-accessible platform.)
2.6 The road angles left, away from the creek.
3.4 Continue straight. (A gravel path leads to the park office.)
4.2 Go left and follow the paved path.
5.0 Arrive back at the parking area.

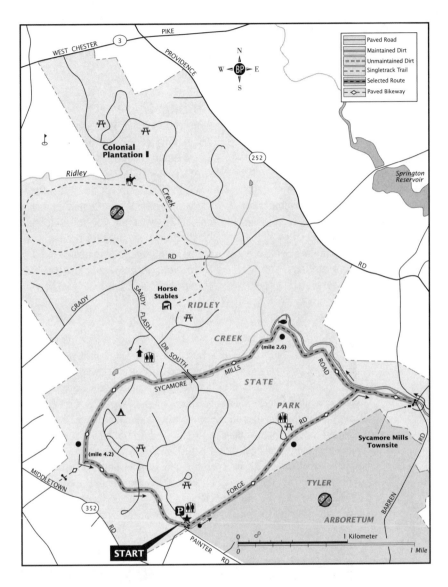

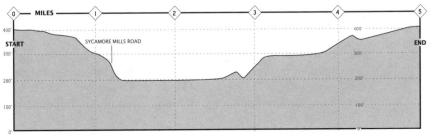

Valley Forge National Historical Park

Ride Specs

Start: From the Washington Headquarters parking area
Length: 6.7-mile loop
Approximate Riding Time: 45 min.–1 hour
Difficulty Rating: Easy, with no technical sections or major hill climbs
Terrain: Asphalt path
Elevation Gain: 432 feet
Land Status: National Park Service
Nearest Town: King of Prussia, PA
Other Trail Users: Hikers and joggers

Getting There

From Philadelphia, PA: Drive west on I-76 to King of Prussia and U.S. 202. Travel south on U.S. 202 to U.S. 422 west. Follow U.S. 422 west for 1.6 miles to PA 23. Go left on PA 23. Pass the Valley Forge Visitor Center. Continue on PA 23 west for 2.4 miles to the Washington Headquarters parking area on the right. Park here to begin the ride.
DeLorme: Pennsylvania Atlas & Gazetteer: Page 81 D-7

T his 6.7-mile loop is not so much a bike ride as it is a journey through history. Valley Forge, aside from its historic significance, is a beautiful spot for hiking, jogging, biking, kite-flying, and even cross-county skiing. Still, the main attraction here is undoubtedly the winter encampment of General George Washington.

While passing through the park, one can only begin to imagine the conditions Washington's troops had to endure that winter of 1777-78. Small, crowded huts and meager rations, combined with a harsh and deadly winter, made camp-life almost unbearable. Over 2,000 men perished from typhoid, pneumonia, dysentery, and other diseases over the course of the winter. You can spend the better part of a day trying to see what the entire park has to offer. My suggestion would be to ride the bike path, bring a lock for your bike, and stop at the many historical sights along the path.

Your ride starts from the parking lot at Washington's Headquarters. From the parking area, go left and head up the bike path toward the visitor center. Please obey all signs and stay on your side of the path. This path sees a lot of foot traffic, so be courteous to other trailusers. Rolling terrain brings you to Pennsylvania 23 and a statue of Von Steuben. Incidentally, Von Steuben was a former Prussian army veteran who was appointed Acting Inspector General by General Washington. He took the dispirited troops and trained them in Prussian military techniques, and within 6 months, the troops were better disciplined, battle-ready, and reinvigorated. Follow the path past the Washington Memorial Chapel and then make a nice downhill run past the nature center on the right to a paved road. Cross over the road and continue up to the visitor center.

Beyond the visitor center, the path cuts through an open field. Be on the lookout for grazing deer. At the 2.8-mile mark, you pass some soldier huts. Stop here and check out the conditions the soldiers had to live in during that harsh winter. Continue straight to the National Memorial Arch, where the path goes to Wayne's Woods. At the 4.8-mile mark your ride goes right and passes several picnic areas and roads. Continue along an open field and follow the path back up to the Von Steuben statue and Pennsylvania 23. Cross the road and head back to the parking area.

MilesDirections

0.0 START by pedaling back up to PA 23. Go left on the well-marked walking/bike path. Begin a gradual climb up, passing several monuments and soldier huts to PA 23.

0.7 Cross PA 23 (with caution) and veer left onto the bike path, passing the Von Steuben statue.

1.2 Washington Memorial Chapel is on the left; continues straight.

1.3 Cross over a paved road.

1.8 Roll down a steep hill. Control your speed through this section.

2.1 Cross a road and make a short climb up to the visitor center.

2.4 The trail veers left past the visitor center and then breaks out into an open field. Be on the lookout for deer in this area.

2.8 Reach a cluster of soldier cabins.

3.3 National Memorial Arch is on the left. The trail goes right to Wayne's Woods and a picnic area.

4.0 Arrive at Wayne's Woods.

4.8 The trail splits. Go right and head up a short hill. The path then drops down to a picnic area. Use caution through this area. There are many paved road crossings and stop signs.

5.9 Arrive back at the Von Steuben statue. Cross over PA 23 to the bike path. Go left on the bike path and head down to Washington Headquarters parking area.

6.6 Go right into the parking area.

Ride Information

❋ Trail Contacts:
Valley Forge National Historical Park, PA 23 and N. Gulph Rd., Valley Forge, PA (610) 783-1077 or *www.nps.gov/vafo – visitor center is open 9:00 A.M. to 5:00 P.M.*

◷ Schedule:
6:30 A.M. to sunset

❓ Local Information:
The Valley Forge Convention and Visitors Bureau, 600 W. Germantown Pike, Ste. 130, Plymouth Meeting, PA (610) 834-1550 or *www.valleyforge.org*

♀ Local Events/Attractions:
Schuylkill Center for Environmental Education, 8480 Hagy's Mill Road,

Philadelphia, PA; (215) 482-7300 or *www.schuylkillcenter.org – offers a variety of outdoor and indoor natural history and environmental science programs* • **Hopewell Furnace National Historic Site,** 2 Mark Bird Lane, Elverson, PA; (610) 582-8773; *www.nps.gov/hofu/newweb/home.ht ml* • **King of Prussia Mall**, U.S. 202 and I-76, King of Prussia, PA – one of the worlds largest

Ⓝ Maps:
USGS maps: Valley Forge, PA • **Valley Forge National Historical Park** map – *available from the park office*

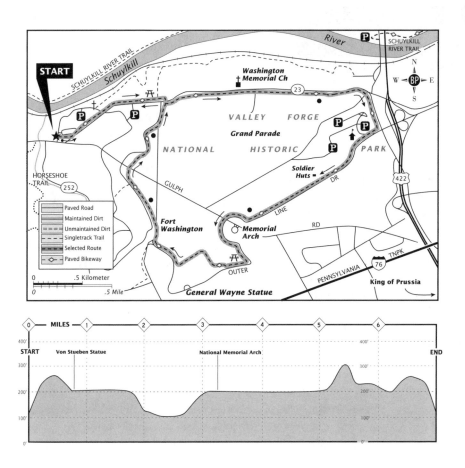

Schuylkill River Trail

Ride Specs

Start: From the Betzwood Bridge parking area

Length: 6.3-mile loop

Approximate Riding Time: 45 min.–1 hour

Difficulty Rating: Easy, due to the non-hilly terrain and lack of technical difficulty

Terrain: Wonderful riding through open fields and dense woods, along the scenic Schuylkill River Trail

Elevation Gain: 229 feet

Land Status: National Park Service

Nearest Town: King of Prussia, PA

Other Trail Users: Hikers, joggers, and horseback riders

Getting There

From Philadelphia, PA: Drive west on I-76 to King of Prussia and U.S. 202. Travel south on U.S. 202 to U.S. 422 west. Follow U.S. 422 west for 2.2 miles to PA 363. Go left on PA 363 (west). Drive 0.3 miles to Betzwood Lane and turn right into the Betzwood Bridge parking area. *DeLorme: Pennsylvania Atlas & Gazetteer:* Page 81 D-7

This is one of the best-kept secrets in the Philadelphia area. Part of Valley Forge National Historical Park, the ride is located across the Schuylkill River from the main attractions of the park—hence, it sees very little traffic except from hikers, joggers, and cyclists. This particular portion of the park is where General George Washington positioned his commissary. Out of these stone buildings blacksmiths, leather workers, wheelwrights, and other skilled laborers produced wagons, cannonballs, muskets, ammunition, and other goods to support Washington's encampment.

The Schuylkill River played an important role in Washington's strategy during the winter of 1777-78. The river was a major supply route and was also the northern defense for Philadelphia. Food was shipped on the river from farms in the outlying area to feed the soldiers at the encampment. The clay from the riverbanks was used as mortar in the wooden huts used by the soldiers.

Your ride starts at the parking area near the Betzwood Bridge. From the parking area, go east on a wide gravel path. After a short distance, make a left onto an old railroad grade. The paved path continues straight under the Betzwood Bridge and can be ridden all the way to the Art Museum in Philadelphia. Your ride follows the old railroad grade past some power lines. Pedal under a dense canopy of trees to a gate. Pass the gate and make a left onto a gravel singletrack trail which leads down

to an open field. Here, on a late evening ride, I must have spotted 25 whitetail deer grazing. Go right here and follow the trail along a farmer's field to a bridge.

Cross the bridge over a small stream, leaving the woods. Pass the Washington's Commissary on the right. Take a left onto a wide, gravel road. Pass a gate and then continue straight to a singletrack trail that lies just before a private home. At the 3.2-mile mark, your ride drops down to the Schuylkill River and the Schuylkill River Trail. Go left on this well-maintained trail and pass several bridges. If it's hot out, here's a chance to enjoy the shade as you pedal under the canopy of large oak, walnut, and sycamore trees. Many benches are located along the Schuylkill River Trail if you want to stop and enjoy the tranquility of the river.

At the 5.1-mile marker you come to a large rock marking the site of General Sullivan's Bridge. Sullivan built the bridge to allow for a quick evacuation for the troops in case of a British siege. The bridge didn't last long; the British destroyed it the following year. The ride continues straight, past an old stone house in ruin and a locked gate, into the parking area.

MilesDirections

0.0 START from the Betzwood Bridge parking area. Pick up the paved bike trail and make an immediate left onto an old, grassy railroad grade–the tracks and ties have been removed. Continue straight to intersection.

0.7 Arrive at a trail junction. Your ride continues straight.

0.8 Reach the power lines. Continue straight as the trail passes under a thick canopy of trees.

1.4 Pass a gate. Go 500 ft. to a gravel singletrack trail on the left. Take the left and pass another gate. Fly down to the power lines.

1.7 Come to a trail junction at the power lines. Go right on the Hikers Trail. The Hikers Trail weaves alongside an open field to a bridge.

2.3 Cross over a small bridge to the Commissary Trail. The Commissary Trail goes through an open meadow with a large stone buildings on the right. This was the location of General Washington's Commissary.

2.6 Arrive at a gravel road. Go left on the road and follow it to trail junction, just before a private home.

3.2 Go left and head down the Connector Trail to the Schuylkill River Trail.

3.4 Go left on the Schuylkill River Trail. Follow the trail over several well-maintained footbridges.

5.1 A spur trail goes left at a large rock, marking the site of the General Sullivan's Bridge. Continue straight on smooth tread.

6.0 Cross over a small bridge and pass an old stone building on the left.

6.1 Come to a locked gate. Continue straight to the parking area.

6.3 Arrive at the parking area.

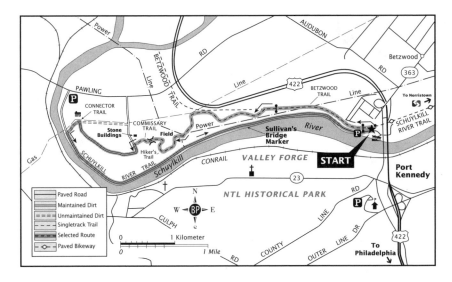

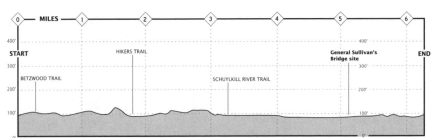

Ride Information

📞 Trail Contacts:
Valley Forge National Historical Park, PA 23 and N. Gulph Rd., Valley Forge, PA (610) 783-1077 or *www.nps.gov/vafo* – visitor center is open 9:00 A.M. to 5:00 P.M.

⏰ Schedule:
6:30 A.M. to sunset

❓ Local Information:
[see Ride 8: Valley Forge National Historical Park]

📍 Local Events/Attractions:
[see Ride 8: Valley Forge National Historical Park]

🗺 Maps:
USGS maps: Valley Forge, PA • **Valley Forge National Historical Park map** – *available from the park office*

10

Tohickon Creek

Ride Specs

Start: From the High Rocks/Climbers parking area

Length: 3.8-mile loop

Approximate Riding Time: 30 min.–1 hour

Difficulty Rating: Moderate, with some very technical sections on rocky tread

Terrain: Singletrack, doubletrack, paved and pack-dirt roads

Elevation Gain: 325 feet

Land Status: Pennsylvania State Parks/ Bucks County Parks

Nearest Town: Doylestown, PA

Other Trail Users: Hikers, joggers, rock climbers, and horseback riders

Getting There

From Doylestown, PA: Travel north on PA 611 for 3.2 miles to Silo Hill Road. Go right on Silo Hill Road and drive to Point Pleasant Pike. Go left on Point Pleasant Pike and travel to the village of Point Pleasant, PA. At Point Pleasant go left on River Road (PA 32) and drive to Cafferty Road. Go left onto Cafferty Road and travel 1.8 miles to Tory Road. Go left on Tory Road and travel 1 mile to where the road forks. Go left onto a gravel road and drive to the High Rocks parking area on the right. **DeLorme: Pennsylvania Atlas & Gazetteer:** Page 82 A-3

This short loop, one of the few trails open to mountain bikers in Bucks County, is a wonderful ride past some spectacular terrain above Tohickon Creek. The creek gets its name from the Lenni-Lenape Indian word "To-Hick-Hanne," meaning "deer bone creek." To this day, deer and other wildlife are abundant in the area. The creek is very popular with whitewater enthusiasts and offers a very challenging course during times of high water. A boat launch is located at the bridge over the creek in Ralph Stover Park. Noted author James A. Michener donated land known as the "High Rocks" to the park system. These shale cliffs above the creek are very popular with rock climbers and offer challenging fifth-class climbing to experienced climbers.

Your ride starts at the High Rocks parking area. Cross the road and go left onto the white-and-red-blazed trail. At mile 0.1 there's an overlook from the cliffs of Tohickon Creek. The cliffs are over 200 feet high here, so be careful. Many injuries and deaths have occurred in this area. There is a safety fence along the trail to protect people from any missteps. Continue straight, following the red and white blazes, past some rocky tread on tight singletrack.

Beginning at the 1.4-mile mark the trail becomes very rocky, as you pedal past a stand of hemlock trees. Crank up a short, steep hill to a trail junction. Go right and follow the red and white blazes to a trail junction at a gate. Go left at the gate and then left again. Follow a road through the camping area. Continue straight to a trail located between campsite 21 and 22. Follow the sweet single-track back into the woods past a short, rocky, technical section. The trail weaves back up to a trail junction at the 3.1-mile mark. Go right here, still on nice singletrack. The trail goes right again at the 3.4-mile mark. Pedal past a field following tight singletrack up to Tory Road. Go left on Tory Road and head back to the parking area and your car.

This ride is very short, but combined with all the other activities in the area, it's well worth the effort to locate. While in the area, be sure to visit one of Bucks County's many fine restaurants and quaint bed and breakfasts.

Ride Information

🔋 Trail Contacts:
Ralph Stover State Park Office, 6011 State Park Rd., Pipersville, PA; (610) 982-5560 • **Bike Line**, 73 Old Dublin Pike, Doylestown, PA; (215) 348-8015 or *www.bikeline.com*

🕐 Schedule:
8.00 A.M. to sunset

❓ Local Information:
Bucks County Conference and Visitors Bureau, 115 W. Court St., Doylestown, PA; (215) 345-4552 or 1-800-836-BUCK or *www.bctc.org*

📍 Local Events/Attractions:
Mercer Museum, 84 S. Pine St., Doylestown, PA; (215) 345-0210 or *www.libertynet.org/bchs/MMuseum.h tm* • **Moravian Pottery and Tile Works**, 130 Swamp Rd., Doylestown, PA (215) 345-6722; *www.libertynet.org /bchs/ TileWork.htm*

• **Peddler's Village,** at the junction of U.S. 202 & PA 263, Lahaska, PA; (215) 794-4000 or *www.peddlersvillage.com – over 70 specialty shops and restaurants* • **James A. Michener Art Museum**, 138 S. Pine St., Doylestown, PA; (215) 340-9800; *www.michenerartmuseum.org*

😊 Accommodations:
Six rental cabins are available for weekly rental from the second Friday in April until late December. Daily, half-week, and weekly rentals are available for the spring and fall season. Contact the park office for cabin information.

⊗ Maps:
USGS maps: Bucks County, PA • **Ralph Stover State Park/PA State Parks** – *available from the park office*

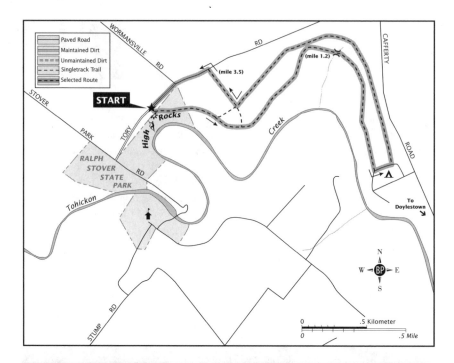

Map Legend:
- Paved Road
- Maintained Dirt
- Unmaintained Dirt
- Singletrack Trail
- Selected Route

START

High Rocks

WORMANSVILLE RD
RD
CAFFERTY
STOVER
TORY
PARK
RD
RALPH STOVER STATE PARK
Tohickon
Creek
(mile 3.5)
(mile 1.2)
ROAD
To Doylestown
STUMP RD

N
W ⬤BP⬤ E
S

0 .5 Kilometer
0 .5 Mile

MilesDirections

0.0 START from the High Rocks/Climbers parking lot and cross over the road to a well-marked singletrack trail. Go left on tight tread.

0.1 To the right is an overlook of Tohickon Creek.

0.3 The tread becomes rocky. Go right at the fork.

0.8 The trail becomes very rocky as you head up a short, steep hill.

1.0 Pedal past a stone wall.

1.2 Cross over a small stone bridge.

1.4 The trail becomes very rocky—there's no shame in pushing here.

1.5 Crank up a short, steep hill.

1.7 Trail forks; go right.

1.8 Go left at the gate. Hug the edge of an open field and turn left onto a road leading through the campground.

2.1 Pick up a singletrack trail in between campsites 21 and 22. The trail curves past some great tight singletrack sections.

3.1 Go right.

3.4 Go right and head up into a field.

3.5 Reach Tory Road. Go left and head back to the parking area.

3.8 Arrive back at the parking area. Go do a couple loops for a great workout.

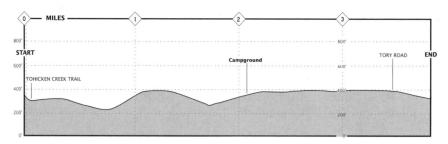

MILES

START
TOHICKEN CREEK TRAIL
Campground
TORY ROAD
END

Wharton State Forest

11

Ride Specs

Start: From Batsto Village parking area

Length: 11.9 miles

Approximate Riding Time: 1½ hours

Difficulty Rating: Easy, with no hills and no technical difficulties

Terrain: Doubletrack and soft, sandy roads

Elevation Gain: 322 feet

Land Status: New Jersey Department of Environmental Protection

Nearest Town: Hammonton, NJ

Other Trail Users: Hikers and 4-wheelers

Getting There

From Philadelphia, PA: Travel east on 1-76 across the Walt Whitman Bridge to NJ 42. Follow NJ 42 to the Atlantic City Expressway. Take the Expressway to exit 28. Go east on NJ 54 to NJ 542. Take NJ 542 and follow the signs to Wharton State Forest and the Batsto Village parking area. *DeLorme: New Jersey Atlas & Gazetteer: Page 64, E8*

Wharton State Forest's 110,000 acres form the largest single tract of land in the New Jersey State Park System, but Wharton is part of a much larger system, one that stretches over one million acres in southern and central New Jersey, an area known as the Pine Barrens. Swedish emigrants gave the region its misleading name because it wouldn't support familiar crops, but the Pine Barrens are far from barren. Within this lengthy ecological belt are 850 plant species and over 350 species of birds, mammals, reptiles, and amphibians. Amidst this diversity are rare, and in some cases threatened, plants and animals, such as the curly grass fern, the broom crowberry, the timber rattlesnake, and the Pine Barrens tree frog. The ecological value of the Pinelands prompted Congress in 1978 to create the New Jersey Pineland Reserve—America's first National Reserve. In 1983 the United Nations acknowledged the Pinelands global significance by designating it an International Biosphere Reserve.

Travel back 10,000 years and you wouldn't have recognized the place. But that's when humans came on the scene. The region's first inhabitants enjoyed a far less hospitable, almost tundra-like environment. It wasn't until about 5000 BC that the region took on characteristics we'd deem familiar. Just prior to European invasion, in the mid-to-late 1600s, the Pinelands were inhabited by the Lenni-Lenape Indians, who thrived on the areas vast fish and wildlife reserve. The first European settlers stuck to the coast and were generally whalers and shipbuilders. It wasn't until the 1760s that the Europeans turned to the interior for their livelihood, first looking to bog iron deposits. The area's abundance of raw materials made paper and glass production profitable businesses. By the mid-1800s, however, the various rural industries had declined dramatically—to the point where entire villages had vanished. Fortunately, railroads began laying track through Barrens, forever altering the economic landscape. Berry production became, and still is, a major Pinelands industry. And, of course, the rails brought tourism. It was soon after the arrival of the railroads that coastal resorts began springing up. Today, berry production and recreational tourism make up the bulk of the Pinelands' economy.

Batsto Village, a former bog iron and glass making industrial center, is a wonderful example of an early Pine Barrens village. Consisting of 33 historic buildings, the village includes a restored post office, gristmill, sawmill, mansion, and general store. How Batsto Village managed to survive, where other villages simply disap-

peared, is in part thanks to Joseph Wharton, a Philadelphia businessman, who purchased the land in 1876. When Wharton died in 1909, his holdings consisted of about 96,000 acres. In 1954 the state purchased the land and named the newly formed state forest after Wharton whose former property comprises the better part of the park.

Your ride starts at the parking area at Batsto Village. From the parking area, pedal back to Batsto-Washington Road. Your mileage starts here. Go left on the paved road and pass the Batona Trail (off-limits to cyclists). Continue straight past the fire tower to where the road bends to the right. Continue straight on the soft, sandy, washboard road. At the 2.3-mile marker go left into the woods. At mile 2.5 there's a four-way intersection. Go right on the firm tread and head to another four-way intersection.

Ride Information

● Trail Contacts:
Wharton State Forest Park Office, RD # 9 Batsto, Hammonton, NJ (609) 561-0024 – *open 9:00 A.M. to 4:00 P.M.* • **Pro Pedals Bike Shop,** 682 S. White Horse Pike, Hammonton, NJ; (609) 561-3030 or *www.propedals.com*

● Schedule:
Sunrise to sunset

● Fees/Permits:
$3 parking fee during the summer weekends

● Local Information:
New Jersey Pinelands Commission, 15 Springfield Rd., New Lisbon, NJ; (609) 894-7300; *www.state.nj.us/ pinelands – they oversee the management of the entire Pinelands preserve*

● Local Events/Attractions:
Batsto Village Historic Site, on NJ

542 in Wharton State Forest, Hammonton, NJ (609) 561-0024 • **Edwin B. Forsythe National Wildlife Refuge,** Great Creek Rd., Oceanville, NJ; (609) 652-1665 – *protects more than 40,000 acres of southern New Jersey Coastal Habitats and tidal wetlands.*

● Accommodations:
Campgrounds and cabins are available in the park. Call the park office at (609) 561-0024 for reservations.

● Other Resources:
A field guide to the Pine Barrens of New Jersey. By Boyd, HP. Plexus Publishing, Medford, NJ. 1991. 423 pages.

● Maps
Wharton State Forest, *New Jersey Department of Environmental Protection* – *available at the park office*

When you're in the remote area of the park, you begin to get a feel for the size of the Pine Barrens. It seems as if the pine trees and scrub oaks go on forever—they do! At the 2.7-mile marker, go left on a straight, soft sand road. Follow this to a beautiful open area with a four-way intersection at mile 4.0. Here is a great place to stop and enjoy some snacks. At the 4.7-mile marker, go left and follow an overgrown doubletrack road. Pass through a beautiful stand of pitch pines. At mile 5.6, the trail terminates at a flat white sand area. Turn around here and return to the 4.7-mile mark. Once you've reached this mark, go left and then right on good tread leading up to an intersection at a wide sandy road. Your odometer should read 7.3 miles. From this point, retrace your route back to Batsto Village and the parking area.

This is a complex area. Many roads lead nowhere and even the most experienced cyclist can get lost. I have given you only a small sampling of the roads open to mountain biking. If you're willing to explore the area, go for it. Just keep in mind that most of the roads that are fine for hiking and four-wheeling are horrendous for mountain biking because of the soft, inches-deep sugar-sand. For all you hikers out there, the 50-mile Batona Trail connects Lebanon, Wharton, and Bass River state forests for a beautiful hiking tour through the heart of the Pine Barrens.

MilesDirections

0.0 START from the parking area. Pedal out to Batsto-Washington Road. Go left on the paved Batsto-Washington Road.

0.2 Take notice of Batona Trail as it crosses the road. The trail is off-limits to bikes.

0.4 A large fire tower is off to the left.

0.9 The paved road ends and the road turns too sandy, washboards tread.

2.3 Go left onto a flat, soft, sand road.

2.5 Turn right to a four-way intersection.

2.7 Turn left on a good flat, pine covered sand road to a four-way intersection at an open area.

4.0 Continue straight to spur road on the left.

4.7 Veer left here onto an overgrown, doubletrack road. Follow this to a flat, white, sandy area where the trail ends. Go back to the trail junction at 4.0 miles.

6.5 Go left, then right on good tread up to wide, sand road. Feel free to explore any of the roads in this area. I turn around here and retrace my route back to the village.

11.9 Arrive back at the entrance to Batsto Village.

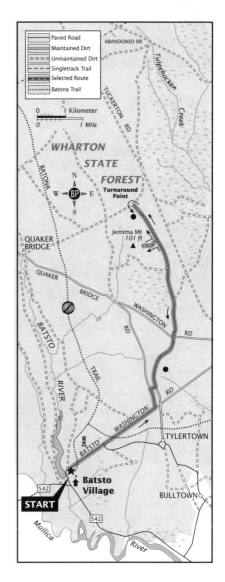

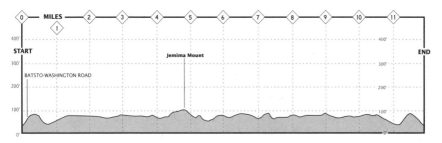

Lebanon State Forest

Ride Specs

Start: From the park office
Length: 11 miles
Approximate Riding Time: 1½ hours
Difficulty Rating: Easy, with no hills and no technical difficulties
Terrain: Singletrack, doubletrack, and soft, sandy roads
Elevation Gain: 129 feet
Land Status: New Jersey Department of Environmental Protection
Nearest Town: Medford, NJ
Other Trail Users: Hikers, birdwatchers, school groups, and fishermen

Getting There

From Philadelphia, PA: Travel east on 1-76 across the Walt Whitman Bridge to I-295. Go north on I-295 to NJ 70 east. Follow NJ 70 to NJ 72 south. Take NJ 72 south for 1 mile to the park entrance on the left. Park at the park office. *DeLorme: New Jersery Atlas & Gazetteer:* Page 56, D12

L ebanon State Forest once supported one of the largest stands of Atlantic white cedar on the East Coast, and then in stepped Lebanon Glass Works. Production at the glass works began in 1851 and proved quite successful, thanks to the wealth of natural resources in the area: quality sand and wood. But within 16 years, the majority of the trees in the area had been harvested and the land was nearly bare. Having depleted the cedar resource, the furnace was abandoned. The state of New Jersey slowly began to acquire the land that in 1908 would become Lebanon State Forest. Through natural regeneration, reforestation by the Civilian Conservation Corp, and proper management practices, the site has now begun to rebound. Today Lebanon State Forest protects a robust and diverse forest of oak, maple, pine, gum, and Atlantic white cedar. Deer, wild turkey, fox, and raccoon are just a few animals that make Lebanon State Forest their home.

Your ride starts just past the park office on a small connector trail. Cross over Four-Mile Road to the well-marked Red Trail and continue straight to a gate. Pedal on smooth tread following the Red Trail. As you make your way to a dirt road, the trail curves past stands of beautiful pitch pine. Go left on the wide dirt road and pass a swamp area with dense stands of Atlantic white cedar. At the 1.8-mile mark, your ride goes right onto a gravel hiking/biking path. Continue following the red blazes. At the 2.2-mile mark the trail splits and you go left on the well-marked White Trail. Follow the White Trail past a gate and a four-way intersection. The trail goes left at mile 2.9, onto a very sandy road. Don't worry, the tread becomes firmer in a short distance.

The Jersey Devil

No story about the Pine Barrens would be complete without mentioning the Jersey Devil. Legend has that a beast with a forked tail, horns, and bat wings was born to a Mrs. Leeds in the year 1735. Known as the Jersey Devil, the beast is believed still to terrorize the local inhabitants of the Pine Barrens, doing everything from burning barns to causing cows to dry up. Many are convinced he affects the weather. Anyone who's spent any time camping in the Pinelands is sure to have heard tales around the campfire about the Jersey Devil. The Devil is so famous, in fact, that New Jersey made him the state demon in 1939—and you know the competition was stiff. While your riding out in the wilds of the Pinelands, be on the lookout for the little devil.

If you're interested in more Pinelands lore, visit the Pineylore web site at www.telplus.net/~lopez. Author Lilli Lopez has compiled a fascinating book of local history and legends, which her daughters have turned into a wonderful web site. The site also will link you to a wealth of similar information.

At the 3.1-mile mark you go left and pass some cranberry bogs—here's where the beauty of the Pine Barrens becomes apparent. Tall marsh grasses, scrub oak, water lilies, and bogs contribute to a most stunning ecosystem. Continue straight past several spur roads, still following the white blazes, to a trail at the 3.6-mile mark. Go left here on a wonderfully tight pine-lined trail and head up to a trail junction. At mile 4.1 your ride crosses over a paved road and begins a great section of tight singletrack riding. At the 4.3-mile mark the trail makes a quick left, then a right, still following the White Trail. Be careful here as it's easy to get lost. At the 4.6-mile mark you come to a four-way junction. Continue straight, following the White Trail. This section of the trail cuts through thick scrub oak and dense stands of pitch pines. At mile 5.2 go left, still following the White Trail. Head to a wide dirt road, Mount Misery (on the left), and the 5.5-mile mark. Turn around here and retrace your route back to the park office. To enrich your experience in the Pine Barrens, take some time on your way back to explore some of the roads around the bogs.

Pedaling past the Cranberry Bogs.

Presidential Lakes.

Ride Information

📞 Trail Contacts:
Lebanon State Forest Office, off NJ 72, (609) 726-1191 – *open 8:00 A.M. to 4:00 P.M.* • **Mount Holly Bicycles**, 1646 NJ 38, Mount Holly, NJ; (609) 267-6620 • **Bike Line**, 185 NJ 70, Medford, NJ; (609) 654-6868 or *www.bikeline.com*

🕐 Schedule:
8:30 A.M. to sunset

❓ Local Information:
[see Ride 11: Wharton State Forest]

💡 Local Events/Attractions:
[see Ride 11: Wharton State Forest]

🛏 Accommodations:
Campground and cabins are available in the park. Call the park office at (609) 726-1191.

🍴 Restaurants:
Red Lion Diner, 1753 U.S. 206, South Hampton, NJ; (609) 859-2301 – *for classic New Jersey diner cuisine*

🗺 Maps:
Lebanon State Forest map – *available from the forest office*

MilesDirections

0.0 START from the parking area and locate the short connector trail. Cross over Four-Mile Road to a gate and the well-marked Red Trail.

0.6 Go right and follow the Red Trail.

0.9 Go left on the well-marked Red Trail.

1.2 Go left.

1.8 The trail forks. Go right.

2.2 The Red Trail goes right. Your ride goes left and follows the well-marked White Trail.

2.6 Reach a gate and a four-way intersection. Continue straight.

2.9 Go left onto a very sandy road. The tread becomes firmer after a short distance.

3.1 Go left and follow the White Trail past cranberry bogs.

3.4 A spur road goes right. Continue straight to a singletrack trail on the left.

3.6 Go left on a tight, pine tree-lined single-track trail.

4.0 Go right at the three-way junction.

4.1 Cross a paved road. Continue straight on wonderful, tight, curving singletrack.

4.3 Go left and then right, following the White Trail.

4.6 Reach a trail junction. Continue straight.

4.7 Go left at the three-way junction.

4.8 The Yellow Trail is on the right. Continue straight.

5.2 Go left and follow the White Trail.

5.3 Go right and follow the White Trail as it turns back into a singletrack trail.

5.5 The trail goes past some houses and ends at a dirt road with Mt. Misery on the left. Turn around here and retrace your route back to the parking area.

11.0 Return to the parking area and your car.

A nearby Amish farm.

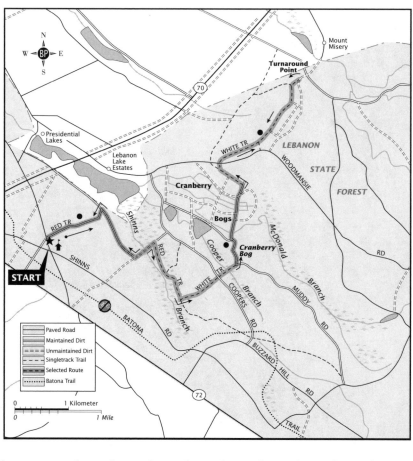

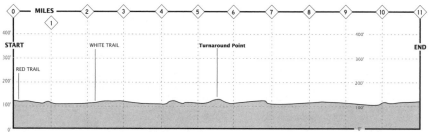

Southern

Honorable Mentions
A. Woodlawn Wildlife Refuge

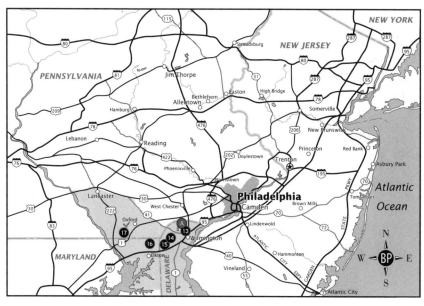

Philadelphia
Area

Brandywine Creek State Park

Ride Specs

Start: From the intersection of Garden of Eden Road and U.S. 202

Length: 795-acre park with over 14 miles of trails.

Approximate Riding Time: 1-1½ hours

Difficulty Rating: Moderate, with a few short hills

Terrain: Singletrack, doubletrack, dirt, and paved roads. Mostly tight singletrack, with some short rocky sections and wide doubletrack trails. Pass rolling hills and farmland. Connects with Woodlawn Land Trust.

Land Status: Delaware State Parks and Woodlawn Land Trust

Nearest Town: Wilmington, DE

Other Trail Users: Hikers, joggers, and equestrians

Getting There

From Chadds Ford, PA: Go south on U.S. 202 for 5.1 miles (from where it intersects U.S. 1) to Garden of Eden Road. Turn right on Garden of Eden Road. Park on the right in a lot at the recycling center. *DeLorme: Maryland/ Delaware Atlas & Gazetteer:* Page 63 A-5

The lovely Brandywine Creek weaves its way through Chester County, Pennsylvania, and Delaware to join the Delaware River. Along the way the creek has created a valley of stunning natural beauty. Rolling hillsides, charming fieldstone houses, back-country roads, and rural open lands, all contribute to the charm of this lovely area. Over the years, the river has seen more than 100 mills on its banks, producing everything from flour, paper, black powder, snuff, and textiles. Today, the Brandywine River Valley is a major tourist area, attracting visitors from all across the United States to its beautiful rural landscape and its rich history.

The area's historical fate was sealed during the American Revolution when, in 1777, under the direction of General Howe, the British landed on the banks of what is today Elkton, Maryland. Their intention was to seize control of the American colonies' political center, Philadelphia. General Washington, anticipating the invasion, positioned his men in such a way as to force a battle in Chadds Ford, Pennsylvania. General Howe got word of Washington's trap and chose a more northern route. By the time Washington became aware of Howe's new movements and repositioned his men, it was too late and Howe's troops easily pushed back the unprepared Continental Army.

The so-called Battle of Brandywine proved a critical loss in the defense of Philadelphia. Two weeks later, Howe's forces marched into Philadelphia uncon-

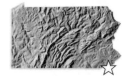

tested. It was at the Battle of Brandywine that Washington's friend, the young Frenchman Marquis de Lafayette, saw his first action in the American Revolution. Brandywine Battlefield Park preserves the headquarters of both Generals Washington and Lafayette, as well as various other historical buildings. Stop by their visitor center and check out the interpretive displays.

Moving forward, two present-day names have become synonymous with this region, Wyeth and du Pont. Both of these families have left their mark on the area—the Wyeths with their powerful and beautiful paintings and the du Ponts with their industrial achievements and civic contributions. The 795-acre Brandywine Creek State Park, in which this ride takes place, was originally a dairy farm owned by the du Pont family. The gray stone walls that divide the park are vestiges of the du Pont's original farm.

Crossing Ramsey Run.

Just down U.S 1 from Brandywine Battlefield Park is the world-renowned Brandywine River Museum. The museum, a converted Civil War-era gristmill, has an outstanding collection of paintings by the Wyeth family and other local artists. If you're in the mood for a little wine tasting, head just a little farther south on U.S. 1 to the Chaddsford Winery. You can taste a variety of wines and tour the facility with a guide who will explain the winemaking process. These are just a few of the activities to be found in the Brandywine River Valley.

Ride Information

🚲 Trail Contacts:
Woodlawn Land Trustees, 2201 W. 11th, Wilmington, DE (302) 655-6215 • **Alan's Bicycles**, 4723 Concord Pike, Wilmington, DE (302) 478-0990 – *they also offer local group rides*

🕐 Schedule:
Sunrise to sunset

❓ Local Information:
Greater Wilmington Convention and Visitors Bureau, 100 W. 10th St., Wilmington, DE 1-800-422-1181 • **Brandywine Valley Tourist Information Center**, 300 Greenwood Road, Kennett Square, PA (410) 388-2900 or 1-800-228-9933 or *www.brandywinevalley.com*

💡 Local Events/Attractions:
Brandywine Battlefield Park, U.S. 1, Chadds Ford, PA (610) 459-3342 or *www.ushistory.org/march/phila/bran dywine.htm* • **Brandywine River Museum**, on U.S. 1 just west of DE 100, Chadds Ford, PA (610) 388-2700 or *www.brandywine-museum.org* • **Brandywine Creek State Park**, Talleyville, DE (302) 577-3534 • **Chaddsford Winery**, 632 Baltimore Pike, Chadds Ford, PA (610) 388-6221 or *www.chadds-ford.com* • **Delaware Museum of Natural History**, 4840 Kennett Pike, Greenville, DE (302) 652-7600 or *www.delmnh.org* • **Hagley Museum**, DE 141 (between DE 100 & U.S. 202), Wilmington, DE (302) 658-2400 or *www.hagley.lib.de.us* • **Winterthur Museum**, DE 52, Winterthur, DE (302) 888-4600 or *www.winterthur.org*

🛏 Accommodations:
Inn at Montchanin Village, DE 100 & Kirk Road, Montchanin, DE 1-800-269-2473 or.*www.montchanin.com*

🍴 Restaurants:
Brew Ha Ha Coffeehouse, 3636 Concord Pike, Wilmington, DE (302) 478-7227 • **LaTolteca Mexican Restaurant**, 2209 Concord Pike, Wilmington, DE (302) 778-4646

👥 Organizations:
Delaware Trail Spinners, 334 Grey Bull Dr., Bear, DE 19701 (302) 834-1133 • **White Clay Bicycle Club**, 3 Yale Rd., Wilmington, DE (302) 994-2990 or *www.delanet.com/~wcbc*

Ⓝ Maps:
USGS maps: Wilmington North, *DE* • **Woodlawn Wildlife Refuge map** – *available by calling* (302) 655-6215

The off-road trails within Brandywine State Park offer some of the best singletrack riding in the book-and it's just a short drive from Philadelphia and Wilmington. There are many spur trails that connect with the main blaze trails, including the Brandywine Bike Trail that follows along Brandywine Creek, so feel free to explore these trails to add more riding time.

MilesDirections

Cyclists are encouraged to explore the trails within the park or travel north along Brandywine Creek in search of additional singletrack north of Smithbridge Road near Woodlawn Land Trust. If you choose to head north, start from the parking area, and head down Garden of Eden Road. You travel on a wide dirt trail past a gate. Fly down a fast, steep, rocky hill to a bridge. Now you're in the park. From here, you can follow the white blazes north toward Thompson's Bridge Road and cruise along the dirt path to an intersection with Smithbridge Road—Brandywine Creek is on your left. Crossing the road here leads to more singletrack and Woodlawn Trust Land. The trails up here continue to roll through open fields and dense wooded areas before looping back to Smithbridge Road. At Smithbridge Road, you can turn right and head back to Brandywine Creek, retracing your route back to the parking area.

Nala, the biking dog.

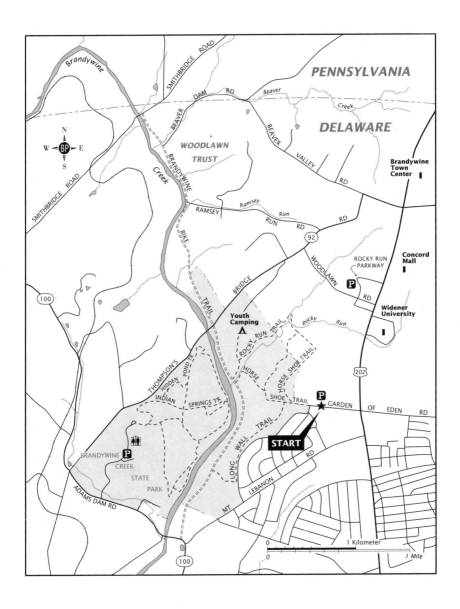

14

Middle Run Natural Area

Ride Specs

Start: From the Middle Run Natural Area day-use parking lot
Length: 7.1 miles
Approximate Riding Time: 1 hour
Difficulty Rating: Moderate, with a few short hills
Terrain: Moderate, tight singletrack riding with some short sections of gravel road
Elevation Gain: 712 feet
Land Status: New Castle County Parks
Nearest Town: Newark, DE
Other Trail Users: Hikers, joggers, and horseback riders

Getting There

From Wilmington, DE: Drive south on I-95 to DE 273. Go west on DE 273. Turn right on Paper Mill Road. Drive 2.1 miles and turn right on Possum Park Road. Go 0.5 miles and turn left on Possum Hollow Road. Notice the park entrance on the left. Turn left into the park's day-use parking area. The ride starts here.
DeLorme: Maryland/Delaware Atlas & Gazetteer: Page 78 A-3

lose to both Philadelphia and Wilmington, Middle Run Natural Area is 850 acres of rolling hills, open fields, deciduous forests, and small streams. Flowing through the park is Middle Run Creek, a tributary of the White Clay Creek. Identified as a critical natural area, Middle Run Natural Area came about through the hard work of many private and public groups in the New Castle area. Established in 1975, Middle Run Natural Area is a relative newcomer to the New Castle County Park System. Amidst a sea of urban sprawl, the park has managed to maintain a rare and pristine setting. While you're riding or hiking in the park, it's hard to remember that you're so close to a major urban area.

As you ride through the park, you'll appreciate the well-marked and well-maintain trails, as well as the handy wooden footbridges. You can thank New Castle County and a number of private local groups for these. The park system has received a number of awards for the Middle Run Natural Area—and deservedly so. This is a prime example of private and public agencies working together for the preservation of open space.

This excellent short ride takes a tour around the Middle Run Natural Area on the Lenape Trail. There are many spur trails that connect with the main trail. Feel free to explore these trails to add riding time. First time users can easily get confused with all the spur trails shooting off from the main trail, but don't worry. It's hard to get lost in the park since all of the trails are well-marked and eventually funnel back to the Lenape Trail.

Your ride starts at the day-use parking area. Go left into the woods on the well-marked Lenape Trail. Follow the blazes along the tight singletrack through dense forests and open fields to Fox Den Road. At the 2.4-mile mark, the ride skirts along the banks of Middle Run Creek. The trail pulls away from the creek briefly but then returns, leading you across the stream at the 4.1-mile mark to more singletrack riding.

At the 4.4-mile mark, the trail cuts through a stand of tall pine trees. Make a nice downhill run to the Double Horseshoe Trail. Follow the Double Horseshoe Trail up to Possum Hollow Road. Go left on Possum Hollow Road and make a quick right back onto dirt. From here, follow the trail back to the parking area and your car. Feel free to explore the many side trails in this biker-friendly area. You can spend the better part of the afternoon on all the trails in the park.

MilesDirections

0.0 START from the parking and go left on the Lenape Trail.

0.4 Go right and pass an open field.

0.9 Go right and pass several wooden footbridges.

1.2 Cross over a small stream.

1.4 Come to an open field.

1.6 Cross over Fox Den Road.

1.8 Go left and follow the Lenape Trail.

2.4 Continue straight along the banks of Middle Run Creek.

2.8 Cross over Smith Mill Road.

3.2 A spur trail goes right. Continue straight.

3.5 Go right and head up a short, steep hill.

3.7 Reach a trail junction. Continue straight.

4.1 Turn right and go across Middle Run Creek.

4.4 Go left and follow the Lenape Trail through a stand of tall pine trees.

4.8 Enjoy a nice downhill run.

5.2 Go left down tight, curving singletrack.

5.9 The Lenape Trail breaks out into an open field and turns into the Double Horseshoe Trail.

6.2 Go left, back into the woods.

6.6 Go left on Possum Hollow Road, then make a quick right, and follow the Double Horseshoe Trail back to the parking area.

7.1 Arrive back at the parking area.

Ride Information

Trail Contacts:
New Castle County Parks, 187A Old Churchman's Rd., New Castle, DE; (302) 395-5720 • **Wooden Wheels**, Newark Shopping Center, Main St. Newark, DE; (302) 368-2453 *www.woodenwheels.com – they offer local group rides*

Schedule:
Sunrise to sunset

Local Information:
(see Ride 13: Brandywine Creek State Park)

Local Events/Attractions:
(see Ride 13: Brandywine Creek State Park)

Restaurants:
(see Ride 13: Brandywine Creek State Park)

Organizations:
(see Ride 13: Brandywine Creek State Park)

Maps:
Middle Run Valley Natural Area maps – *available at Wooden Wheels bike shop*

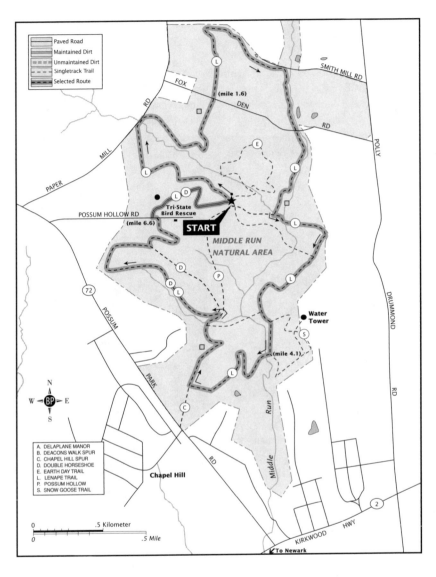

Paved Road
Maintained Dirt
Unmaintained Dirt
Singletrack Trail
Selected Route

A. DELAPLANE MANOR
B. DEACONS WALK SPUR
C. CHAPEL HILL SPUR
D. DOUBLE HORSESHOE
E. EARTH DAY TRAIL
L. LENAPE TRAIL
P. POSSUM HOLLOW
S. SNOW GOOSE TRAIL

MILL RD

FOX

DEN RD

SMITH MILL RD

POLLY

PAPER MILL RD

POSSUM HOLLOW RD

(mile 1.6)

(mile 6.6)

Tri-State
Bird Rescue

START

*MIDDLE RUN
NATURAL AREA*

Water
Tower

DRUMMOND RD

(mile 4.1)

72

POSSUM PARK RD

Middle Run

Chapel Hill

KIRKWOOD HWY

2

To Newark

0   .5 Kilometer
0   .5 Mile

N
W — BP — E
S

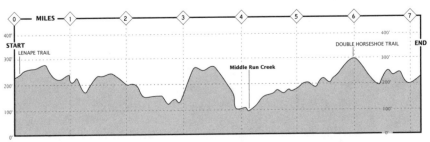

MILES 0 1 2 3 4 5 6 7

400'   400'
START   DOUBLE HORSESHOE
LENAPE TRAIL   TRAIL   **END**
300'   300'

                          Middle Run Creek
200'   200'

100'   100'

0'   0'

15

Iron Hill Park

Ride Specs

Start: From the Iron Hill Park parking area

Length: Over 15 miles of trails

Approximate Riding Time: Rider's discretion

Difficulty Rating: Moderate, with a few short hills

Terrain: Mostly tight singletrack and wide doubletrack trails, with some short, rocky sections. Some wild BMX-type sections are off the main trails.

Land Status: New Castle County Parks

Nearest Town: Newark, DE

Other Trail Users: Hikers and joggers

Getting There

From Wilmington, DE: Go south on I-95 to DE 896 north. Go north on DE 896 to Welsh Tract Road. Go left on Welsh Tract Road and drive for 1 mile. Go left on Whitaker Road and drive to the park entrance on the left. Turn left into the first parking area. The ride starts here.

DeLorme: Maryland/Delaware Atlas & Gazetteer: Page 78 B-2

The park's convenient location, close to both Philadelphia and Wilmington, makes it an ideal after-work ride. Once the site of a large mining operation, Iron Hill Park's 334 acres now lie alongside the hustle and bustle of Interstate 95. Many of the old mining pits now offer mountain bikers trails that are laced with roller-coaster hills and BMX jumps. A good example is the Mega-Dip: a 40-foot drop into an old abandoned iron mining pit.

This is an excellent short ride. There are many spur trails that connect with the main blaze trails. Feel free to explore these if you want to add riding time. This ride takes a tour around the longer trails in the park. First time visitors can easily get confused with all of the spur trails shooting off from the main trails. But don't worry; it's very hard to get lost in park. The spur trails either dead-end or eventually lead back to the main trails.

The New Castle County Park System manages Iron Hill and Middle Run Natural Area and is currently working on connecting the two trail systems, giving cyclists a ride of over 20 miles on mutli-use trails. Hats off to the park system for keeping the trails open for mountain biking in this crowded urban area.

Ride Information

🌜 Trail Contacts:
New Castle County Parks, 187A Old Churchman's Rd., New Castle, DE (302) 395-5720 • **Wooden Wheels**, Newark Shopping Center, Main St. Newark, DE (302) 368-2453 or *www.woodenwheels.com—they offer local group rides*

🕐 Schedule:
Sunrise to sunset

❓ Local Information:
(see Ride 13: Brandywine Creek State Park)

🌐 Local Events/Attractions:
Iron Hill Mountain Bike Race, in October, Newark, DE; call the Delaware Trail Spinners for information at (302) 834-1133 • *(see Ride 13: Brandywine Creek State Park)*

🍴 Accommodations:
(see Ride 13: Brandywine Creek State Park)

🍽 Restaurants:
(see Ride 13: Brandywine Creek State Park)

👥 Organizations:
(see Ride 13: Brandywine Creek State Park)

🅝 Maps:
USGS maps: Newark West, DE-PA-MD

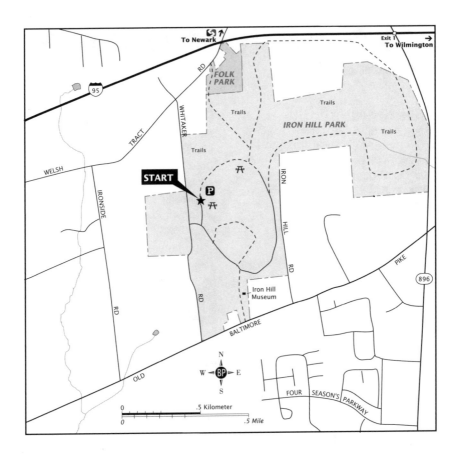

MilesDirections

Bordered by Interstate 95 to the north and DE 896 to the east, this system of trails covers over 15 miles and spans over 300 acres. It'll be tough to get lost, so go where your bike will take you and have a great time!

Fair Hill
Natural Resources
Management Area

Ride Specs

Start: From parking area at the intersection of Black Bridge Rd. and Appleton Road
Length: 8-mile loop
Approximate Riding Time: 1-2½ hours
Difficulty Rating: Moderate, with some steep hills
Terrain: Singletrack, doubletrack, dirt and paved roads
Elevation Gain: 243 feet
Land Status: Maryland Department of Natural Resources
Nearest Town: Newark, DE
Other Trail Users: Hikers, joggers, and horseback riders

Getting There

From Philadelphia, PA: Travel south on I-95 to the DE 273 exit (Newark, DE). Drive 8 miles west and turn right on Appleton Road. Travel one mile to a large parking area on the left.
DeLorme: Maryland/Delaware Atlas & Gazetteer. Page 78 A-1

Located in the northeast corner of Cecil County, Maryland, the Fair Hill Natural Resources Management Area covers 5,622 acres of gentle rolling hillsides, lush forests, wandering streams, and fertile hayfields. The park boasts over 40 miles of singletrack trails. Add to that the dirt roads and paved sections and you have a treasure for mountain bikers in the tri-state area.

This is one of my favorite rides in the book. If you love singletrack riding, this is the place to go. Fair Hill has a complex trail system, with trails shooting off in all sorts of directions. If you follow the directions closely and use your odometer, you should be fine. There is a park map available at the park office for two dollars. It's worth the money. The map will help you locate all the new trails in the park. Once you get to know the area, you can really add up the miles.

Fair Hill is a pro-mountain bike area. In fact, park officials encourage the use of mountain bikes on the park's many trails. Just remember that when riding your bike, you're sharing the trails with other users. Be courteous and yield the right of way to all hikers and horseback riders.

The Fair Hill Natural Resources Management Area is also well known for its racehorse training center as well as its racetrack. Both steeplechase and flat races are frequently held on the grounds here. If you're a gambler, you'll be happy to know that pari-mutuel betting is allowed. Fair Hill also hosts mountain bike races, Civil War reenactments, equine and canine events, and

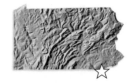

the Cecil County Fair. Check with the park office for more information on these and other events.

The Big Elk Creek Covered Bridge is another attraction not to be missed. (Don't worry; you pass it on this ride.) It's one of only five covered bridges left in the state of Maryland. The bridge is located on Tawes Road, near the park office. Also located on Tawes Road is the Fair Hill Nature and Environmental Center. The center offers nature tours, on-going seasonal programs, and a summer day-camp for school-age children. The non-profit Fair Hill Environmental Foundation operates the center. Bring the whole family and enjoy all of the wonderful activities this great park has to offer.

Recently, Fair Hill was chosen as the location for Oprah Winfrey's 1998 movie *Beloved*. In 1997, while flying concentric circles from Philadelphia in search of a movie set location, producers for the movie noticed a large and secluded parcel of land marked by vast open fields ccombined with deep wooded sections. Upon further investigation and several ground visits, Oprah and company would choose this area as one of their primary filming locations. The movie, which is based on the 1988 Pulitzer Prize winning novel by Toni Morrison, stars Oprah Winfrey and Danny Glover.

Chosen to depict 19th Century rural Cincinnati, it is here that Sethe Bluestone's (Oprah's character) roadhouse was built. In an effort to accurately reproduce 19th Century living, the film producers hired local contractors and craftsmen to build the movie set. In addition, they trucked in several additional buildings bought from a broker in South Carolina.

Intended as temporary structures, the buildings still stand and line part of your ride. Local interest and hundreds of visitors each year prompted the managers of Fair Hill to keep the structures standing. In addition, and for their support of the movie and use of the land, the Fair Hill Natural Management Area received well over one million dollars in much needed revenue.

Ride Information

Trail Contacts:
Fair Hill Natural Resources Management Area Office, 376 Fair Hill Drive, Elkton, MD; (410) 398-1246 • **Wooden Wheels,** Newark Shopping Center, Main St. Newark, DE; (302) 368-2453 or *www.wooden-wheels.com – they offer local group rides*

Schedule: .
Sunrise to sunset

Local Information:
(see Ride 13: Brandywine Creek State Park)

Local Events/Attractions:
(see Ride 13: Brandywine Creek State Park)

Accommodations:
(see Ride 13: Brandywine Creek State Park)

Restaurants:
(see Ride 13: Brandywine Creek State Park)

Organizations:
(see Ride 13: Brandywine Creek State Park)

Maps:
USGS maps: Newark West, DE-MD-PA • **Fair Hill Natural Resources Management Area map** – *available from the park office*

MilesDirections

0.0 START from the parking area and go right on a dirt road. Pedal to a road on the right.

0.2 Go right and cross the bridge over Appleton Road.

0.3 The trail forks. Go right.

0.7 The trail forks. Turn right into the woods. Follow the trail through a stream crossing. Angle right to a singletrack trail on the right at a post.

1.3 Go right at the post and follow the tight, winding singletrack trail to a doubletrack trail.

1.8 Angle left and then make a quick right back to a singletrack trail. The trail now drops to a small stream.

2.0 Cross the stream and then jam up a short, steep hill.

2.2 A spur trail goes right. Continue straight.

2.4 Go right and pedal up a short, steep hill.

2.5 Angle right back into woods.

2.6 Go right.

2.7 Go right over a small cement bridge. Make a quick left and follow the singletrack along the bank of a stream.

2.9 Splash past a small stream and go up a short, steep hill.

3.1 The trail forks. Go right, down to a small stream.

3.5 Cross the stream and go right on sweet singletrack to a trail junction at a fence line.

3.6 Roll left and head down a steep hill and to a stream crossing. Follow the trail along the fence line.

4.0 Drop down past the fence and go left through Christina River. Continue straight up the hill to a trail junction.

4.6 The trail forks. Go left.

4.7 Turn left over a small wooden bridge. Continue following the singletrack across a small cement bridge.

4.8 Go right and head across a field. Angle left at the trail junction. Follow the singletrack up a hill to a trail junction.

5.0 Go right on a tight singletrack trail and ride to a trail junction.

Multi-use trails.

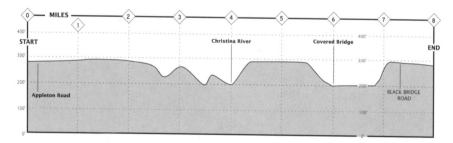

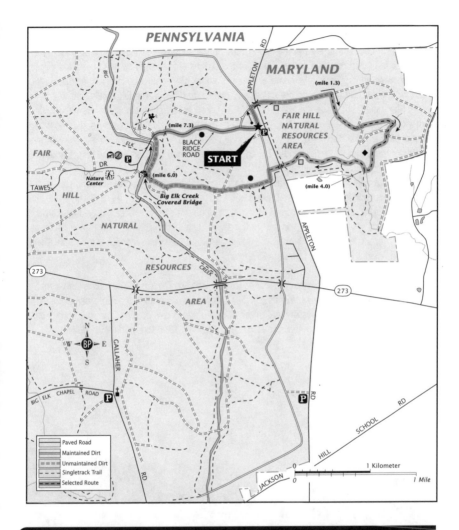

MilesDirections *continued*

5.1 Go left and then make a quick right back onto tight singletrack and go through trees.

5.3 The trail breaks out to an open field. Follow the main trail through an underpass to Appleton Road

5.5 Cross the road to an obvious, gravel trail. Follow the gravel trail straight to an intersection at a large metal barn.

6.0 Continue straight on the main road down to the Big Elk Creek Covered Bridge.

6.3 Turn right onto a singletrack trail. Climb steeply to a trail junction.

7.1 Reach the trail junction. Go left and head down a short hill.

7.2 Go right and ride across small stream, angling right to Black Bridge Road.

7.3 Turn right up Black Bridge Road.

8.0 Arrive back at the parking area.

Another possible route through Fair Hill:

Start from the parking area at the intersection of Black Bridge Road and Appleton Road. From the lot go left down the wide Access Road. At the 0.6-mile mark, the ride heads into the woods on tight, winding singletrack—a prime example of some of the new mountain bike trails in the park. Follow the trail through an open field and then drop down to Big Elk Creek. The trail goes under Maryland 273, along the Big Elk Creek, and then goes right, across some small wooden footbridges back into the woods. At the 3.4-mile mark, the ride goes left and passes some horse jumps. Ride across Maryland 273 on a footbridge and then follow the tight singletrack under a cluster of trees back into the woods. The trail drops down and crosses a small bridge and then rises up a short hill to a trail junction.

At the 7.2-mile mark, the ride travels across Big Elk Creek along a cracked concrete dam—expect to get your feet wet. The trail then climbs up to a gravel road. At the 8.0-mile mark, the trail cuts straight through an old farm in ruin. The trail parallels an old fence line and heads back into the woods. To the right of the trail is the farmhouse used in the motion picture *Beloved*. Continue over a small concrete bridge. The trail goes left through more farm ruins to Access Road. Go left on Access Road back to the parking area.

*[**NOTE:** There are over 100 miles of trails and roads in the Fair Hill Natural Resource Management Area. These loops are only samplings of what this location has to offer. Time permitting, you should explore the many miles of trails in the area. An alternative parking area where additional trails are found is adjacent to Appleton Road. Have fun and keep the rubber side down.]*

Sethe Bluestone's roadhouse from the movie *Beloved* starring Oprah Winfrey.

104

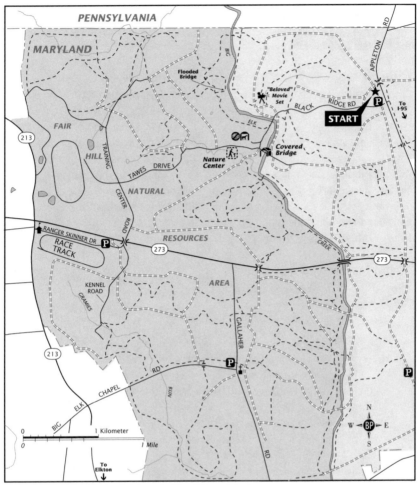

The other side of Fair Hill, "Fair Hill West" contains the horse track and dozens of miles more singletrack.

Nottingham Park

Ride Specs

Start: From the parking area below the park office
Length: 6.1-mile loop
Approximate Riding Time: 45 min.–1½ hours
Difficulty Rating: Easy with a few hills
Terrain: Singletrack, doubletrack, and dirt roads
Elevation Gain: 445 feet
Land Status: Chester County Park System
Nearest Town: Nottingham, PA
Other Trail Users: Hikers, joggers, and horseback riders

Getting There

From Philadelphia, PA: Take U.S. 1 south to PA 272 (Nottingham, PA, exit). Follow the signs for Nottingham Park. Turn left into park. Just after the Ranger Station, take a left into the parking lot and park near the bathrooms.
DeLorme: Pennsylvania Atlas & Gazetteer: Page 94 C-2

Early settlers called this area the Barrens because the thin, dry soil would not support plants commonly found in the surrounding hills. What do grow in the park are pitch pines, prairie grasses, serpentine chickweed, and mosspink—plants which may look out of place but actually thrive in the heavy-metal, nutrient-poor soil in and around the park. This area is also unique in that it's one of just three areas in North America with outcroppings of rare, light green serpentine rock. Riding through the park you'll notice many sinkholes and mine openings, evidence of the feldspar and chromite mining activity in the area from the late 1800s to the 1930s.

This is a relatively small park, just 651 acres, and it's tucked away in the southern part of Chester County, Pennsylvania. Farms still dominate the landscapes—as do Amish and Mennonites families. Known as the Plain People because of their simple dress and lifestyle, these two religious groups choose to live without many of our modern conveniences. They still work their farms with horse-drawn plows and drive horse-drawn carriages. Nearby Lancaster County has the highest concentration of Mennonites and Amish in the world. The park is also located near Kennett Square and the world-renowned Longwood Gardens. The community of Kennett Square, interestingly enough, has been deemed the mushroom growing capital of the world.

For an extra treat for the family, stop by the Herr's Potato Chip factory, located on Herr Drive just before you enter the park. Pennsylvania is ranked first in the production of potato chips, and the Herr factory is one of the largest in the country. So stop by for a great tour and some delicious, fresh potato chips. The factory

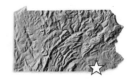

gives free tours Monday through Thursday, 9 A.M. to 3 P.M., and Fridays, 9 A.M. to 11 A.M., starting from the Herr's Visitor Center.

Nottingham Park offers a lot of recreational activities in its 651 acres. You and your family can enjoy camping, fishing in the 2.6-acre MacPherson Lake, picnicking, and hiking. You'll also find ball fields and a playground. This ride is excellent for beginner riders looking to test their skills. Your ride starts at the parking area below the park office. The course takes in a mixture of singletrack, doubletrack, and dirt roads, all of which run along the perimeter of the park. The riding is never difficult, but you can expect a few short, steep hills, as well as tight singletrack trails and stream crossings. Be courteous to all trail users and keep your speed in check around horses and hikers.

Ride Information

● Trail Contacts:

Nottingham Park Office, 150 Park Road, Nottingham, PA; (610) 932-2589 • **Chester County Parks and Recreation Dept.**, 601 West Town Road, Ste. 160, West Chester, PA; (610) 344-6415 • **Wooden Wheels**, Newark Shopping Center, Main St. Newark, DE; (302) 368-2453; *www.woodenwheels.com – they offer local group rides*

● Schedule:

8:00 A.M. to sunset

● Local Information:

Brandywine Valley Tourist Information Center, 300 Greenwood Road, Kennett Square, PA; (410) 388-2900 or 1-800-228-9933 or *www.brandywinevalley.com*

● Local Events/Attractions:

Herr's Snack Factory Visitor Center, 20 Herr Drive, U.S. 1 & PA 272, Nottingham, PA; (610) 932-6400 or 1-800-284-7488 or *www.herrs.com* •

Longwood Gardens, off U.S. 1 and PA 52, Kennett Square, PA; (610) 388-1000 or *www.longwoodgardens.org* • **Northbrook Canoe Company,** 1810 Beagle Road, West Chester, PA; (610) 793-2279 or 1-800-898-2279 • *(see Ride 13: Brandywine Creek State Park)*

● Accommodations:

Cornerstone Bed & Breakfast, 300 Buttonwood Rd., Landenberg, PA; (610) 274-2143 or *www.belmar.com /cornerstone*

● Restaurants:

Hanks Place, U.S. 1 and PA 100, Chadds Ford, PA; (610) 388-7061 – *excellent home-style cooking overlooking Brandywine Creek*

● Organizations:

(see Ride 13: Brandywine Creek State Park)

● Maps:

Nottingham Park map – *available from the park office*

MilesDirections

0.0 START just beyond the bathrooms on Chrome Trail. Follow this up to the trail junction.

0.2 Turn right onto Doe Trail.

0.4 Turn left on Lonesome Pine Trail and climb up to a trail junction.

0.7 Pedal left and follow Buck Trail. Fly down a short hill and then climb up to a trail junction.

1.1 Continue straight to another trail junction.

1.7 Turn left on a newly cut trail. Continue straight to a trail junction.

2.1 Turn left.

2.2 Pass a radio tower.

2.3 Go left on the wide Buck Trail. Climb up a short, steep hill to a trail junction.

2.7 Go left and then right, still following Buck Trail. Pass Ridge Trail on the left and then fly down a steep hill to a trail junction.

3.0 A spur trail goes right. Continue straight to a trail junction.

3.4 Continue straight to trail junction.

3.7 Go right and junction with Feldspar Trail.

3.8 Go left on Buck Trail. Pass a road on the left. Continue straight down a hill and over waterbars. Follow the trail along Black Run Creek.

4.5 Pedal left up a short, steep hill to a trail junction.

4.7 Go left to a trail junction.

4.9 Go right on Buck Trail.

5.0 Take a left on Feldspar Trail and ride down to a trail junction at a fence.

5.2 Pedal right and head down to a bridge. Cross the bridge to trail junction.

5.4 Take a right on Doe Trail and cross a bridge. Follow the trail to a junction.

5.6 Lonesome Pine Trail is on the right, but you want to continue straight.

5.9 At the trail junction, go left on Chrome Trail.

6.1 Arrive back at the parking area.

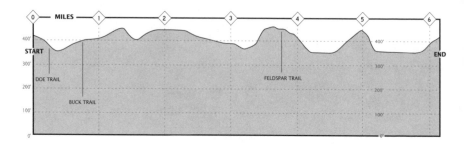

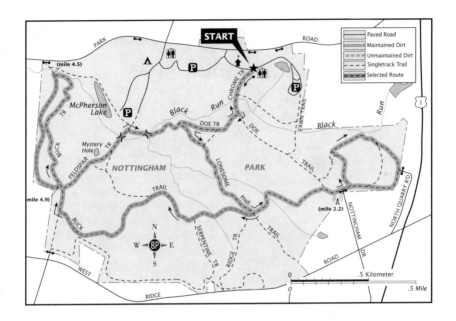

Honorable Mentions

Southern Philadelphia Area

Listed here is one of the great rides in the Southern Philadelphia Area that didn't make the A-list this time around but deserves recognition. Check it out and let us know what you think. You may decide that this ride deserves higher status in future editions or, perhaps, you may have a ride of your own that merits some attention.

(A) Woodlawn Wildlife Refuge

Off-road bicycling in the Woodlawn Wildlife Refuge follows many excellent singletrack trails that weave up, down, and along the valley. The rolling hills, pastoral farmlands, small wandering creeks, and dense wooded tracts of land create a wonderful riding experience. This is a great place for riding in the area. For a longer ride, you can easily hook-up with other trails in nearby Brandywine Creek State Park *(see Ride 13)*.

To get there from Chadds Ford, PA, go south on U.S. 202 for 4.5 miles (from where it intersects U.S. 1) to Rocky Run Pkwy. Turn right on Rocky Run Parkway and park in the large Brandywine Commons parking lot between TGI Friday's and Homewood Suites. The trail starts to the left of Homewood Suites at the edge of the woods. Woodlawn Wildlife Refuge map – available by calling (302) 655-6215. *DeLorme: Maryland/Delaware Atlas & Gazetteer:* Page 63 A-5; *DeLorme: Pennsylvania Atlas & Gazetteer:* Page 95 B-6

Western

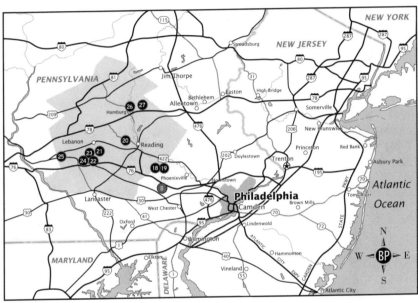

Philadelphia

French Creek State Park/Red & White Loop

Ride Specs

Start: From the parking area at the junction of PA 345 and Shed Road

Length: 6.2-mile loop

Approximate Riding Time: 1½ hours

Difficulty Rating: Moderate, with a few strenuous sections

Terrain: Hilly, rocky, technical singletrack and doubletrack

Elevation Gain: 926 feet

Land Status: Pennsylvania State Parks

Nearest Town: Birdsboro, PA

Other Trail Users: Hikers, joggers, horseback riders, and hunters (in season)

Getting There

From Philadelphia, PA: Go west on U.S. 30 to Exton, PA, and PA 100. Go north on PA 100 for 7.8 miles. Go west on PA 401 for 6.4 miles to PA 345. Go north on PA 345 for 5.6 miles, past the park entrance, to Shed Road and a pull-off/parking area on the right.

DeLorme: Pennsylvania Atlas & Gazetteer: Page 81 C-4

Nearby Hopewell Lake.

French Creek State Park offers a wide variety of outdoor activities for the general public. The park has two Disc Golf courses that weave through dense forests close to Hopewell Lake. The courses attract Frisbee golfers of all ages and abilities. On weekends there are many locals on the courses who are more than willing to offer a bit of advice to first-timers. Maps and score cards can be obtained from the park office. Orienteering—the art of map and compass reading—is another popular sport in the park. Some consider the park the orienteering capital of America. The park has a self-guided course that's open to the public—maps are available at the park office.

Fishing is a big sport at the park, and anglers can be seen year-round on Scotts Run Lake and Hopewell Lake. Bass, Northern pike, panfish, trout, and chain pickerel are some of the species of freshwater fish in the lakes. A swimming pool is open at Hopewell Lake from 11 A.M. to 7 P.M., Memorial Day to Labor Day. And if that's not enough, you can rent boats, wooded campsites, and cabins. Just call the park office for more information.

For the mountain biker, there are over 22 miles of trails in the park where cyclists can hop logs, crank up steep hills, get wet crossing streams, and pedal through dense forests on some of the best terrain for mountain biking in Eastern Pennsylvania. But that could change. Mountain bikers need to get involved with

maintaining the trails. The park rangers are pro-mountain biking, and with your help, it can stay that way. For more information on trail maintenance, call the Pennsylvania Trail Hands organization (P.A.T.H.) or call the park office.

Your ride starts out on a wide doubletrack trail and climbs gently. Following the white and red blazes, pass some power lines and head up to a trail junction. At the junction, the trail goes left and you make a great run down tight, rocky singletrack tread to Millers Point. At the 2.2-mile mark, the trail goes right, up tight single-

Ride Information

◐ Trail Contacts:
French Creek State Park Office, 843 Park Road, Elverson, PA; (610) 582-9680 • **The Bike Shop**, 2233 Penn Ave., West Lawn, PA; (610) 670-4750 • **P.A.T.H.**, 24 North Field Drive, Downingtown, PA; (610) 970-0812

◐ Schedule:
8:00 A.M. to sunset

❓ Local Information:
Reading and Berks County Visitors Bureau, 352 Penn Street, Reading, PA 1-800-443-6610 or (610) 375-4085 or www.readingberkspa.com

◑ Local Events/Attractions:
Daniel Boone Homestead, 400 Daniel Boone Rd., Birdsboro, PA; (610) 582-4900 • **VF Outlet Village**, Penn Ave. & Park Rd., Reading, PA; 1-800-772-8336 or www.vffo.com • **Hopewell Furnace National Historic Site**, 2 Mark Bird Lane, Elverson, PA; (610)582-8773; www.nps.gov/hofu /newweb/home.html • **The Rodale Institute Experimental Farm**, 611 Siegfriedale Rd., Kutztown, PA (610) 683-1400; www.rodaleinstitute.org

▬ Accommodations:
Adamstown Inn, 62 W. Main St., Adamstown, PA; (717) 484-0800 or 1-800-594-4808
www.adamstown.com

🍴 Restaurants:
Jimme Kramer's Peanut Bar, 332 Penn St., Reading, PA; (610) 376-8500 – *great American food with Middle Eastern and vegetarian dishes, grilled meat and fish dinners* • **Gregory's Diner**, 668 Ben Franklin Hwy., Birdsboro, PA; (610) 385-7900 – *excellent diner food and fresh baked goodies*

🏢 Organizations:
Pennsylvania Trail Hands (P.A.T.H.), 24 North Field Drive, Downingtown, PA; (610) 970-0812

Ⓝ Maps:
USGS maps: Berks County, PA • **French Creek State Park map** – *available at the park office*

track, and crosses over Mill Creek on very rocky, technical tread. At the 2.9-mile mark, the trail curves right and leads up a long, steep, strenuous hill. Staying in low gear will help as you try to pick the right line through this difficult section.

You have just made it through a couple of the hardest sections of the ride. You still have one hard climb to go. At the 3.5-mile mark the ride goes right onto wonderful, tight singletrack. Enjoy it because at the 4.3-mile mark you hit another steep, low-gear climb on loose, rocky tread. Crank past this section and you're home free on a great downhill run back to the parking area.

MilesDirections

0.0 START from the parking area at the junction of PA 345 and Shed Road. Go left on Shed Road, for a short distance, to a trailhead on the right at a gate. Pedal up the wide, rocky doubletrack trail.

0.3 A spur trail goes right. Continue straight on smoother tread and come to a trail junction.

1.1 Go left on narrow singletrack. The tread becomes rockier as you pick up speed on this great downhill section.

1.9 Reach a steep downhill section. Be on your toes.

2.1 Reach a trail junction. Go left and head down a short, steep hill to a trail junction.

2.2 Go right and head up rocky single-track, past two small crossings.

2.7 Cross the streams on rocky tread. Continue straight, passing the Raccoon

Trail on the right, and come to another stream crossing. Continue straight to a trail junction.

2.9 Go right and head up a long, steep, loose, strenuous hill on rocky tread to trail junction.

3.5 Pedal right and go down a short hill. Weave your way on tight singletrack. Bunny-hop past log jumps on tight singletrack. Jam up a short hill to level tread. Continue straight and head down a short hill to a trail junction.

4.3 Go right and pass the Raccoon Trail. Continue up strenuous, steep, loose, rocky tread to a trail junction.

5.1 Reach the trail junction. Continue straight on a wide and fast doubletrack trail and head back down to Shed Road.

6.2 Cruise into the parking area.

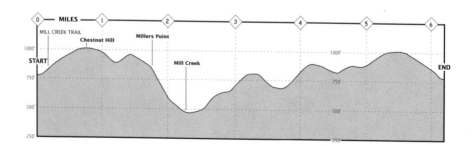

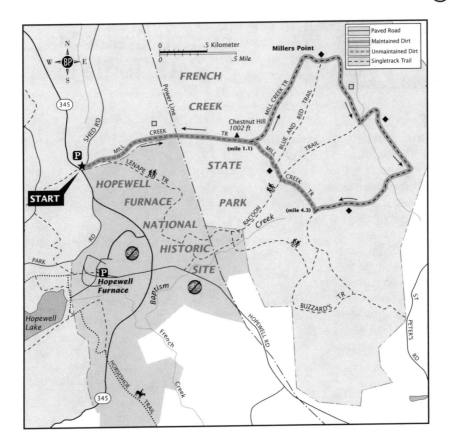

Weekly French Creek Trail Maintenance Schedule:

Tuesdays at 6:00 PM, Meet at the Park's Naturalist's Office.

The French Creek trail maintenance program is critical to preserving mountain biking at French Creek State Park. Please attend as often as possible. The Pennsylvania Trail Hands (PATH) urge you to help. We mountain bikers need to increase participation at the weekly maintenance sessions. We know that you are busy, but please try to attend two or three times a year. This is a small price to pay for the excellent riding provided by the park. Don't assume somebody will do all the work, get involved.

For More information contact:

Eagle Cycle and Accessories: (610) 458-9951
(ask for John)
Jamie Theurkauf: (610) 363-9570Path/MCMBA
(610) 754-6163
Pennsylvania Trail Hands (PATH) Montgomery County Mountain Bike Association (MCMBA)

French Creek State Park/Turtle Loop

Ride Specs

Start: From the parking area at the junction of PA 345 and Shed Road

Length: 10.9-mile loop

Approximate Riding Time: 1½–2½ hours

Difficulty Rating: Moderate with a few strenuous sections

Terrain: Singletrack, doubletrack, dirt and paved roads

Elevation Gain: 822 feet

Land Status: Pennsylvania State Parks

Nearest Town: Birdsboro, PA

Other Trail Users: Hikers, joggers, horseback riders, and hunters (in season)

Getting There

From Philadelphia, PA: Go west on U.S. 30 to Exton, PA, and PA 100. Go north on PA 100 for 7.8 miles. Go west on PA 401 for 6.4 miles to PA 345. Go north on PA 345 for 5.6 miles, past the park entrance, to Shed Road and a pull-off/parking area on the right.

DeLorme: Pennsylvania Atlas & Gazetteer: Page 81 C-4

rench Creek State Park, one of the crown jewels of the Pennsylvania State Park system, offers up 7,339 acres of opportunity for the outdoor enthusiast. Located approximately 14 miles southeast of Reading, Pennsylvania, the forested hills of the park not only provide habitat to animals and plant life, but they also house over 32 miles of trails. Portions of the trails are open to mountain bikes and have become quite popular.

As you ride through the park's rich forests, try to imagine large tracts of the park timbered completely off. That's pretty much how it looked at the close of the nineteenth century. By the late 1700s, America had grown increasingly hungry for

steel. Iron production required large quantities of iron ore, limestone, and charcoal. French Creek State Park was the site of one of the major players in the iron-producing industry, Hopewell Furnace. From 1771 to 1883, nearby Hopewell Furnace supplied America's growing demand with resources drawn directly from the surrounding hardwood forests. Colliers placed hearths throughout these woods (which in many cases can still be seen) in order to render charcoal fuel for the rapacious Hopewell Furnace. Visit the Hopewell Furnace National Historic Site during the summer months and costumed interpreters will tell you the story of Hopewell's iron-making years and what life was like in the workers' village. The historic site is located just off Pennsylvania 345, before the entrance to French Creek State Park.

Your ride starts from the parking area at Pennsylvania 345 and Shed Road. Cross Pennsylvania 345 to the green-blazed Lenape Trail. Pedal up the wide doubletrack trail to a paved road. The Contact Station is to the left. Cross the road, following the green blazes. Go right onto the green and blue-blazed trail and pass several technical rocky sections. At the 0.8-mile marker you cross over a small boulder field—there's no shame in walking through this section. At the 0.9-mile mark there's a trail junction. Continue straight. Make an immediate left, then right, and follow the orange blazes. The tread becomes smoother as you pedal

down tight singletrack. At mile 1.3, go left on tight singletrack and head to a trail junction. At mile 2.0, go left down rocky tread and ride to a gravel road. Continue straight up to a paved road. If you make it this far and are feeling good, continue with confidence.

Cross the road and following the Blue Trail down through a thick pine grove, past several wooden bridges and up to a trail junction. Go right here and pass two more wooden bridges. At the 3.5-mile mark the Blue Trail goes left and follows yellow and white blazes down to a paved road. Cross the road and get ready for some hard riding. At mile 4.4, crank up some loose rocky tread to a trail junction. At mile 5.0, the trail goes right, through some difficult technical sections. At this point you can go into cruise control and enjoy a wonderful singletrack run. At mile 6.9, continue straight past a trail on the left. Drop down some rocky tread to a trail junction. Go right and head down some tight rocky singletrack to the Park Road. Had enough yet?

Go left on the road and pedal past the park headquarters to the green-blazed Lenape Trail at the 8.8-mile mark. Go left here onto smooth doubletrack and head up past Scotts Run Lake. Go right and follow green blazes up past a gnarly, rocky, steep hill to a road. Cross the road to the trail and crank up to a trail junction at mile 10.0. You're almost home. Go right and retrace your route back to the parking area.

Ride Information

Trail Contacts:
French Creek State Park Office, 843 Park Road, Elverson, PA; (610) 582-9680 • **The Bike Shop**, 2233 Penn Ave., West Lawn, PA; (610) 670-4750 • **P.A.T.H.**, 24 North Field Drive, Downingtown, PA; (610) 970-0812

Schedule:
8:00 A.M. to sunset

Local Information:
[see Ride 18: French Creek/Red & White]

Local Events/Attractions:
Hopewell Furnace National Historic Site, 2 Mark Bird Lane, Elverson, PA (610) 582-8773;

www.nps.gov/hofu/newweb/home.html • [see Ride 18: French Creek/ Red & White]

Accommodations:
[see Ride 18: French Creek/Red & White]

Restaurants:
[see Ride 18: French Creek/Red & White]

Organizations:
[see Ride 18: French Creek/Red & White]

Maps:
USGS maps: Berks County, PA • **French Creek State Park map** – available at the park office

MilesDirections

0.0 START by crossing PA 345 (use caution) and access the green-blazed Lenape Trail. Pedal on good tread to Park Road.

0.4 Cross the road to the Lenape Trail. Pedal to a trail junction. Go right onto the green and blue-blazed trail and crank past some rocky tread to a trail junction.

0.9 Continue straight for a short distance. Make a sharp left, then a right, onto the orange-blazed Six Penny Trail. Follow this sweet singletrack to a trail junction.

1.3 Reach the trail junction. Go left onto the tight singletrack and head to another trail junction.

2.0 Pedal left down steep, loose, rocky tread to a service road.

2.3 Go right onto the wide road and follow the blue-blazed Boone Trail to Fire Tower Road.

2.4 Cross the road, following the Boone Trail. Weave your way down to Fire Tower Road. Cross Fire Tower Road again. Pedal past two bridges to a 3-way trail junction.

3.2 Go right onto rocky tread and head to a spur trail. Bend right and crank down to a paved road.

3.5 The Boone Trail goes left. Go right past several wood-plank bridges.

3.7 Cross a service road to the yellow-blazed Turtle Trail. Continue straight to a trail junction.

4.4 Go left onto singletrack and up loose, rocky tread to a trail junction.

5.0 Go right onto the white and yellow-blazed Turtle Trail. Crank up several loose, rocky sections. Continue straight on good tread to a spur trail.

6.9 The Horseshoe Trail goes left. Continue straight down very rocky tread.

7.0 Turn right onto very rocky tread and head down to Park Road.

7.5 Go left on Park Road. Pedal past the park office. Look for the Lenape Trail on the left.

8.8 Go left on the Lenape Trail to a trail junction.

9.1 Turn right and follow the Lenape Trail. Make a sharp right turn and crank up a steep rocky hill to Scotts Run Road.

9.4 Cross Scotts Run Road. Follow the Lenape Trail to a trail junction.

9.6 Encounter a very steep rocky uphill.

10.0 Turn right and pedal through very rocky tread up to Park Road.

10.5 Cross the road. Follow the Lenape Trail back to PA 345.

10.9 Cross PA 345 (with caution) to your car.

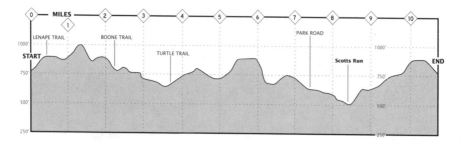

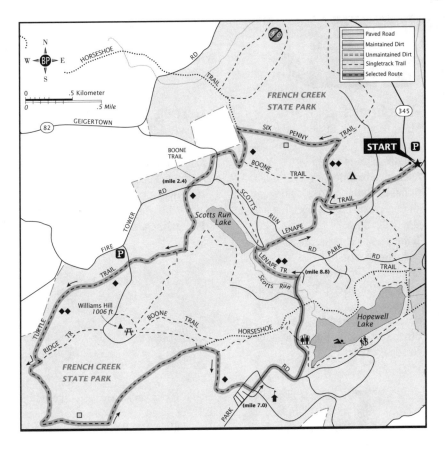

Blue Marsh Lake

Ride Specs

Start: From the Stilling Basin parking area
Length: 20.8-mile loop
Approximate Riding Time: 2–4 hours
Difficulty Rating: Strenuous: there is a lot of climbing on this ride. The hills are steep, but short.
Terrain: Singletrack, doubletrack, dirt and paved roads
Elevation Gain: 978 feet
Land Status: The U.S. Army Corps of Engineers
Nearest Town: Reading, PA
Other Trail Users: Hikers, joggers, and horseback riders

Getting There

From Reading, PA: Go west U.S. 422 to PA 183. Travel north on PA 183 for 5.6 mile to Palisade Road. Go left on Palisade Road to Stilling Basin Road. Turn right on Stilling Basin Road and into the parking area. *DeLorme: Pennsylvania Atlas & Gazetteer:* Page 80 A-2

I could rave all day about this fantastic loop around Blue Marsh Lake. It's easily one of the best rides around. The singletrack trails are tight and the terrain offers a number of short, steep hills and stream crossings. The trail is never very difficult, so you can really crank out the miles. If you're in the Reading area only for a short time, this is the ride I would recommend. And IMBA agrees. They called this one of the best mountain bike trails in America. Ride it and find out why. Expert riders will spend most of ride in their middle chain ring.

When you're driving along the back roads around Reading, try to notice the beautiful farms, especially those with hex signs decorating the barns. Hex signs are a familiar sight along the back roads of Berks County and are one of the more visible displays of Pennsylvania Dutch folk art. There are many theories on the symbolic meaning of the hex signs, but more than likely the geometric designs are placed on barns either to bring luck or to ward off evil.

Currently known for its many outlet malls, the city of Reading has enjoyed a rich and diverse past. Thomas and Richard Penn, sons of the state's founder William Penn, laid out the old town. The city used the Schuykill River as its focal point, spreading out alongside its banks. Reading and other nearby towns quickly became major producers of iron and steel goods. Reading's arms manufactures supplied a good majority of the cannons, rifles, and ammunition used by the Continental Army in the Revolutionary War.

Ride Information

🕿 Trail Contacts:
Blue Marsh Lake Ranger Station, 1268 Palisades Drive, Leesport, PA; (610) 376-6337 or *www.nap.usace. army.mil/sb/bm_guide.htm* • **The Bike Shop**, 2233 Penn Ave., West Lawn, PA; (610) 670-4750

🕘 Schedule:
8:00 A.M. to sunset

❓ Local Information:
Reading and Berks County Visitors Bureau, 352 Penn Street, Reading, PA 1-800-443-6610 or (610) 375-4085 or *www.readingberkspa.com*

💡 Local Events/Attractions:
[see Ride 18: French Creek/Red & White]

🛏 Accommodations:
[see Ride 18: French Creek/Red & White]

🍴 Restaurants:
[see Ride 18: French Creek/Red & White]

👥 Organizations:
To volunteer, call the ranger station and ask for the volunteer coordinator.

Ⓝ Maps:
USGS maps: Berks County, PA • **The Blue Marsh National Recreation Area map** – *available from the ranger station*

By the mid-1800s the iron industry began to fade. Textile mills took hold of the local economy. Today the town still relies on the textile trade to fuel its economic growth. Outlet malls dominate the area. Companies such as London Fog, Ralph Lauren, Laura Ashley, Jockey, and other high-end retailers, all offer their goods to the general public with discounts of up to 70 percent. So for all you power shoppers, bring your checkbook.

MilesDirections

0.0 START by taking the Blue Marsh Lake Trail. Follow the well-marked singletrack trail up a hill and past a spillway to a trail junction.

1.2 Go right on the main trail and head to a trail junction.

1.3 Go right on the unmaintained road.

1.4 Go left on singletrack. Follow the trail to a parking area. Cross the parking area to the Squirrel Trail.

2.3 Go left on the Squirrel Trail and pedal to a trail on the right.

2.5 Go right and then cross a stream. Crank up a short, steep hill to a bridge.

3.1 Pedal over the bridge and then go right on singletrack.

4.6 Cross over a paved road (Sterners Hill Road), and crank down a fast hill to a trail junction.

5.5 Take the singletrack trail that weaves along the edge of the lake to a steep hill.

6.4 Crank up a steep, loose, low-gear hill. Hit the top and fly down fast singletrack to a small bridge.

7.2 Go right on sweet singletrack.

7.8 Go left on a wide gravel road. Cross a paved road and then crank up a short hill, with great views of the lake.

8.1 Go left up the wide gravel road.

8.6 Go left up a steep hill.

8.7 Bear right. Follow the trail to yellow gate.

9.0 Go right on singletrack and head past a gate to a bridge.

9.6 Cross over the bridge to a trail junction.

9.7 Continue straight on singletrack.

10.0 Cross a bridge over Crane Creek and follow the trail through another stream crossing.

10.4 Pedal through yet another stream, then crank up a short hill that leads to Lamm Road.

10.5 Cross Lamm Road to a wide doubletrack trail. Follow this down a fast hill to an intersection.

11.4 Go right on the unmaintained road.

11.5 Go left on sweet singletrack. Float across a small stream and then crank up a short hill to where the trail forks.

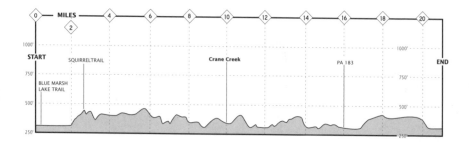

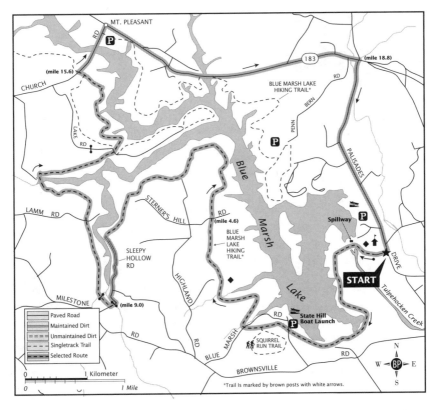

Paved Road
Maintained Dirt
Unmaintained Dirt
Singletrack Trail
Selected Route

0   1 Kilometer
0   1 Mile

*Trail Is marked by brown posts with white arrows.

MilesDirections *continued*

12.1 Go left and head to a paved road.

12.2 Go left on the paved road and head to a trail on the right.

12.3 Go right. Pass a spur trail on the left. Continue straight on wide tread and head to a trail on the left.

13.2 Pedal left through an open area. Crank up a hill to a trail junction.

13.9 Go right and head down sweet singletrack that winds through a dense forest to a bridge.

14.7 Pedal past three wooden bridges to a trail junction.

15.0 Continue straight on singletrack and head to a trail junction.

15.1 Go straight on fast singletrack and head down to a trail junction.

15.4 Pedal left and head up to Church Road.

15.6 Turn right on Church Road. Pedal straight to PA 183.

16.0 Pedal right onto PA 183. Watch for vehicular traffic as you pedal to Palisade Road.

18.8 Turn right on Palisade Road. Follow the road to Stilling Basin and the Blue Marsh Lake Trailhead.

20.8 Cruise into the parking area.

21

Pumping Station

Ride Specs

Start: From the parking area at U.S. 322 and Pumping Station Road

Length: 5.6-mile loop

Approximate Riding Time: 1–2 hours

Difficulty Rating: Moderate, with a few strenuous sections

Terrain: Singletrack, doubletrack, and gravel roads, rocky. Rocky sections on tight singletrack. Fast downhills on rocky tread.

Elevation Gain: 656 feet

Land Status: Pennsylvania State Game Lands and Boy Scouts of Lancaster/Camp Mack Boy Scout Camp

Nearest Town: Lebanon, PA

Other Trail Users: Hikers, horseback riders, and Boy Scouts

Getting There

From Philadelphia, PA: Take I-76 west to Exit 20. Follow PA 72 north to U.S. 322. Go east on U.S. 322 for 5.5 miles to Pumping Station Road and a large parking area on left. Park here.

DeLorme: Pennsylvania Atlas & Gazetteer: Page 79 B-6

I n the 19th Century, Pennsylvania was the leading producer of iron in the United States. The hills and valleys of Pennsylvania provide an abundance of iron ore, limestone, charcoal, and waterpower—the four ingredients needed to produce iron. Most of the early mills used a cold-blast furnace process, which required a tremendous amount of materials. The furnaces had to be fed around the clock. The temperature in the core of the furnace could reach up to 3000 degrees Fahrenheit.

Entire villages were built around the mills. Supporting the furnaces were miners, molders, colliers, teamsters, housewives, and woodcutters. The king of the hill was the iron-master, who managed the forge. These forges were some of America's first factories and signaled the beginning of the American Industrial Revolution. Touring one of these forges, one can only imagine the unbearable conditions workers had to endure—the extreme heat, the noise, the soot-filled air.

The old-fashioned cold-blast furnaces were soon replaced by the larger, steam powered hot-blast furnaces. Generally located in large cities near rail yards, the hot-blast furnaces all but put an end to old, rural way of iron making.

While in the area, check out the Cornwall Iron Furnace. Located in the serene village of Cornwall, the furnace was in operation from 1742 to 1883. The visitor center contains exhibits on mining, charcoal making, and iron making. Take a

drive down Boyd Street and into Minersvillage for a look at the attractive stone houses which have been occupied by local miners since the 1860s.

This ride offers excellent technical riding on both singletrack and doubletrack trails. The singletrack section, along Walnut Run, is just beautiful. Both bike and rider can take a hammering on this one. The climb up to the Horseshoe Trail will test both your lungs and your legs. The downhill section on the Horseshoe Trail will test the skills of the best downhill riders. This is a short ride, but to make it longer, hook-up with the many different trails in the area that start from the Pumping Station parking area. A short section of this ride is on Camp Mack property, so obtain a free permit from the Boy Scouts of Lancaster before departing. *(See the Ride Info for more information.)* Also, mountain biking is not allowed on Camp Mack lands from June through August.

MilesDirections

0.0 START from the parking area. Turn right on Pumping Station Road and go over a small bridge to a trail on the left.

0.1 Go left and pass through a small parking area to the trailhead. Go straight on beautiful tread along Walnut Run.

0.4 A spur trail goes right. Continue straight.

0.8 Cross a small stream, then cruise down to Walnut Run.

0.8+ Go left across Walnut Run. Pick-up a singletrack trail through an often-wet section. Cross another small stream and begin climbing on tight, rocky tread up to U.S. 322.

1.3 A spur goes right. Continue straight up to U.S. 322. Cross over U.S. 322 (with caution) to a trail at the end of a guardrail. Begin a steep climb up to the Horseshoe Trail.

1.4 The trail forks. Turn right up steep, rocky, tight singletrack.

1.5 The trail forks. Turn right up the tight singletrack.

1.8 The tread becomes very steep and rocky. There's no shame in pushing your bike through this section.

1.9 Go left and follow the orange blazes up more steep tread to the Horseshoe Trail.

2.1 Go left on Horseshoe Trail and follow the yellow blazes.

2.4 The trail forks. Turn right and follow yellow blazes down a tight, rocky, technical, winding, don't-go-over-the-handlebars downhill to Pumping Station Road.

3.5 Go left on Pumping Station Road and head to U.S. 322.

3.7 Go right on U.S. 322. Cross a bridge and head to the Horseshoe Trail, which is on the left.

3.8 Pedal left on the Horseshoe Trail, as beautiful Hammer Creek drops-off to your left.

4.0 A spur trail goes left. Continue straight on a wide and rocky singletrack trail.

4.1 Horseshoe Trail goes right. Continue straight on often-wet tread.

4.4 A spur trail goes left. Continue straight on wide tread and go up a series of short, steep switchbacks.

4.7 Go left on Big Rock Trail. Drop down a short hill and then climb up to a trail junction.

4.9 The State Game Lands trail goes right. Continue straight and head down to the power lines.

5.0 Trail goes left at the power lines. The trail weaves past large boulders on tight tread and leads down to a stream and the Horseshoe Trail.

5.3 Turn right on the Horseshoe Trail.

5.5 Turn right on U.S. 322.

5.6 Cruise into the parking area.

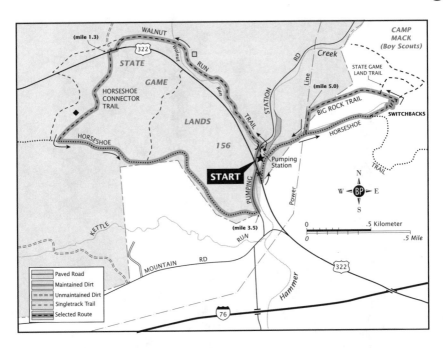

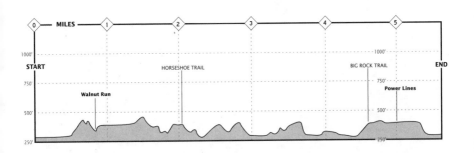

Ride Information

📞 Trail Contacts:
Southeast Pennsylvania Game Commission, RD 2, Reading, PA; (610)-926-1966 or *www.pgc.state.pa.us* • **Boy Scouts of Lancaster/Camp Mack Boy Scout Camp,** 630 Janet Ave., Lancaster, PA; (717) 394-4063 • **KOM Cycles,** 1111 Walnut St., Lebanon, PA; (717) 273-9499 or *www.komcycles.com*

🕐 Schedule:
Sunrise to sunset. *Mountain biking is not allowed on Camp Mack lands from June through August.*

💲 Fees/Permits:
There's no fee, but permits are required to ride on Camp Mack lands. They can easily be obtained by calling (717) 626-8711.

❓ Local Information:
Lebanon Valley Tourist and Visitor Bureau, 625 Quentin Rd., Ste. 4, Lebanon, PA; (717) 272-8555 or *www.parainbow.com*

📍 Local Events/Attractions:
Palmyra (Seltzer's) Bologna Company, 230 N. College St., Palmyra, PA; 1-800-282-6336 or (717) 838-6336 or *www.seltzersbologna.com – offer a video tour of the smokehouses and packing facilities* • **Union Canal Canoe Rental,** Blackbridge Rd. Bellegrove, PA; (717) 838-9580 • **Ephrata Cloister,** 632 W. Main St., Ephrata, PA; (717) 733-6600 or *www.cob-net.org/cloister.htm – one of America's earliest communal societies*

• **Landis Valley Museum,** 2451 Kissel Hill Rd., Lancaster, PA; (717) 569-0401 • **Julius Sturgis Pretzel House,** 219 E. Main St., Lititz, PA; (717) 626-4354 or *www.sturgispretzel.com* • **Cornwall Iron Furnace Historic Site,** SR 2001, Cornwall, PA; (717) 272-9711 • **Hershey's Chocolate World,** 800 Park Blvd., Hershey, PA; (717) 534-4900 or *www.hersheyschocolateworld.com* • **Zoo America, Park Blvd.,** Hershey, PA; (717) 534-3860 or *www.800hershey.com/attractions/zooamerica/zoo_homepage.html*

🛏 Accommodations:
Mt. Gretna Inn/Bed and Breakfast, Kauffman and Pine, Mt. Gretna, PA; 1-800-277-6602 or (717) 964-3234 or *www.mtgretna.com*

🍴 Restaurants:
Mt. Gretna Hideaway, Boulevard Street, Mt. Gretna, PA; (717) 964-3170

🚲 Mountain Bike Tours:
gretnabikes.com, 767 Mine Road, Lebanon, PA; (717) 964-1836 or *www.gretnabikes.com – they offer local and foreign tours and promote races*

🅝 Maps:
USGS maps: Lebanon County, PA • **Pennsylvania State Game Lands No. 156 map,** Lancaster & Lebanon Counties – *available from the Pennsylvania Game Commission for $1.00*

Walnut Run

Ride Specs

Start: From the parking area at U.S. 322 and Pumping Station Road
Length: 10.1 out-and-back
Approximate Riding Time: 1½–2½ hours
Difficulty Rating: Moderate, with a few strenuous sections
Terrain: Rocky singletrack, doubletrack, and gravel roads—a number of log jumps, stream crossings, fast downhills and steep uphills.
Elevation Gain: 1,710 feet
Land Status: Pennsylvania State Game Lands
Nearest Town: Lebanon, PA
Other Trail Users: Hikers and horseback riders

Getting There

From Philadelphia, PA: Take I-76 west to Exit 20. Follow PA 72 north to U.S. 322. Go east on U.S. 322 for 5.5 miles to Pumping Station Road and a large parking area on left. Park here.
DeLorme: Pennsylvania Atlas & Gazetteer: Page 79 B-6

The name Hershey is synonymous with that wonderful sweet-stuff that majority of Americans constantly crave. Chocolate. Before there was a Hershey Park or a Chocolate World there was the factory town of Hershey. The place we now know as Hershey was once a working class factory town, complete with butcher shops, grocery stores, five & dime stores, and other supply businesses. The town has since been turn into a theme park, of sorts, with restaurants, hotels, golf courses, a zoo, botanical gardens, and museums.

Hershey Park and the chocolate factory are the brainchild of Milton Hershey. With previous successful candy businesses in New York and Philadelphia, Milton returned to his hometown of Hershey, first as a caramel producer. He later converted his plant into what would become the world's leading manufacturer of chocolate candy. If you want to make a family outing to Hershey, bring the kids—and a fat wallet—to enjoy all the sites this tourist attraction has to offer.

Your ride starts east of Hershey at the parking area on U.S. 322 and Pumping Station Road. Walnut Run is a great ride, covering a lot of varying terrain in its 10 miles. Single and doubletrack trails, stream crossing, log jumps, and technical sections make this a ride for the mountain bike connoisseur. The first part of the ride follows Walnut Run creek on a beautiful trail, riding toward U.S. 322. The ride

Ride Information

🔋 Trail Contacts:
Southeast Pennsylvania Game Commission, RD 2, Reading, PA (610) 926-1966 or www.pgc.state.pa.us • KOM Cycles, 1111 Walnut St., Lebanon, PA; (717) 273-9499 or www.komcycles.com

🕐 Schedule:
Sunrise to sunset

❓ Local Information:
Lebanon Valley Tourist and Visitor Bureau, 625 Quentin Rd., Ste. 4, Lebanon, PA; (717) 272-8555 or www.parainbow.com

💡 Local Events/Attractions:
[see Ride 21: Pumping Station]

🛏 Accommodations:
[see Ride 21: Pumping Station]

🍴 Restaurants:
[see Ride 21: Pumping Station]

🚵 Mountain Bike Tours:
[see Ride 21: Pumping Station]

🅽 Maps:
USGS maps: Lebanon County, PA • Pennsylvania State Game Lands No. 156 map, Lancaster & Lebanon Counties – available from the Pennsylvania Game Commission for $1.00

then breaks right, away from the highway. Travel up some steep, technical terrain to the power lines. From here the ride climbs up to White Oak Hill on a mixture of single and doubletrack trails. These are some of the best trails in the area, so enjoy. The ride then follows an abandoned power line on some excellent singletrack riding. The ride is an out-and-back, so at the 6.5-mile mark, turn around and retrace your tracks back to the start.

MilesDirections

0.0 START from the parking area, and turn right on Pumping Station Road.

0.1 Go left. Pass a small parking area and head to the trailhead. The trail follows beautiful tread along Walnut Run.

0.4 A spur trail goes right. Continue straight.

0.8 Cross over a small stream and then cruise down to Walnut Run.

0.8+ Go left across Walnut Run. Take the singletrack trail across a small stream and begin climbing on tight, rocky tread, leading to U.S. 322.

1.3 Go right on a wide dirt trail. Cross over a stream and begin a gradual uphill to the power lines.

1.8 The trail forks at the power lines. Go right and head down a tight singletrack trail. Pedal past an often-wet section. Cross over a small stream and climb up a short, steep, rocky hill. Follow beautiful singletrack to a three-way trail junction.

2.4 Go left and head up a singletrack trail.

2.6 The tread becomes steep and rocky.

2.7 A spur trail goes left. Continue straight.

2.9 Cross over a service road. Continue straight on a game land road.

3.0 Go right onto the white-blazed Deer Trail—the turn is near a private home.

3.1 The white-blazed trail goes left. The ride continues straight on wonderful singletrack and goes over several log jumps down to a trail junction.

3.6 Go left and head down the fast Powerline Trail. Be cautious of loose rocks and tree limbs on the trail.

4.3 Go left at a major trail junction.

4.8 The trail forks. Go right and head down the tight Creek Trail. Crank past several log jumps and head down to a small stream crossing.

5.1 Cross the stream. Crank over several downed trees on tight tread and head up to the Powerline Trail.

5.4 Go right and head up to a trail junction.

5.7 Reach a trail junction. Continue straight.

6.5 Go right on singletrack. From here (you're at the original 3.6-mile mark), retrace your route back to the parking area.

10.1 Hit the brakes! You're home.

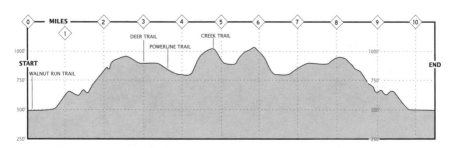

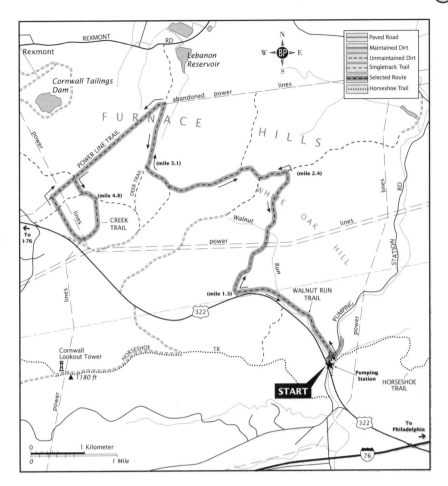

Horseshoe Trail

Ride Specs

Start: From the parking area at U.S. 322 and Pumping Station Road
Length: 7.6-mile loop
Approximate Riding Time: 1½–2½ hours
Difficulty Rating: Moderate, with a few strenuous sections
Terrain: Rocky singletrack, doubletrack, and gravel roads
Land Status: Pennsylvania State Game Lands and Camp Mack Boy Scout Camp
Nearest Town: Lebanon, PA
Other Trail Users: Hikers, horseback riders, and Boy Scouts

Getting There

From Philadelphia, PA: Take I-76 west to Exit 20. Follow PA 72 north to U.S. 322. Go east on U.S. 322 for 5.5 miles to Pumping Station Road and a large parking area on left. Park here.
DeLorme: Pennsylvania Atlas & Gazetteer: Page 79 B-3

This ride takes in a small section of the 120-mile long Horseshoe Trail. The Horseshoe Trail starts in Valley Forge Historical Park at the Woolman Memorial Marker on the south bank of Valley Creek and takes a meandering line west to where it intersects with the Appalachian Trail on Sharp Mountain, just northeast of Hershey, Pennsylvania. The trail passes through Hopewell Village National Historical Site and the adjoining French Creek State Park. From French Creek State Park the trail cut west through the Furnace Hills, hugging the Lebanon and Lancaster County Line. The main trail is clearly marked with yellow blazes and all side trails are marked with white blazes. Sections of the trail are open to mountain biking and offer some very steep and technical riding. For more information on the Horseshoe Trail, contact the Horseshoe Trail Club.

Pennsylvania is blessed with a number of "long trails" that crisscross the state. The most famous of these "long trails" is, of course, the Appalachian Trail. The Appalachian Trail extends from Maine to Georgia and follows the ridge of the Appalachian Mountains through twelve states. The 222-mile section through Pennsylvania starts near the Delaware Water Gap in the northeastern part of the state, and takes a southerly line down to Rouezerville, Pennsylvania, near the Maryland state border. The trail passes through five Pennsylvania State Parks, as well as National Park lands. Well-maintained cabins and shelters are located along the trail and offer refuge for weary hikers. For more information on the Appalachian Trail, contact The Appalachian Trail Conference.

Other "long trails" of interest to hikers and cyclists in the state are the 58-mile Loyalsock Trail, located north of Williamsport, Pennsylvania; the 45-mile Warrior Trail, near Greensboro, Pennsylvania; the 70-mile Potomac Heritage National Scenic Trail, near Ohiopyle, Pennsylvania; and the 119-mile North County National Scenic Trail, located in the Allegheny National Forest in northwest Pennsylvania.

Your ride starts at the Pumping Station parking area and follows the Horseshoe Trail into Camp Mack Boy Scout lands. (Mountain biking is not allowed on Camp Mack lands from June through August, and a permit is required at other times. See below for permit information.) This ride is a wonderful mixture of tight singletrack trails, wide dirt roads, and technical rocky sections that will demand the attention of most riders. The downhill section on the Horseshoe Trail is steep, rocky, and technical. Once down the hill the ride loops back to the Pumping Station parking area and calmer waters. Please respect the wishes of the Camp Mack Land Owners and obey all rules and restrictions. These folks have been more than considerate in allowing mountain biking on their property. Many folks in the Lebanon area have established a wonderful rapport with the Camp Mack folks, so don't blow it!

Ride Information

📞 Trail Contacts:

Southeast Pennsylvania Game Commission, RD 2, Reading, PA (610)-926-1966 or *www.pgc. state.pa.us* • **Boy Scouts of Lancaster/Camp Mack Boy Scout Camp,** 630 Janet Ave., Lancaster, PA; (717) 394-4063 • **KOM Cycles,** 1111 Walnut St., Lebanon, PA (717) 273-9499 or *www.komcycles.com*

🕐 Schedule:

Sunrise to sunset. *Mountain biking is not allowed on Camp Mack lands from June through August.*

💲 Fees/Permits:

There's no fee, but permits are required to ride on Camp Mack lands. They can easily be obtained by calling (717) 626-8711.

❓ Local Information:

Lebanon Valley Tourist and Visitor Bureau, 625 Quentin Rd., Ste. 4, Lebanon, PA; (717) 272-8555 or *www.parainbow.com*

💡 Local Events/Attractions:

Appalachian Trail Conference, 799 Washington St., Harpers Ferry, WV; (304) 535-6331 or *www.atconf.org* • *[see Ride 21: Pumping Station]*

🍴 Restaurants:

[see Ride 21: Pumping Station]

👥 Organizations:

Horseshoe Trail Club, 509 Cheltena Ave, Jenkintown, PA

🅝 Maps: USGS, Lebanon County, PA

• **Pennsylvania State Game Lands No. 156 map,** Lancaster & Lebanon Counties – *available from the Pennsylvania Game Commission for $1.00*

MilesDirections

0.0 START from the parking area and turn left on U.S. 322. Cross the bridge over Hammer Creek to the Horseshoe Trail, on the left.

0.1 Pedal left onto the yellow-blazed Horseshoe Trail. Hammer Creek drops off to the left.

0.3 A spur trail goes left. Continue straight on the Horseshoe Trail.

0.4 The Horseshoe Trail goes left. Continue straight up through an often-wet section.

0.7 A spur trail shoots off to the left. Continue straight up, past a series of steep switchbacks.

0.9 The Big Rock Trail goes left. Continue straight up to a trail junction.

1.0 Go left and fly down past several Kelly humps to Hammer Creek. Follow wide tread along Hammer Creek to a trail junction.

1.5 The Knob Hill Trail goes left. Continue straight past several spur trails to the Shooters Trail, on the right.

2.1 Go right on the Shooters Trail. Weave along wonderful, tight single-track to the shooting range.

2.4 Continue straight past the range. Jam it up a short, steep, rocky hill to a dirt road.

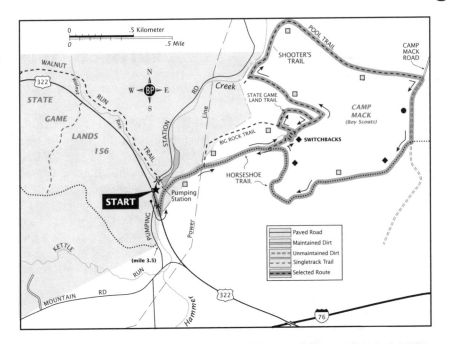

MilesDirections *continued*

2.6 Go left, on the wide dirt road. The trail goes past the pool to road junction.

2.7 Go right on the Pool Trail. Pedal up past the Chapel to a trail junction.

2.8 Go left on Pool Trail. The trail goes through a large camping area to a water tank.

3.2 Continue straight, passing the water tank. Fly down a short hill to Camp Mack Road.

3.4 Go right on Camp Mack Road. Climb up short hill, passing a road on the right. Continue straight to a trail junction.

3.8 Light Trail goes left. Continue straight for 50 feet to Horseshoe Trail on the right. Go right on the Horseshoe Trail. Climb up steep, rocky tread. At the top of hill, catch your breath and begin an extended downhill, past several technical rocky sections, down to the Big Timber Trail.

4.9 Keep left, on the Horseshoe Trail. The trail still has several technical sections as you fight your way to a trail junction.

5.3 Turn right and head back up to the Big Rock Trail.

5.9 Go left onto the Big Rock Trail. Climb up a short hill to the Game Land Trail, on the right.

6.1 Roll right onto the Game Lands Trail. Fly down tight, smooth singletrack.

6.2 A spur trail goes right. Continue straight on tight singletrack.

6.4 Reach a familiar trail junction. Turn right onto wide tread. Fly down the switchbacks retracing your route back to the trailhead.

7.3 Go right and head across U.S. 322.

7.6 Take a right into the parking area.

Furnace Hills

Ride Specs

Start: From the parking area at U.S. 322 and Pumping Station Road

Length: 8.1-mile loop

Approximate Riding Time: 1½–2½ hours

Difficulty Rating: Moderate, with a few strenuous sections

Terrain: Rocky single and doubletrack trails and gravel roads

Elevation Gain: 1,086 feet

Land Status: Pennsylvania State Game Lands

Nearest Town: Lebanon, PA

Other Trail Users: Hikers and equestrians

Getting There

From Philadelphia, PA: Take I-76 west to Exit 20. Follow PA 72 north to U.S. 322. Go east on U.S. 322 for 5.5 miles to Pumping Station Road and turn right. Travel 0.2 miles and turn right on Mountain Road. Go 0.5 miles to a state game land parking area on the right. Park here. The ride starts here. *DeLorme Pennsylvania Atlas & Gazetteer,* Page 79 B-7

W hen I first started this book, I heard there was some good riding in the Lebanon area. All I had to do was find it—not an easy thing to do if you're unfamiliar with the area. The first thing I did was call *gretna-bikes.com* in Lebanon to get some information. Little did I know I had tapped into one of the best resources for mountain biking in the region. Bill, the owner of *gretnabikes.com*, is one of the most knowledgeable riders in the area. Bill and his staff are very involved in the local mountain biking scene. They are more than willing to give you information on the rides in the Lebanon area—an area which, I feel, has some of the best riding in Eastern Pennsylvania. Bill and his staff have sponsored downhill and cross-county racing teams and are also responsible for promoting the annual Mount Gretna Mountain Bike Race. Bill has been a great voice in the Lebanon area for keeping trails open. If you're in his neck of the woods and would like to talk mountain biking, give Bill a call or visit his terrific website.

Your ride starts at the State Game Lands No. 156 parking area 1.5 miles from U.S. 322. The ride follows a wide dirt road for a short distance and then goes right along Kettle Run. The trail along Kettle Run is tight, rocky, and technical. This is a difficult patch and can easily be avoided by walking. The next part of the ride climbs up a wide dirt road, passing several State Game Land food plots as it leads you up to the top of a ridge and to the radio towers. Just past the towers the trail

drops steeply down a tight singletrack trail back to Kettle Run. At the bottom of the steep hill the ride goes right and leads out to wide dirt road. It then flies back to the parking area and the comforts of your car.

I just loved the riding around the Lebanon area. The trails are extremely challenging and are by far some of the best mountain biking trails in the state. From the Pumping Station parking area you can do several of the rides in the west section of this book, or you can customize a ride from the many trails in the region. Whatever you do, if you're riding in the Lebanon area, you're sure to have a wonderful time.

Ride Information

Trail Contacts:
Southeast Pennsylvania Game Commission, RD 2, Reading, PA; (610)-926-1966 or *www.pgc.state.pa.us* • **KOM Cycles,** 1111 Walnut St., Lebanon, PA; (717) 273-9499 or *www.komcycles.com*

Schedule:
Sunrise to sunset

Local Information:
Lebanon Valley Tourist and Visitor Bureau, 625 Quentin Rd., Ste. 4, Lebanon, PA; (717) 272-8555 or *www.parainbow.com*

Local Events/Attractions:
[see Ride 21: Pumping Station]

Accommodations:
[see Ride 21: Pumping Station]

Restaurants:
[see Ride 21: Pumping Station]

Maps:
USGS, Lebanon County, PA • **Pennsylvania State Game Lands** No. 156 map, Lancaster & Lebanon Counties – *available from the Pennsylvania Game Commission for $1.00*

MilesDirections

0.0 START from the parking area. Pedal up the gravel road a short distance to a trail on the right.

0.1 Turn right and follow the trail through rocky sections down to a stream crossing.

0.3 Cross Kettle Run and then follow the faint singletrack trail through several rocky sections.

0.5 Cross Kettle Run again and crank up rocky tread, passing several log jumps and technical sections to a trail junction.

1.1 Go left and head up steep, wide tread.

1.3 A spur trail goes right. (Make a mental note of this trail junction. You'll be coming down this trail on your way back.) Continue straight down the rocky road.

1.5 Go right and head up wide gravel.

1.8 Spur trail goes left; continue straight.

2.0 Spur trail goes left; continue straight.

2.6 Spur trail goes left, continue on the road.

3.7 Spur road goes left; continue climbing up to a road junction.

4.3 Roll right and head up a wide road.

4.5 Pedal past a gate and a state game lands parking area on the right. Begin a nice climb up through a pine forest to the radio towers.

6.0 Arrive at the towers. Continue straight on the road.

6.1 A singletrack trail goes right. Continue straight past several towers to a trail junction on right.

6.5 Go right onto the white-blazed singletrack trail.

6.6 The trail forks. Go right and head down awesome, tight, rocky singletrack trail.

7.1 Go right—you're back at the 1.3-mile mark—down to a road.

7.3 Go left onto a wide gravel road. Fly down fast tread back to the parking area.

8.1 Hit the brakes! You're home.

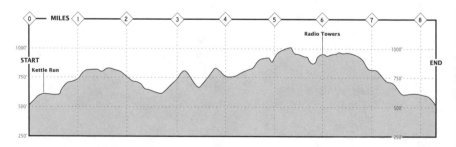

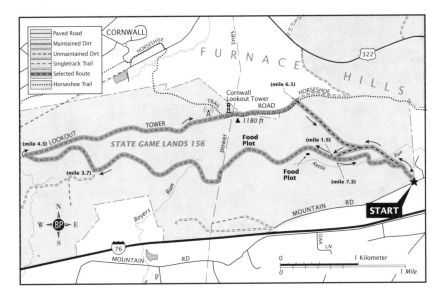

145

Mount Gretna

Ride Specs

Start: From the parking area on PA 117
Length: 7.6-mile loop
Approximate Riding Time: 1½–2½ hours
Difficulty Rating: Moderate, with a few strenuous sections
Terrain: Rocky single and doubletrack trails and gravel roads
Elevation Gain: 1,239 feet
Land Status: Pennsylvania State Game Lands
Nearest Town: Lebanon, PA
Other Trail Users: Hikers and equestrians

Getting There

From Philadelphia, PA: Take I-76 west to Exit 22. Follow PA 72 north to PA 117. Go west on PA 117 for 0.8 mile to pullout/parking on the left at a gate.
DeLorme: Pennsylvania Atlas & Gazetteer: Page 79 B-6

Mt. Gretna Inn/Bed & Breakfast.

The Pennsylvania Chautauqua Society founded the quaint small village of Mount Gretna in the 1890s. The Society was attracted to the area's tranquil feel and natural beauty. Walking or driving through the village, one comes to realize that little has changed in the last 100 years. It's as charming as ever.

The word "Chautauqua" was given to a lake in upstate New York by the local Seneca Indians. The lake was also the site of the original Chautauqua Assembly in 1874. The original Assembly was established to promote culture, education, and entertainment in a resort-like setting. At the height of their popularity, over 10,000 different assemblies were located throughout the United States. Concerts and lecture series were sponsored for the cultural advancement of the community, along with popular public figures who spoke on current issues of the day. With the advent of radio and television, popularity of the assemblies declined as Americans looked to other venues for current events and entertainment. Only four assemblies remain in the United States today.

The houses in the village of Mount Gretna are mostly of Victorian design, and many have been restored to their original state. The village offers an array of activities during the summer months, including the well-known Timbers Dinner Theatre that stages Broadway caliber plays throughout the summer. For more information on all the activities in the Mount Gretna area, call the Mount Gretna Arts Council.

The Mount Gretna Inn is a beautifully restored Victorian home located just a few hundred yards from some of the best mountain bike trails in the area. The rooms in

the inn have been tastefully decorated from the Victorian period. The inn has reasonable prices and offers a package deal that includes mountain bike rentals and guided trips from Mount Gretna Bike Tours in Lebanon. If you're looking for a great get-
away that includes awesome mountain biking and a wonderful place to be pampered
after your ride, I highly recommend the Mount Gretna Inn.

Your ride starts at a parking area just off Pennsylvania 117. The first mile is an
uphill grind on a wide doubletrack trail. At the top of the hill, look left for yellow
blazes marking the Horseshoe Trail. Turn left here and go down some tight, technical singletrack. The trail passes through an often-wet section and leads to a trail junction. Turn right at the junction, then right again, riding on a new singletrack trail.
The trail makes a short loop, going along Pennsylvania 72 for a short distance. After
this section, the ride heads out toward Pennsylvania 117, skirts along the village of
Mount Gretna, and then climbs up to the Governor Dick Tower. The tower is an old
fire tower that was used to spot forest fires in the surrounding hills. Leave your bike
outside, go into the tower, and climb the stairs to the top for some great views of the
surrounding Furnace Hills. Make a great downhill run back toward Pennsylvania 117
and follow the trail back to the parking area and your car.

Ride Information

📞 Trail Contacts:
**Southeast Pennsylvania Game
Commission,** RD 2, Reading, PA;
(610)-926-1966 or *www.pgc.state.
pa.us* • **KOM Cycles,** 1111 Walnut
St., Lebanon, PA; (717) 273-9499 or
www.komcycles.com

🕐 Schedule:
Sunrise to sunset

❓ Local Information:
**Lebanon Valley Tourist and Visitor
Bureau,** 625 Quentin Rd., Ste. 4,
Lebanon, PA; (717) 272-8555 or
www.parainbow.com • **Mt. Gretna
Arts Council,** Mt. Gretna, PA; (717)
964-0554

💡 Local Events/Attractions:
Timbers Dinner Theatre, 350 Timber
Road, Mt. Gretna, PA; (717) 964-

3601 or *www.mtgretna.com/timbers*
• *[see Ride 21: Pumping Station]*

🍽 Accommodations:
Mt. Gretna Inn/Bed and Breakfast,
Kauffman and Pine, Mt. Gretna, PA;
1-800-277-6602 or (717) 964-3234
or *www.mtgretna.com*

🍴 Restaurants:
[see Ride 21: Pumping Station]

🚵 Mountains Bike Tours:
[see Ride 21: Pumping Station]

🅝 Maps:
Pennsylvania State Game Lands No.
156 map, Lancaster & Lebanon
Counties – *available from the
Pennsylvania Game Commission for
$1.00*

MilesDirections

0.0 START by pedaling past the gate. Crank up a steep gravel road.

0.6 A spur trail goes left. Continue straight.

0.6+ A spur trail goes left. Continue straight, on the wide road, to a yellow-blazed trail on the left.

0.8 Go left on Horseshoe Trail (lined with yellow blazes). Drop down on tight, rocky singletrack to a log bridge.

1.4 Continue straight, past the log bridge to a trail junction.

1.7 Go right, on tight singletrack, to a trail junction.

1.8 Roll right, on tight, rocky tread, past several short technical sections that lead down to a log bridge.

2.5 Continue straight, past the bridge. The trail rolls left and runs parallel to PA 72 and eventually leads to a trail junction.

2.6 Go left, up some tight, rocky, technical singletrack.

2.9 The trail becomes steep, narrow, and rocky. Continue on rocky tread, down a steep hill, to a trail junction.

3.5 Reach the trail junction. Continue straight.

3.6 Pedal right and then left, onto wider tread. Crank up a short hill to the parking area.

4.0 Pedal straight, past the parking area, to a singletrack trail. Follow the winding singletrack trail to a junction at a yellow gate.

4.4 Go left, up smooth, wide trail.

4.6 A spur trail goes left; continue straight.

4.8 A spur trail goes left; continue straight to a gate.

5.2 Pedal straight, past a gate and several houses, to a trail junction on the right.

5.4 Go right, on singletrack, to a trail junction.

5.6 Go left.

5.7 Grunt left up steep tread, past several logs and rocky sections, to a wide dirt road.

5.9 Cross the road to a singletrack trail—most riders will walk this section. Ride or walk up the steep, rocky tread to the Governor Dick Tower. Climb up the tower to enjoy the views.

6.0 Go left, on a wide dirt road. Turn left and then left again, finally to singletrack on the right.

6.1 Roll right, down fast and rocky tread, to a trail junction.

6.7 Go left to a trail junction.

6.8 Go right, on wide tread, to a yellow gate.

7.2 Roll right, on singletrack. Crank up a short, steep hill to the parking area.

7.6 Cruise into the parking area.

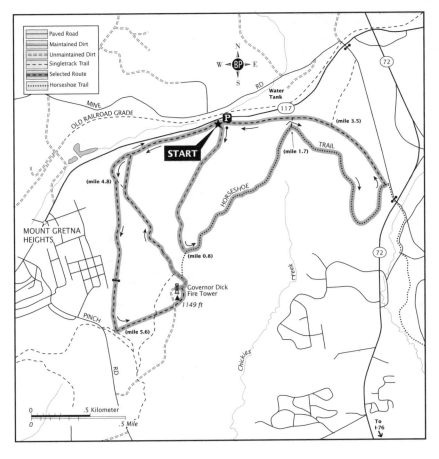

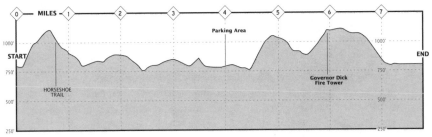

Weiser State Forest

Ride Specs

Start: From the parking area just off PA 61
Length: 10.8 miles out-and-back
Approximate Riding Time: 1½–2½ hours
Difficulty Rating: Strenuous, with a good climb to start the ride
Terrain: Singletrack, doubletrack, and dirt roads
Elevation Gain: 1,746 feet
Land Status: Pennsylvania State Forest and Pennsylvania State Game Lands
Nearest Town: Port Clinton, PA
Other Trail Users: Hikers, vehicular traffic, and hunters (in season)

Getting There

From Allentown, PA: Go west on I-78 to PA 61 north. Travel 3.2 miles north on PA 61 to a pullout/parking area at a Weiser State Forest sign. Park here.
DeLorme: Pennsylvania Atlas & Gazetteer: Page 66 D-2

S
o, who is the Weiser in Weiser State Forest? Almost forgotten in modern history books, Conrad Weiser's accomplishments as a diplomat made him a legend in his day. Born in New York in 1696, Weiser became an expert on Iroquois languages and customs. When Weiser moved to the Pennsylvania frontier at the age of 33 to homestead, he was constantly sought out as a Native American negotiator. Through his treaties, travels, and land deals, he kept the area peaceful for both Native Americans and whites. After the French and Indian War in 1754, the area became more hostile. The situation worsened considerably after Weiser's death in 1760. Relations between Native Americans and whites were never the same.

If you are in the Reading area stop by the Conrad Weiser Homestead. The 26-acres park is nestled between gentle rolling hills in Berks County. Located in the park are a visitor center, several restored buildings, a monument to Weiser, as well as his gravesite. Stop into the visitor center to learn about Weiser and his efforts to keep the Pennsylvania frontier peaceful.

Another good reason to visit the area is the Yuengling Brewery, located in the town of Pottsville, Pennsylvania. The brewery is America's oldest, and it still produces some of the finest beer around. Tours are given on a daily basis. There's a museum and gift shop on the premises. At a time when micro-breweries tend come and go—and are rarely "micro"—it's refreshing to see Yuengling Brewery plugging away, producing excellent beers since 1829. My personal favorites are the dark Porter, the smooth Lager, and the Chesterfield Ale.

Your ride starts from the parking area on Pennsylvania 61. The immediate climb up to the radio towers is long and strenuous, but once you arrive, the trail

Ride Information

🕯 Trail Contacts:
Weiser State Forest Park Office, Gordon Nagle Trail, Cressona, PA; (570) 385-7800 • **Southeast Pennsylvania Game Commission**, RD 2, Reading, PA (610)-926-1966 or *www.pgc.state.pa.us* • **Spokes Bike Shop**, 4125 Pottsville Pike, Hamburg, PA; (610) 562-8900

🕐 Schedule:
Sunrise to sunset

❓ Local Information:
Berks County Visitors Bureau, 352 Penn Street, Reading, PA; 1-800-443-6610 or (610) 375-4085 or *www.readingberkspa.com* • **Schuylkill County Visitors Bureau**, 91 South Progress Ave. Pottsville, PA; 1-800-765-7282 or (570) 622-7700 or *www.schuylkill.org*

💡 Local Events/Attractions:
Conrad Weiser Homestead, U.S. 422, Womelsdorf, PA (610) 589-2934 •**Yuengling Brewery**, 5th and Mahantongo, Pottsville, PA; (570)

628-4890 or *www.yuengling.com* – *call for tours or just stop by for a beer* • **Pennsylvania Dutch Folk Culture Center**, off U.S. 222, Kutztown, PA; (610) 683-1589 – seasonal • **The Museum of Anthracite Mining**, 17th and Pine streets, Ashland, PA; (570) 875-4708 • **Pioneer Tunnel Coal Mine and Steam Locomotive**, Ashland, PA; (570) 875-3850 – *seasonal* • **Locust Lake State Park**, RR 1, Barnesville, PA; (570) 467-2404 • **Tamaqua Farm Markets**, PA 54 and PA 309, Tamaqua, PA – *every Wednesday, year-round*

🔵 Accommodations:
The Kaier Mansion, 729 E. Centre St., Mahanoy City, PA; (570) 773-3040

Ⓝ Maps:
USGS maps: Hamburg, PA • **Weiser State Forest map** – *available from the Weiser State Forest park office* • **Pennsylvania State Game Lands No. 106 map** – *available from the Pennsylvania Game Commission for $1.00*

drops down a steep hill to a stream crossing. The ride then climbs up another steep hill to the Weiser Trail. The Weiser Trail is a two-mile long singletrack and doubletrack trail that cuts through a beautiful section of Weiser State Forest. At the trail end, your ride turns left and heads down a fast, steep hill back to the parking area. Remember to keep your speed in check on the downhill. There are a couple of sharp turns where you can easily lose control. Watch for the loose gravel. There's a lot of good mountain biking in the Hamburg area. Feel free to explore the trails that weave through the State Game Lands and Weiser State Forest.

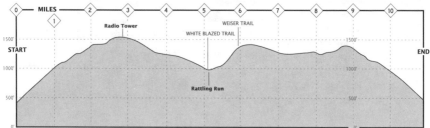

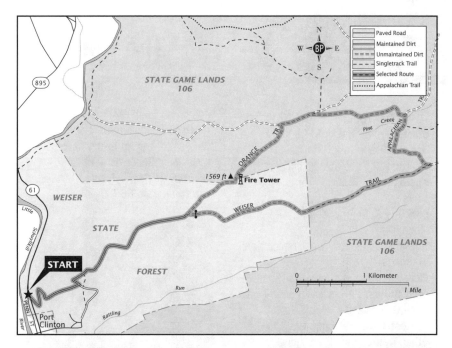

MilesDirections

0.0 START from the parking area. Pedal up a steep, wide dirt road. Maintain a steady pace. There's a lot of climbing ahead.

1.2 The grade eases, for the moment.

1.9 Arrive at a road intersection. Turn left and climb up to the radio towers.

2.6 A spur trail goes right; continue straight.

2.7 A spur road goes left; continue straight to the towers.

3.0 Radio towers are on the left. Continue straight to the fire towers.

3.1 Reach the fire towers. Go left down the orange-blazed trail and pass some Kelly humps.

3.8 A spur trail goes left; continue straight down wide tread.

4.1 Go right on wide, rocky tread and head down to a white-blazed trail.

5.1 Go right on the white-blazed trail.

5.2 Cross over Rattling Run. Begin a steep climb on loose, rocky tread, through beautiful stands of hemlocks and mountain laurels.

5.8 The grade eases.

5.9 Arrive at a trail junction. Turn right onto the Weiser Trail.

6.2 The tread becomes rockier.

7.1 Reach a sign marking the Weiser State Forest boundary. What a beautiful trail!

7.7 The grade becomes steep as you climb up to a gate.

8.3 Arrive at a gate and a service road. Turn left and head down the dirt road.

8.9 Turn right and head down a wide, dirt road. Use caution as you fly down this fast hill.

10.0 Use caution on this steep, loose, gravel downhill section.

10.8 Cruise into the parking area.

The Pinnacle

Ride Specs

Start: From the parking area at Hamburg Reservoir
Length: 8.2 miles out-and-back
Approximate Riding Time: 1½–2½ hours
Difficulty Rating: Moderate, with a few steep hills
Terrain: Singletrack, doubletrack, and dirt roads
Elevation Gain: 868 feet
Land Status: Private and Pennsylvania State Game Lands
Nearest Town: Hamburg, PA
Other Trail Users: Hikers, joggers, and hunters (in season)

Getting There

From Allentown, PA: Go west on I-78 to PA 143. Go north on PA 143 for 0.9 miles to Mountain Road. Go left on Mountain Road for 2.4 miles to Reservoir Road. Turn right on Reservoir Road and travel up to the parking area at Hamburg Reservoir. Park here.
DeLorme: Pennsylvania Atlas & Gazetteer: Page 66 D-3

This ride has the feeling of being bigger than it is. The hill climb up to the helipad is steep in sections and the tread is very rocky along the way. You really feel like your deep in the mountains even though you're only a few miles from Interstate 78. The ride takes you on an uphill climb through stands of lovely mountain laurel and pine and then along beautiful Furnace Creek. The last section to the Pinnacle is very rocky and technical. It's also very short-lived and can be easily walked. Once on top of the Pinnacle you're rewarded with great views overlooking Hawk Mountain, the Lehigh Valley, and Blue Rocks. The top of the Pinnacle is also a great place to view hawks riding the wind currents along Kittatinny Ridge.

Hawk Mountain Sanctuary, just north of this ride, encompasses 2,226 acres along the spine of Kittatinny Mountain, near the small village of Eckville, Pennsylvania. The majority of its visitors come to see the various birds of prey that seasonally descend upon the mountain. Two lookouts in the sanctuary provide an opportunity for birders to watch thousands of raptors, representing over 14 species. The hawks use the mountain as a landmark when passing through the area during

their seasonal migrations. During the cool autumn months hundreds of people come to Hawk Mountain to the watch the flights of these beautiful birds.

The birds' dependable routine almost led to their downfall. They would appear each year at the same time, and just as routinely, hawk hunters would come prepared to shoot. The killing of these birds became sport. The hunters reasoned that they were performing a service to the area by eliminating from the air these "horrible flying killers." Bird carcasses—sometimes hundreds of them—would be lined in rows along the ground. Proud hunters would even snap pictures with their kill. One such photograph made its way into the hands of Rosalie Edge, an environmental activist from New York. Edge was so outraged that in 1934 she saw to it that the world's first sanctuary for birds of prey was established on Hawk Mountain, forever ensuring safe passage for these beautiful birds.

The lookouts are open every day, and there's a small admission fee. The visitor center has a museum, art gallery, bookstore, and restrooms. The sanctuary offers a number of nature programs, lectures, and workshops for groups and schools. The South Lookout is a few hundred yards from the visitor center. The North Lookout involves a challenging quarter-mile hike, but you're rewarded with panoramic views overlooking Kittatinny Ridge. Be sure to check it out.

Ride Information

Trail Contacts:
Southeast Pennsylvania Game Commission, RD 2, Reading, PA; (610)-926-1966 or *www.pgc. state.pa.us* • **Spokes Bike Shop,** 4125 Pottsville Pike, Hamburg, PA; (610) 562-8900

Schedule:
Sunrise to sunset

Local Information:
Berks County Visitors Bureau, 352 Penn Street, Reading, PA; 1-800-443-6610 or (610) 375-4085 or *www.readingberkspa.com* • *[see Ride 26: Weiser State Forest]*

Local Events/Attractions:
Hawk Mountain Sanctuary Association, 1700 Hawk Mountain Rd., Kempton, PA (610) 756-6961 or *www.hawkmountain.org* • *[see Ride 26: Weiser State Forest]*

Accommodations:
Hawk Mountain Bed & Breakfast, Kempton, PA; (610) 756-4224

Maps:
USGS maps: Hamburg, PA • *Pennsylvania State Game Lands No. 106* – available from the park office for $1.00

MilesDirections

0.0 START from the Hamburg Reservoir parking area. Go straight through a gate and head up a wide dirt road with Furnace Creek on the right.

0.4 The Appalachian Trail goes left. Turn right and go over a bridge. Then go left, following the blue blazes.

0.6 A service road goes right. Continue straight up to Hamburg Reservoir.

0.8 Pedal through a gate. Continue past the reservoir on a wide dirt road.

1.0 The grade becomes steep and the tread gets rockier as you climb past mountain laurels, pines, and ferns. Furnace Creek is on the left.

1.4 The grade eases.

1.5 Encounter a short steep hill.

1.6 Arrive at a trail junction. Turn right.

1.7 A spur trail goes right. Continue straight.

2.1 Begin a steep climb up to the helipad.

2.4 Arrive at a trail junction and the helipad—a large open, level area. Turn right and follow the white blazes on a rocky, beautiful doubletrack trail.

3.8 The trail turns to singletrack. The trail becomes very rocky and technical as you pedal toward the Pinnacle.

4.1 Arrive at a trail junction. Follow the blue blazes that lead to the Pinnacle. Hop off your bike and walk 150 yards to the Pinnacle and spectacular views of Hawk Mountain and the Lehigh Valley. Go back to your bike and retrace your route back to the parking area. Watch your speed on the downhills back to the parking area. Be on the lookout for hikers and other trail users.

8.2 Cruise into the parking area.

Two of my best biking buddies, Adam D. and Nala.

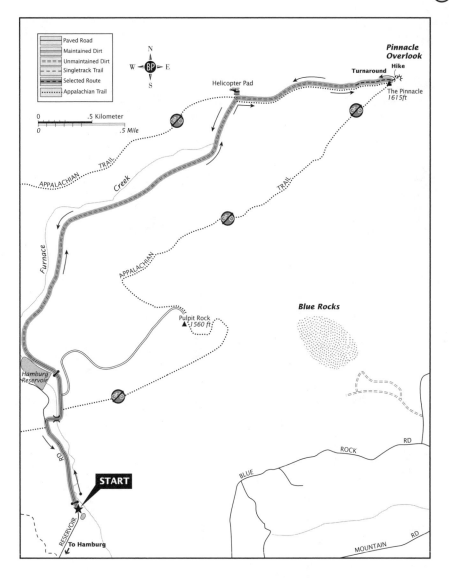

Map Legend:
- Paved Road
- Maintained Dirt
- Unmaintained Dirt
- Singletrack Trail
- Selected Route
- Appalachian Trail

N
W — BP — E
S

0 — .5 Kilometer
0 — .5 Mile

Pinnacle Overlook

Turnaround — Hike

The Pinnacle
1615ft

Helicopter Pad

APPALACHIAN TRAIL

Creek

TRAIL

Furnace

APPALACHIAN

Blue Rocks

Pulpit Rock
▲1560 ft

Hamburg
Reservoir

ROCK   RD

BLUE

START

RD

RESERVOIR

MOUNTAIN   RD

To Hamburg

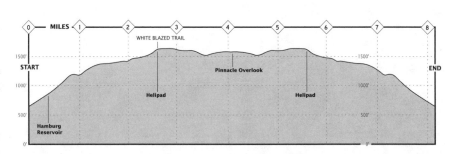

MILES 0 1 2 3 4 5 6 7 8

WHITE BLAZED TRAIL

1500'
Pinnacle Overlook
1500'

START
1000'
1000'

Helipad   Helipad
END

500'
500'

Hamburg
Reservoir

0'
0'

The Inn at Jim Thorpe in downtown Jim Thorpe.

Jim

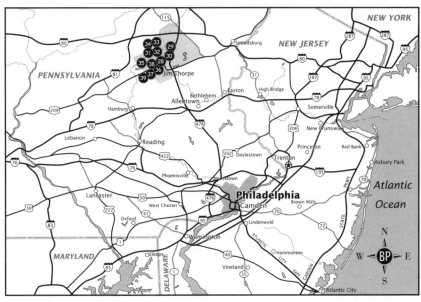

Thorpe

So how did two small mining towns in Northeast Pennsylvania come to be associated with Jim Thorpe? The towns in question were Upper Mauch Chunk and East Mauch Chunk, two communities, one Irish and the other German, which lay on opposite sides of the Lehigh River. The story begins in the early 1920s when the coal mining industry in Northeast Pennsylvania crashed—so too did the economies of Upper Mauch Chunk and East Mauch Chunk. For the next 30 years the towns struggled to recover.

Joe Boyle, the son of a local newspaperman, decided to save the towns with a nickel drive. What began as a somewhat futile attempt to bail out a depressed economy became, in time, a potential savior. By 1953 Boyle had garnered some $30,000. This amazing achievement earned him a great deal of recognition.

While visiting in Philadelphia, Pat Thorpe, the third wife of famed athlete Jim Thorpe, heard about Boyle's humble project—and his tidy sum. Her husband Jim had recently died in California and was interred in his home state of Oklahoma. But Pat wasn't exactly happy with the treatment her husband got from Oklahoma. It seems that Jim was buried in a rather nondescript grave with little fanfare.

Pat Thorpe approached Joe Boyle with the peculiar idea of using the $30,000 to build a memorial to her late husband. In exchange for this—and changing the town's name—she promised not only to have Thorpe's remains moved to Mauch Chunk, but also that she would see to it that Mauch Chunk got the soon-to-be-formed Football Hall of Fame, as well as a new hospital. In May of 1954, the voters of the two boroughs voted unanimously to approve the merger of the two communities under the name Jim Thorpe. As you may well know, the Hall of Fame ended up in Canton, Ohio. And though it has only been 40-some years, it doesn't seem likely that the town will get its hospital. But what they do have is a very strange story to tell.

Since 1954 the locals have done a wonderful job of revitalizing and preserving this beautiful Victorian town. Today Jim Thorpe is a destination for tourists who come to enjoy the town's restored Victorian buildings, quaint shops, and clean mountain air. The area is also popular with outdoor enthusiasts who flock to the area to raft on the Lehigh River, mountain bike in the surrounding forests, and hunt on the state game lands.

Getting to Jim Thorpe:

Jim Thorpe, PA is located at the western edge of the Pocono Mountains. It is reached via the NE Extension of the PA Turnpike (I-476). From Exit 34, follow US. 209 south through Lehighton to Jim Thorpe.

For more information about the town of Jim Thorpe and Old Mauch Chunk go to *mauchchunkmuseum.org*.

Lehigh Gorge State Park

Ride Specs

Start: From the Glen Onoko Access parking area
Length: 21.3 miles one-way
Approximate Riding Time: 1½–2½ hours
Difficulty Rating: Easy
Terrain: Abandoned railroad grade
Elevation Gain: 1,837 feet
Land Status: Pennsylvania State Parks
Nearest Town: Jim Thorpe, PA
Other Trail Users: Hikers and hunters (in season)

Getting There

From Jim Thorpe, PA: Travel south on U.S. 209 to PA 903. Go right on PA 903 and travel across the Lehigh River to a stop sign. At the stop sign, go straight onto Coalport Road. Go 0.4 miles to the park entrance. Turn left at the entrance gate and travel 1.5 miles to the Glen Onoko Access parking area. *DeLorme: Pennsylvania Atlas & Gazetteer:* Page 67 A-5

The Lenni-Lenape Indians called it "the stone that burns." Nearly 200 years ago, while out tracking game near present-day Summit Hill, Philip Ginder picked up a piece of shiny black rock and stashed it in his pocket, thinking it might be "the stone that burns." Later, Ginder took the stone to Colonel Jacob Weiss, a Revolutionary War veteran with strong business connections in Philadelphia. The stone was sent to scientists in Philadelphia for examination. What they had found was anthracite coal. Recognized as a clean-burning fuel, anthracite coal quickly became the fuel-of-choice for both domestic and industrial use. In no time, its production launched the America Industrial Age.

Anthracite coal is found in very few places on earth. Northeastern Pennsylvania has three of the largest deposits in the world. Anthracite coal became the fuel that stoked the young nation's furnaces. Northeastern Pennsylvania, with over 500 square miles of anthracite fields, was producing over 75 million tons of anthracite coal by the end of the 19th Century. This high yield lead to the many furnaces that dotted the countryside. By the close of the 19th Century, most of America's steel and iron was being produced in Pennsylvania.

Though the mineral was abundant, the mining and transporting of it created many headaches. Unlike the soft bituminous coal, which lies close to the surface and can be mined easily with picks and shovels, anthracite coal resides deep in the ground and has to be blasted out. And once out of the ground, the coal had to be transported, sometimes hundreds of miles from the mine. In those days you had two options for transport, river or rail. Often, it required both.

Lehigh River Gorge.

In order to transport the anthracite coal efficiently, Josiah White and Erskine Hazard developed the Lehigh River Navigational System in the early 1800s. The system, which stretched from White Haven in the north to the Delaware River in the south, was a series of locks, dams, inclined planes, and railroad connections that transported huge amount coal to Philadelphia and beyond. The lower portion of the system, just below Jim Thorpe, continued to transport coal until 1942. The route you'll be following on this ride was, in fact, an old railroad line used mainly for transporting anthracite coal.

The Lehigh Valley railroad parallels the Lehigh River through the stunning and scenic Lehigh River Gorge. The Lehigh Gorge State Park is a narrow area consisting of 4,548 acres along the Lehigh River. The park is popular among hikers, joggers, cyclists, cross-country skiers, and rafters. The two most popular sports are clearly rafting and cycling. The Lehigh River happens to be one of the most popular whitewater rivers in the country. And the Lehigh River Gorge is equally renown as one of Pennsylvania most popular mountain bike rides.

Your ride starts at the Glen Onoko Access parking area and follows the old Lehigh Valley railroad line to the town of White Haven—which is a great place to hang out and grab a bite to eat. The ride, overall, is flat and is suitable for both hybrid and mountain bike. The course is clean and presents few difficulties, except in terms of sheer distance. So go out there and ride what *Outside Magazine* calls "Pennsylvania's Best Biking."

Ride Information

📞 Trail Contacts:
Lehigh Gorge/Hickory Run State Park, RR 1, White Haven, PA; (570) 443-0400 • **Blue Mountain Sports**, 34 Susquehanna St., Jim Thorpe, PA; (570) 325-4421 or *www.bikejimthorpe.com – they offer local group rides and tours*

🕐 Schedule:
Sunrise to sunset

❓ Local Information:
Carbon County Tourist Promotion Agency, Railroad Station, Jim Thorpe, PA; 1-888-546-8467 or (570) 325-3673 or *www.jtasd.k12.pa.us/index.html* • **Pocono Mountains Vacation Bureau,** 1004 Main St., Stroudsburg, PA 1-800-762-6667 or *www.poconos.org*

💡 Local Events/Attractions:
Jim Thorpe Mountain Bike Festival, *held in June,* Jim Thorpe, PA – *send a SASE to: MBW '00, c/o Dave Boucher, 634 South Spruce St., Lititz, PA 17543* • **Mauch Chunk** 5 & 10, 9 Broadway, Jim Thorpe, PA – *last of a dying breed, check it out* • **The Old Jail Museum,** 128 W. Broadway, Jim Thorpe, PA; (570) 325-5259 – *seasonal* • **Asa Packer Mansion,** Hazard Square Extension, Jim Thorpe, PA; (570) 325-3229 - *seasonal* • **Mauch Chunk Museum &**

Cultural Center, 41 W. Broadway, Jim Thorpe, PA; (570) 325-9190 or *www.mauchch-unkmuseum.org* • **Mauch Chunk Lake Park,** 625 Lentz Trail Highway, Jim Thorpe, PA; (570) 325-3669 • **Mauch Chunk Historical Society**, 200 Broadway, Jim Thorpe, PA; (570) 325-4439 • **Carbon County Environmental Education Center,** 151 E. White Bear Dr., Summit Hill, PA; (570) 645-8597 • **Eckley Miner's Village,** 3 mi. off 940, Eckley, PA; (570) 636-2070 – *19th Century mining town*

🛏 Accommodations:
The Inn at Jim Thorpe, 24 Broadway, Jim Thorpe, PA; 1-800-329-2599 or (570) 325-2599 or *www.innjt.com*

🍴 Restaurants:
Sunrise Diner, 3 Hazard Square, Jim Thorpe, PA; (570) 325-4093 – *for a great breakfast* • **Black Bread Café,** 45-47 Race Street, Jim Thorpe, PA; (570) 325-8957 – *fresh, innovative food in bistro style setting*

Ⓝ Maps:
USGS maps: Carbon County, PA • **Lehigh Gorge/Hickory Run State Park maps** – *available from the park office* • **Pennsylvania State Game Lands** No. 141 map – available from the Pennsylvania Game Commission at (570) 675-1143 for $1.00

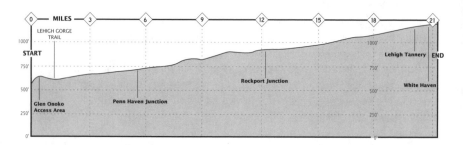

Map 1

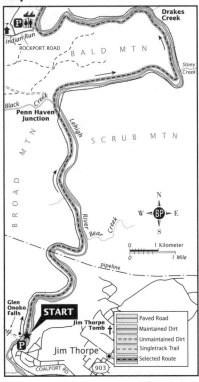

Continued on Map 2

Map 2

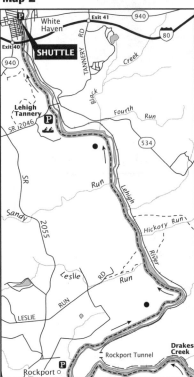

MilesDirections

0.0 START at the far end of the Glen Onoko Access parking area. Go through the gate and travel north on a dirt trail along the Lehigh River.

3.3 Come to Bear Creek.

5.8 Reach Penn Haven Junction. Cross the railroad tracks, then head left over a small bridge.

8.9 Reach Stony Creek.

10.0 Reach Drakes Creek.

12.4 Reach the village of Rockport Junction. Restrooms are on the left.

The ranger's office is located up the Access Road.

15.2 Reach Mud Run.

16.0 Reach Leslie Run.

17.2 Reach Hickory Run.

18.1 Reach Sandy Run.

18.8 Reach Hayes Creek.

20.0 Reach the Lehigh Tannery Gate, a parking area, and an access to SR 2046.

21.3 Arrive at the town of White Haven.

Drake's Creek

Ride Specs

Start: From the parking area on Unionville Road

Length: 14.6-mile loop

Approximate Riding Time: 2½–4 hours

Difficulty Rating: Moderate, with a very rocky, strenuous, and technical uphill

Terrain: Singletrack, doubletrack, paved and dirt roads

Elevation: 1,376 feet

Land Status: Pennsylvania State Game Lands

Nearest Town: Jim Thorpe, PA

Other Trail Users: Hikers, 4-wheelers, vehicular traffic, and hunters (in season)

Getting There

From Jim Thorpe, PA: Follow PA 209 south to PA 903. Follow PA 903 north for 9.5 miles to Unionville Rd. Go left for 0.75 miles to a Pennsylvania State Game Lands parking area just past a stop sign. Park here. (You can also start the ride from the parking lot just past the 1.7-mile marker. This eliminates the road riding at the beginning and end of the ride.) *DeLorme: Pennsylvania Atlas & Gazetteer:* Pages 67 A-5

The Pocono Mountain Range extends roughly from the Delaware Water Gap in the north to Allentown, Pennsylvania, in the south. Given the name Pohoqualine ("a river between two mountains") by the Lenni-Lenape Indians, the region is home to over 100 tree varieties, 21 state game lands, nine state parks, 12 ski resorts, numerous environmental educational centers, and three major rivers. It's no wonder the Nature Conservancy called the Poconos one of the "Last Great Places" in America.

Tourist attractions abound in the area, and so do golf courses, ski resorts, and honeymoon getaways. Morris B. Wilkins started the region's honeymooner craze when he built the first heart-shaped bathtub for two at his Cove Haven Resort in 1963. Since then the area has been the destination of choice for honeymooners the world over. Caesar's Pocono Palace is perhaps one of the more famous resorts. Here, newlyweds and other lovers can sip champagne and romance the days away in heart-shaped bathtubs, swimming polls, and Jacuzzis.

Still, the major draw to the Poconos is the great outdoors. Wildlife enthusiasts can spot a variety of wild animals, including black bears, wild turkeys, whitetail deer, bobcats, coyotes, hawks, upland birds, and bald eagles. The famous Appalachian Trail wanders through the area, making its way up to the Delaware Water Gap National Recreation Area before leaving Pennsylvania into New Jersey. The Poconos' Hickory Run State Park, near the small village of White Haven, has been called "one of the best state parks in the nation" by the National Commission of State Parks. The Lehigh and Delaware rivers, along with various lakes, streams, and ponds, all provide rafters, canoeists, fisherman, and water

enthusiasts unlimited opportunity to pursue their sport. The Poconos have over 115 established hiking trails scattered throughout the area, including the 25-mile section of the Appalachian Trail. Cross-country ski trails can be found in the many state parks and game lands. Mountain biking is also a popular sport in the area, and most of the state owned lands are bicycle-friendly.

Despite its proximity to the major metropolitan areas of Philadelphia and New York, the Poconos have remained remarkably rural, as have many of its towns. When driving along the narrow roads through many of these picturesque small towns and villages, one gets the feeling that this is a very special area indeed.

The Drake's Creek ride takes you through some interesting terrain in the northeastern section of Pennsylvania State Game Lands No. 141. There is a section of road riding, but there's minimal car traffic—and it's a nice warm-up before the big climb out of Drake's Creek. The climb is very strenuous and demands all of your attention. Once on top, the ride mellows out and the scenery consumes your attention. Thick stands of mountain laurel dominate the landscape, and in the month of June, they're in full, beautiful bloom. If you're lucky, you may see some wild turkeys and other wildlife that inhabit the area.

After the climb, the ride does a loop around Summer Mountain. There are a couple of overlooks that reveal beautiful views down the Lehigh River Gorge. The trail terminates in a meadow, with the Lehigh River down to your left. The great part about the ride back is that you get to go down that big hill. Cross through Drake's Creek again and climb back out to the parking area and your car.

MilesDirections

0.0 START from the parking area. Pedal back to the stop sign. Go left and follow Christmansville Road past Pleasant Valley West to an intersection at a stop sign.

1.7 Continue straight past the stop sign and down the fast, fun dirt road. (There's a parking area down the dirt road if you want to eliminate the first 2 miles of the ride.)

2.9 Turn right and cross Drake's Creek. Begin a hideously steep and rocky climb up some very technical terrain to a trail junction.

3.6 Go right and head to a trail junction at the power lines.

4.0 Go left and head down the dirt road to a yellow gate on the left.

4.6 Go left and pass the yellow gate. Pedal up a short hill to a trail junction.

5.0 Go right on a wide dirt road and head to a trail junction.

5.4 Turn left and cruise down a short hill. Bear right at the sharp turn and crank up a short hill to an intersection.

5.8 Turn left and pedal down a short, rocky section.

Ride Information

🌐 Trail Contacts:
Northeast Pennsylvania Game Commission, Dallas, PA; (570) 675-1143 or *www.pgc.state.pa.us* • **Blue Mountain Sports,** 34 Susquehanna St., Jim Thorpe, PA; (570) 325-4421 or *www.bikejimthorpe.com* – *they offer local group rides and tours*

❓ Local Information:
[see Ride 28: Lehigh River]

📍 Local Events/Attractions:
Lehigh Gorge/Hickory Run State Park, RR 1, White Haven, PA; (570) 443-0400 • **Annual Moscow Country Fair,** in August, Moscow, PA; (570) 842-7278 • **Zane Grey Museum,** Scenic Drive, Lackawaxen, PA; (570) 685-4871 • **Cove Haven Resort,** PA 590, Lakeville. PA; 1-800-233-4141 or (570)226-4506 *www.caesars.com/pocono/win* • **Caesar's Pocono Palace,** U.S. 209, Marshall's Creek, PA; 1-800-233-4141 or (570) 588-6692 *www.caesars. com/pocono/win* • *[see Ride 28: Lehigh River]*

♨ Accommodations:
[see Ride 28: Lehigh River]

🍴 Restaurants:
[see Ride 28: Lehigh River]

Ⓝ Maps:
USGS maps: Carbon County, PA • **Pennsylvania State Game Lands** No. 141 map – *available from the park office at (570) 675-1143*

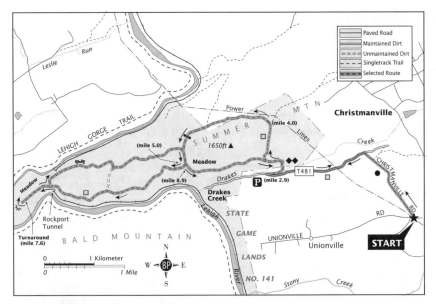

MilesDirections

6.5 A spur road is on the right. Continue straight.

7.1 A spur road is on the right. Continue straight up a short hill. Pass a meadow and head to where the trail ends.

7.6 Turn around and ride 0.5 miles back to the spur road, now on the left.

8.1 Go left and follow the 4WD road. The road becomes very rocky.

8.6 Continue straight up a short, steep, rocky hill to a trail junction.

8.8 Go right and pedal for short distance to a trail junction.

8.9 Go left on a wide dirt road and head to a junction with a meadow on the left.

9.6 Go left. Follow the road to a spur road on the right.

10.1 Continue straight (a left would take you back to the power lines), past beautiful stands of mountain laurel and to a trail junction.

10.8 Turn right. Remember that vicious uphill climb? Well, now you get to ride down it.

11.8 Cross Drake's Creek again and go left.

14.6 Turn right at the stop sign. Continue straight to the parking area and your car.

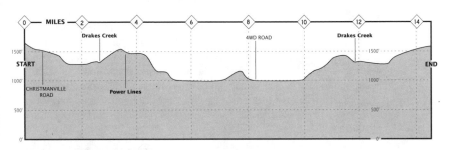

30

Scrub Mountain

Ride Specs

Start: From the parking area on Behren's Road
Length: 8.9-mile loop (or 10.2 out-and-back)
Approximate Riding Time: 1–2 hours
Difficulty Rating: Mostly moderate, with a few steep climbs
Terrain: Singletrack, doubletrack, and dirt roads
Elevation Gain: 426 feet
Land Status: Pennsylvania State Game Lands
Nearest Town: Jim Thorpe, PA
Other Trail Users: Hikers and hunters (in season)

Getting There

From Jim Thorpe, PA: Follow PA 209 south to PA 903. Follow PA 903 for 5 miles to Behren's Road. Go left, following Behren' s Road for 2.6 miles to the PA State Game Lands parking area on the left. *DeLorme: Pennsylvania Atlas & Gazetteer:* Page 67 A-5

This ride offers a couple of good climbs over Scrub Mountain. You can expect some excellent singletrack riding along with a few gradual uphill climbs. You can also hook-up with other trails in the area for a longer ride. There are two options that you can choose from to finish the ride. You can turn around at the 5.1-mile marker or follow the directions to Behren's Road. I recommend turning around at the 5.1-mile marker for a longer and more enjoyable ride. Riding with a friend of mine one warm summer day I had the pleasure of running into—or should I say over—a large Eastern rattlesnake at the 3.3-mile mark—which explains the name, Rattlesnake Alley. Hopefully you won't have the same experience, but if you're lucky, you may see some wild turkeys, whitetail deer, raccoons, or other animals that inhabit Scrub Mountain.

Ride Information

🕭 Trail Contacts:
Northeast Pennsylvania Game Commission, Dallas, PA; (570) 675-1143 or *www.pgc.state.pa.us* • **Blue Mountain Sports,** 34 Susquehanna St., Jim Thorpe, PA; (570) 325-4421 or *www.bikejimthorpe.com* – they offer local group rides and tours

❓ Local Information:
[see Ride 28: Lehigh River]

💡 Local Events/Attractions:
[see Ride 28: Lehigh River]

🛏 Accommodations:
[see Ride 28: Lehigh River]

🍴 Restaurants:
[see Ride 28: Lehigh River]

🅝 Maps:
USGS maps: Carbon County, PA • **Pennsylvania State Game Lands** No. 141 map – *available from the park office at (570) 675-1143*

MilesDirections

0.0 START from the parking area and pedal past a gate on a wide, well-maintain doubletrack road.

0.6 A service road goes left. Stay straight on the main road to a gate and trail on the right.

0.9 Enjoy a nice downhill run.

1.7 Go right and pass a gate. Follow the narrow doubletrack road to a trail junction.

1.9 Tank Hollow Trail goes right. Continue left on main trail.

2.6 A spur trail on right. Turn left and head down a short, rocky hill to a singletrack trail on the left.

2.8 Turn left on a tight, singletrack trail. Crank up a short, moderate hill to a small clearing at a trail junction.

3.3 Turn right on the Rattlesnake Alley Trail. Enjoy a wonderful, sometimes rocky, downhill run to a trail junction.

4.6 Go left and cross over several log jumps and rocky sections. The trail drops down into an open area to a trail junction.

5.1 From this point you have two options. Turn around and retrace your route back to the parking area. Or...Go left on the wide dirt road.

5.5 A spur trail goes left. Continue straight to a gate.

6.0 The trail ends here at Bear Creek Drive. Cruise straight on Bear Creek Drive, past several private homes, to a junction with Behren's Road.

7.5 Go left on Behren's Road.

8.9 Go left into the parking area and you're back at your car.

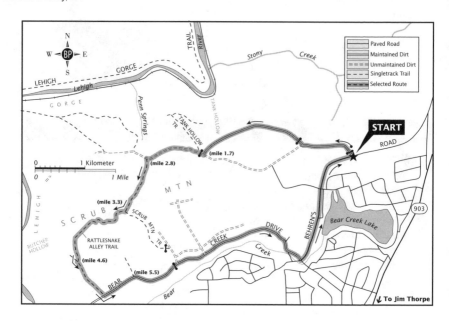

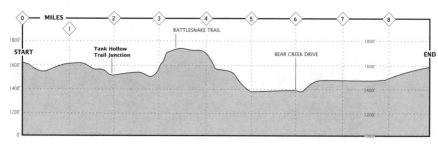

Broad Mountain Loop

Ride Specs

Start: From the Pennsylvania State Game Lands parking area on PA 93
Length: 10.4-mile loop
Approximate Riding Time: 1–2 hours
Difficulty Rating: Easy, with a few short climbs and short, rocky sections
Terrain: Doubletrack and dirt roads
Elevation Gain: 1,023 feet
Land Status: Pennsylvania State Game Lands
Nearest Town: Jim Thorpe, PA
Other Trail Users: Hikers, joggers, and hunters (in season)

Getting There

From Jim Thorpe, PA: Follow PA 209 south for 3 miles to PA 93. Go north on PA 93 for 3.3 miles to a large Pennsylvania State Game Lands parking area on the right. Park here to start the ride. *DeLorme: Pennsylvania Atlas & Gazetteer:* Pages 67 A-4

B road Mountain is a large expanse of mountainous terrain lying smack in the center of Carbon County, Pennsylvania. Within Broad Mountain is the publicly owned Pennsylvania State Game Lands No. 141, an area consisting of 17,048 acres of mountain terrain rich in rhododendron and mountain laurel. The thick deciduous forest stretches east to the Lehigh River and north to Hickory Run State Park. East of the Lehigh River is Scrub Mountain; to the north is the rounded and aptly named Bald Mountain. The town of Jim Thorpe is just a stone's throw away to southeast.

Broad Mountain is quite popular with hunters. The principal game species you'll find are whitetail deer, black bear, wild turkey, ruffed grouse, and gray squirrel. Whitetail deer are particularly plentiful, and come fall, the deer hunters come in droves. Northeast Pennsylvania is also known for its black bear population, the highest concentration in the Lower 48. It's not uncommon for a trophy black bear to weigh in excess of 500 pounds.

But hunters are not the only folks flocking to Broad Mountain. Mountain bikers are coming in equal numbers to enjoy the excellent riding that's available in the area. The Deer Path, Pine Tar Trail, and Broad Mountain Loop are just a few of superb rides you'll find on Broad Mountain. With everything from tight, twisty, rocky singletrack trails to steep climbs and smooth doubletrack trails, Broad Mountain has the terrain to satisfy any skill level. A great thing about biking on Broad Mountain is that after you get to know the area, you'll notice that a number of the trails interconnect—so you can create your perfect ride. A good example of this is the Broad Mountain Connector [see Ride 32], a ride that takes in the best parts of the Deer Path and Pine Tar Trail. Just keep in mind, if you're going to mountain bike or hike on Broad Mountain during hunting season, you'll be sharing the trails with hunters.

Wear bright colored clothing (preferably blaze orange), stay on the main trails, and show common courtesy when coming in contact with hunters and other trail users.

Your ride starts at the main parking area just off Pennsylvania 93. The Broad Mountain Loop is easy riding, except for a few, short, rocky sections. There are exceptional views of the Lehigh River Gorge from the overlooks. You can easily hook-up with other trails for more mileage. This is an excellent ride for the beginner or for the family just looking to get out into the woods.

MilesDirections

0.0 START from the parking area. Pedal past the gate onto a wide doubletrack road. Continue straight to an intersection.

1.1 Continue straight to the power lines.

2.4 Continue straight on good tread. Pass the power lines and come to a "T" intersection.

3.5 Go right and head down a hill on smooth grassy tread to the Overlook Trail 1, on the left.

4.8 Turn left and head down rocky tread to an overlook with great views of the Lehigh River Gorge. Return to the main trail.

4.9 Go left on the main trail and ride to a trail junction.

5.2 Pedal right and head for the power lines.

5.4 Continue straight at the power lines to a trail junction.

5.5 Go right at the junction and ride to Overlook Trail 2, on the left.

5.8 Go left on rocky tread and head down to a spectacular overlook of the Lehigh River Gorge. Return to the main trail.

6.1 Go left on the main trail and head down to Glen Onoko stream.

7.1 Cross the stream. Go right at the trail junction and head up a short hill. Cruise along on rocky tread to Jean's Run.

8.3 Pedal through Jean's Run. Crank up a hill to an intersection.

8.9 Continue straight on wide tread to a gate and PA 93.

9.4 Go right onto PA 93 (watch out for car traffic) and head to the game lands parking area.

10.4 Cruise into parking area.

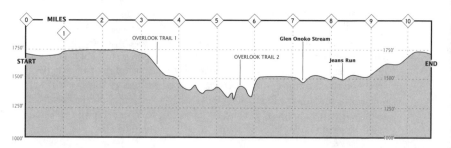

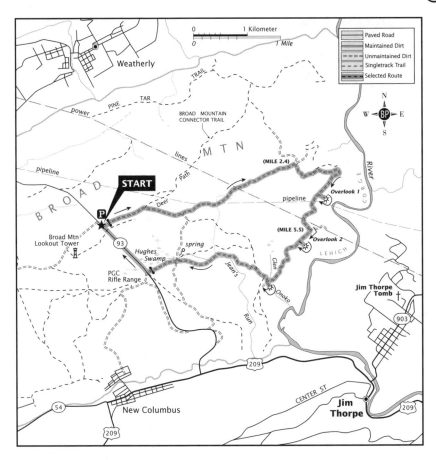

Ride Information

📞 Trail Contacts:

Northeast Pennsylvania Game Commission, Dallas, PA; (570) 675-1143 or *www.pgc.state.pa.us* • **Blue Mountain Sports,** 34 Susquehanna St., Jim Thorpe, PA (570) 325-4421 or ***www.bikejimthorpe.com*** – *they offer local group rides and tours*

❓ Local Information:

[see Ride 28: Lehigh River]

💡 Local Events/Attractions:

Lehigh Gorge/Hickory Run State

Park, RR 1, White Haven, PA; (570) 443-0400 • *[see Ride 28: Lehigh River]*

🛏 Accommodations:

[see Ride 28: Lehigh River]

🍴 Restaurants:

[see Ride 28: Lehigh River]

🅽 Maps:

USGS maps: Carbon County, PA • **Pennsylvania State Game Lands** No. 141 map – *available from the park office at (570) 675-1143*

Broad Mountain Connector

Ride Specs

Start: From the Pennsylvania State Game Lands parking area on PA 93

Length: 12.3-mile loop

Approximate Riding Time: 1–2 hours

Difficulty Rating: Moderate, with a few steep climbs

Terrain: Singletrack, doubletrack trails, and dirt roads

Elevation Gain: 1,440 feet

Land Status: Pennsylvania State Game Lands

Nearest Town: Jim Thorpe, PA

Other Trail Users: Hikers, joggers, and hunters (in season)

Getting There

From Jim Thorpe, PA: Follow PA 209 south for 3 miles to PA 93. Go north on PA 93 for 3.3 miles to a large Pennsylvania State Game Lands parking area on the right. Park here to start the ride. *DeLorme: Pennsylvania Atlas & Gazetteer:* Pages 67 A-4

So you and your family are going to be in Jim Thorpe for several days and you want to check out some of the local attractions? Well here's a brief introduction to some of the many museums and attractions in the Jim Thorpe area that you may find of interest.

Jim Thorpe is an excellent walking town. Most of the sights mentioned here are within a short distance of one another and can be easily access by foot or bike. So park the car and get out and walk around in the clean mountain air and enjoy this very special area.

Start your tour with a stop by the Mauch Chunk Museum and Cultural Center. The museum covers the history of the Jim Thorpe area from the Lenni-Lenape Indian reign to the town's coal mining days to the present. There's also a fine array of old photographs of Jim Thorpe, the man, along with a display of his life and career.

Stone Row, on Race Street in downtown Jim Thorpe, is another interesting attraction. The row consists of 16 stone houses that coal baron and United States Congressman Asa Packer had built for his engineers and foremen. Most of the residences have been restored to quaint shops and restaurants.

The Asa Packer Mansion, located on Hazard Square Extension in downtown Jim Thorpe, is a well-preserved Victorian mansion that has remained virtually unchanged throughout the years. Tours are offered 11:00 A.M. to 4:15 P.M. daily. The mansion suggests the wealth enjoyed by many of the town's early industrialists in the 1850s—considered to be the town's heyday.

If you're looking to be outdoors, the Lehigh River is one of America's most popular whitewater rivers. Guided boat trips will lead you through the scenic Lehigh River Gorge. Depending on the season, these trips can be very challenging. Contact any of the several companies in town that offer guided trips. Contact the Carbon County Tourist Promotion Agency for a list of whitewater guides, local events, and activities in the Jim Thorpe area.

The Broad Mountain Connector is a great ride for the more advanced mountain biker. The ride takes you on a 12-mile loop along beautiful singletrack trails on Broad Mountain. There are some very rocky, technical sections that will test the skills of most riders. The ride offers sections of excellent singletrack riding and gradual uphill climbs. It draws together sections of other choice rides to create a loop that's one of the best in the area.

Ride Information

📞 Trail Contacts:
Northeast Pennsylvania Game Commission, Dallas, PA (570) 675-1143 or *www.pgc.state.pa.us* • **Blue Mountain Sports,** 34 Susquehanna St., Jim Thorpe, PA; (570) 325-4421 or *www.bikejimthorpe.com* – *they offer local group rides and tours*

❓ Local Information:
Carbon County Tourist Promotion Agency, Railroad Station, Jim Thorpe, PA; 1-888-546-8467 or (570) 325-3673 or *www.jtasd.k12.pa.us/index.html [see Ride 28: Lehigh River]*

📍 Local Events/Attractions:
Mauch Chunk Museum & Cultural Center, 41 W. Broadway, Jim Thorpe, PA; (570) 325-9190 or *www.mauchchunkmuseum.org* • **Stone Row,** on Race Street, Jim Thorpe, PA;

Asa Packer Mansion, Hazard Square Extension, Jim Thorpe, PA; (570) 325-3229 - *seasonal* • Lehigh Gorge/Hickory Run State Park, RR 1, White Haven, PA (570) 443-0400 • *[see Ride 28: Lehigh River]*

🛏 Accommodations:
[see Ride 28: Lehigh River]

🍴 Restaurants:
[see Ride 28: Lehigh River]

🗺 Maps:
USGS maps: Carbon County, PA • **Pennsylvania State Game Lands** No. 141 map – *available from the park office at (570) 675-1143*

MilesDirections

0.0 START from the parking area. Pedal past the gate on a wide doubletrack road.

0.7 Turn left over a dirt mound onto the Deer Path. Follow this awesome, twisting singletrack trail through stands of beautiful mountain laurel to the power lines.

1.9 Cross over the road, going straight on the tight Connector Trail. Follow the trail down to a trail junction.

3.1 Go right, still following the Connector Trail.

3.7 Go straight and head down to Uranium Road.

4.0 Pedal left and start a gradual uphill to the Pine Tar Trail.

5.0 Go left up a short hill to the start of the Pine Tar Trail. This is a great singletrack trail.

5.7 The trail becomes very rocky.

6.0 Go right.

6.4 Encounter rocky tread.

6.5 Cross a small stream.

7.0 A spur trail goes right. Continue straight to the power lines.

7.8 Go left at the power lines and head up to the Deer Path.

8.6 Go right onto the Deer Path.

8.8 Go left on singletrack. Cross over a small stream and follow the blue blazes on awesome singletrack up to a trail junction at a wide dirt trail.

10.0 Pedal left. Start a gradual uphill climb, past very rocky tread where the trail turns to singletrack, and go through a boulder field.

11.0 Walk, or ride, over the boulder field. Continue straight on tight, rocky singletrack to a junction with the Deer Path.

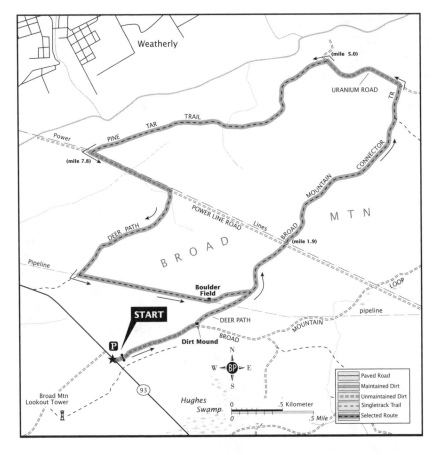

MilesDirections *continued*

11.2 Turn right on sweet singletrack.
11.3 Go right again, back onto the Deer Path.

11.7 Turn right and head back to the parking area.
12.3 Roll into the parking area.

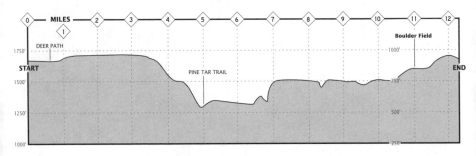

The Deer Path

Ride Specs

Start: From the Pennsylvania State Game Lands parking area on PA 93
Length: 6.8-mile loop
Approximate Riding Time: 1–2 hours
Difficulty Rating: Moderate, with a few steep climbs
Terrain: Singletrack, doubletrack trails, and dirt roads
Elevation Gain: 404 feet
Land Status: Pennsylvania State Game Lands
Nearest Town: Jim Thorpe, PA
Other Trail Users: Hikers, joggers, and hunters (in season)

Getting There

From Jim Thorpe, PA: Follow PA 209 south for 3 miles to PA 93. Go north on PA 93 for 3.3 miles to a large Pennsylvania State Game Lands parking area on the right. Park here to start the ride. *DeLorme: Pennsylvania Atlas & Gazetteer:* Pages 67 A-4

The Deer Path is a great introductory ride along some beautiful singletrack on Broad Mountain. There are some very rocky, technical sections that will test most riders skills. There are some excellent opportunities to link up with other trails on the mountain for a longer or more tailored ride. This short ride is just a small sampling of what's available on Broad Mountain.

Laurel, the author's wife, hanging out atop the boulder field.

Ride Information

Trail Contacts:
Northeast Pennsylvania Game Commission, Dallas, PA; (570) 675-1143 or www.pgc.state.pa.us • Blue Mountain Sports, 34 Susquehanna St., Jim Thorpe, PA; (570) 325-4421 or www.bikejimthorpe.com – they offer local group rides and tours

Local Information:
[see Ride 28: Lehigh River]

Local Events/Attractions:
The Jim Thorpe Mausoleum, on PA 903, 1.5 miles NE of Jim Thorpe, PA • [see Ride 28: Lehigh River]

Accommodations:
[see Ride 28: Lehigh River]

Restaurants:
[see Ride 28: Lehigh River]

Maps:
USGS maps: Carbon County, PA • Pennsylvania State Game Lands No. 141 map – available from the park office at (570) 675-1143

MilesDirections

0.0 START from the parking area. Pedal past the gate on a wide doubletrack road.

0.7 Turn left over a dirt mound onto the sweet, tight Deer Path. Follow wonderful, weaving singletrack, passing along beautiful mountain laurels as you head toward the power lines.

1.9 Go left on wide tread. Pedal down past several towers to a singletrack trail on the left.

3.0 Go left and follow the Deer Path. Pass a very rocky section and head to a trail junction.

3.2 Go left on the singletrack. Cross over a small stream and follow the blue blazes along awesome singletrack up to a trail junction at a wide dirt trail.

4.4 Pedal left. Start a gradual uphill climb, past very rocky tread where the trail turns to singletrack, and go through a boulder field.

5.4 Walk, or ride, over the boulder field. Continue straight on tight, rocky singletrack to a junction with the Deer Path.

5.7 Go right onto the Deer Path.

5.8 Go right again and head back onto the Deer Path.

6.1 Cruise right and head toward the metal gate.

6.8 Roll into the parking area.

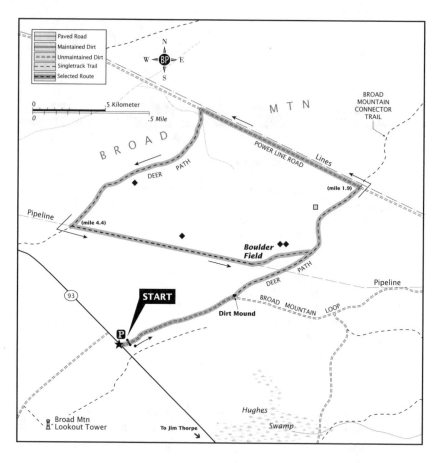

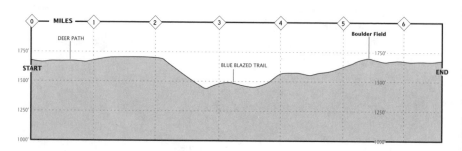

Jim Thorpe—The Man

Wathohuck ("Bright Path") was his native name, but to America, and the world, he was Jim Thorpe, the greatest athlete of his time. Born on May 22, 1887, on the Sac and Fox Indian Reservation, just south of Prague, Oklahoma, James Frances Thorpe, like so many Native Americans of his time, had to be sent off the reservation to be educated. He traveled to Carlisle, PA, to attend the Carlisle Indian Industrial School. An outstanding athlete in school, Jim later went on to break two world records in the decathlon and pentathlon. In the process, he won two gold medals for America at the 1912 Olympics in Stockholm, Sweden. After witnessing Thorpe's performance, King Gustav V of Sweden called Jim Thorpe the greatest athlete in the world. Sadly though, Thorpe's medals were later revoked when it was discovered that he accepted a small sum of money for playing semi-pro baseball while a student at Carlisle. Thorpe went on to play baseball for the New York Giants in the 1913 World Series. He also played for the Cincinnati Reds and Boston Braves.

After that, Thorpe moved on to a 15-year career in professional football. In 1920 he became the first president of the American Professional Football Association (which later became the NFL). In 1950, the Associated Press named Jim Thorpe the greatest athlete of the first half of the 20th Century. He was the first all-around athlete of the 1900s and arguably still ranks as the best. His amazing achievements almost instantly brought him to the level of national folk hero. After his playing days, Thorpe went west to Hollywood to pursue an acting career. Fame and fortune did not materialize, and Jim worked as a laborer until his death in Lomita, California, on March 28, 1953. In a curious, but fitting, twist of fate, Thorpe's Olympic medals were returned to his family on the 30th anniversary of his death.

34

The Pine Tar Trail

Ride Specs

Start: From the Pennsylvania State Game Lands parking area on PA 93
Length: 13.3-mile loop
Approximate Riding Time: 1½–3 hours
Difficulty Rating: Moderate, with several steep, strenuous climbs
Terrain: Singletrack, doubletrack trails, and dirt roads
Elevation Gain: 1,281 feet
Land Status: Pennsylvania State Game Lands
Nearest Town: Jim Thorpe, PA
Other Trail Users: Hikers, joggers, and hunters (in season)

Getting There

From Jim Thorpe, PA: Follow PA 209 south for 3 miles to PA 93. Go north on PA 93 for 3.3 miles to a large Pennsylvania State Game Lands parking area on the right. Park here to start the ride. **DeLorme: Pennsylvania Atlas & Gazetteer:** Pages 67 A-4

I f you're in Jim Thorpe for only a day and you have time for just one ride, this is the ride I would recommend. This course takes you on a beautiful tour around Broad Mountain on a variety of fantastic single and doubletrack trails. The riding is never very difficult, and though the hills are steep, they're short-lived. There are sections of technical riding, but thankfully they're spread out over the entire ride. Intermediate and advanced riders should not have a problem negotiating these difficulties.

Your ride starts at the large state game lands parking area just off Pennsylvania 93. Follow the obvious wide dirt road into the game lands. After a short distance the ride veers left onto the Deer Path. The next mile offers some of the best tight singletrack riding on Broad Mountain. The singletrack section ends at the power lines. Your ride goes left and heads down a long hill, past several towers, to a singletrack trail on the right, just before the tenth tower. Go right onto a fantastically tight, sometimes rocky, and sometimes wet singletrack trail. Enjoy nearly three miles of pure fun, crossing over a couple of streams and pedaling your way to Uranium Road. This section of the ride is one of my favorites in the entire Jim Thorpe area. Go right up Uranium Road to a trail on the right, at a lone pine tree.

The crux of the ride lies ahead and involves some technical riding on very rocky, tight singletrack tread. I found it very hard to clean this section on my first try. You folks with full suspension bikes might find this section just a little bit easier. After this section the ride mellows out, as you loop your way around Broad Mountain and head back to the parking area.

This was the first ride that my son Adam and I did in the Jim Thorpe area. Tom, the proprietor of Blue Mountain Sports in Jim Thorpe, recommended it. And what a good suggestion it was. Adam and I got caught in a beautiful summer rainstorm. The mountain laurels where blooming, the air had a marvelous fragrance, and the cool rain came as a welcomed relief for two very hot riders.

MilesDirections

0.0 START from the parking area. Pedal past the gate onto a wide doubletrack road.

0.7 Turn left. Pedal over a dirt mound onto tight singletrack. Weave your way on wonderfully tight, twisting singletrack to an intersection at the power lines.

1.9 Go left and pedal past nine towers to a singletrack trail before the tenth tower, just past a short uphill section.

2.9 The Deer Path goes left. Continue straight down a dirt road.

3.7 Turn right onto singletrack. Splash through several stream crossings and rocky sections to a trail junction. This section offers 2.4 miles of winding, tight singletrack on excellent tread.

4.1 The tread becomes rocky. Continue straight on sweet singletrack.

4.5 A spur trail goes right and heads back to the towers; continue straight.

5.1 Reach a small stream crossing. The tread becomes rocky and weaves past several short, technical sections.

6.6 Turn right onto the dirt Uranium Road and come to a trail junction.

7.1 A spur trail goes left. Pedal right and head up a short hill to a singletrack trail on the right. There should be a lone 30-ft. pine tree at the beginning of the trail. (Be careful, this is an easy trail to miss.)

7.6 Go right at the pine tree on tight tread and head to a trail junction.

7.9 Go left and weave your way along tight singletrack.

8.6 The singletrack trail ends. Continue straight on a grassy road, past beautiful mountain laurels, to an intersection.

9.5 The trail forks. Go right and head toward the power lines.

10.1 A spur road goes right. Continue straight to the power lines.

10.5 Go right. Follow the road past the power lines.

11.3 Go left onto the Deer Path and retrace your route back to the parking area.

13.3 Cruise into the parking area.

Ride Information

🕭 Trail Contacts:
Northeast Pennsylvania Game Commission, Dallas, PA; (570) 675-1143 or *www.pgc.state.pa.us* • **Blue Mountain Sports,** 34 Susquehanna St., Jim Thorpe, PA; (570) 325-4421 or *www.bikejimthorpe.com – they offer local group rides and tours*

❓ Local Information:
[see Ride 28: Lehigh River]

◑ Local Events/Attractions:
[see Ride 28: Lehigh River]

☎ Accommodations:
[see Ride 28: Lehigh River]

🍴 Restaurants:
[see Ride 28: Lehigh River]

Ⓝ Maps:
USGS maps: Carbon County, PA • **Pennsylvania State Game Lands** No. 141 map – *available from the park office at (570) 675-1143*

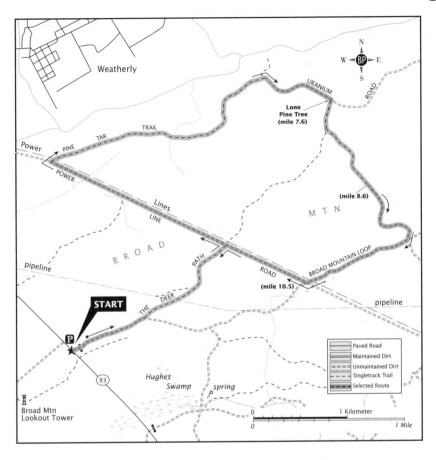

Weatherly

N
W—BP—E
S

URANIUM ROAD

Lone
Pine Tree
(mile 7.6)

Power
PINE TAR TRAIL

POWER

Lines

LINE

(mile 8.6)

M T N

BROAD

PATH

ROAD

BROAD MOUNTAIN LOOP

pipeline

(mile 10.5)

pipeline

START

THE DEER

P

93

Hughes
Swamp   spring

	Paved Road
	Maintained Dirt
	Unmaintained Dirt
	Singletrack Trail
	Selected Route

Broad Mtn
Lookout Tower

0   1 Kilometer
0   1 Mile

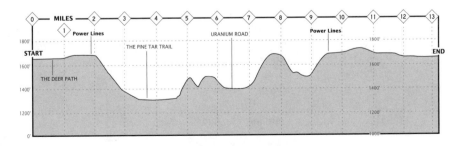

| 0 | MILES | 2 | 3 | 4 | 5 | 6 | 7 | 8 | 9 | 10 | 11 | 12 | 13 |

1 Power Lines

THE PINE TAR TRAIL

URANIUM ROAD

Power Lines

1800'   1800'
START   END
1600'   1600'
THE DEER PATH   1400'
1400'
1200'   1200'
0'   1000'

The American Standard

Ride Specs

Start: From the Pennsylvania State Game Lands parking area on PA 93
Length: 13-mile loop
Approximate Riding Time: 2½–4 hours
Difficulty Rating: Technically difficult and strenuous, requiring advanced riding skills and a high fitness level
Terrain: Singletrack, doubletrack trails, and dirt roads
Elevation Gain: 687 feet
Land Status: Pennsylvania State Game Lands
Nearest Town: Jim Thorpe, PA
Other Trail Users: Hikers, joggers, four-wheelers, and hunters (in season)

Getting There

From Jim Thorpe, PA: Follow PA 209 south to PA 93. Follow PA 93 north for 2.5 miles to a small Pennsylvania State Game Lands parking area on the right, directly across from the Pennsylvania Game Commission shooting range. Park here for the start of ride. *DeLorme: Pennsylvania Atlas & Gazetteer:* Pages 67 A-4

So what are you looking for? Maybe you just bought a new full-suspension bike and you want see if there's really a difference between full-suspension and front-suspension. Maybe you've done most of the rides in the Jim Thorpe area and you're looking to really test your skills and stamina. Or perhaps you've got a big-headed friend who thinks he's God's gift to mountain biking and you simply want to put him in his place. Well, here's the ride for all of the above.

The American Standard is, by far, one of the most technical and difficult rides in Eastern Pennsylvania. Located just off Pennsylvania 93, it follows a loop around the western part of Broad Mountain. Be prepared for a ride that'll test even the best rider's technical skills, endurance, and route-finding ability. A good thing about this ride is that there are several places along the way where you can bail out and retreat back to Pennsylvania 93, should you need to.

Be prepared for tight singletrack trails, very rocky tread, several stream crossings, and some very stiff uphill climbs. The tread in some sections is extremely rocky and unrelenting. At times the underbrush is extremely dense, so wear some protection for your lower legs. Both bike and rider can take a beating, so bring along some tools and extra tubes to repair any mishaps. Also, carry enough food and water to sustain you for a least three hours. Now remember, this ride is for experts. I am not trying to scare anyone away from doing it, but I do want you to know what you're getting into. But if you're up to it, go for it. You'll be rewarded with a challenging but thrilling mountain biking experience.

The author's son "going for it" on the American Standard.

MilesDirections

0.0 START by crossing PA 93. Go south on PA 93 past a large 30-mph sign. Continue straight to a second, smaller 30-mph sign. **0.3** Go right at the sign, over a large dirt mound, to a singletrack trail. Follow the tight, winding, beautiful singletrack trail into the woods.

1.0 Reach a trail junction. Go straight on doubletrack to twisting, tight singletrack.

1.7 Reach a trail junction. Go straight on doubletrack to twisting, tight, rocky singletrack.

2.0 Cross doubletrack to more tight, rocky tread.

2.4 Go left on often-wet, wide, grassy doubletrack.

3.9 Go left on beautiful wide tread.

4.1 Go right on tight singletrack. Don't miss it.

4.5 Go left and head down to Deep Run. Cross Deep Run, following the paint and blaze trail past several log jumps and rocky sections.

5.1 Go right on the singletrack trail and follow the white blazes.

5.3 Go left and head down a smooth, soft singletrack trail. Enjoy it, it doesn't last long.

6.0 Make a sharp right onto a tight, singletrack trail. Climb up to the toilet bowl.

6.2 Go left at the toilet bowl (which, incidentally is what this ride is named for). Follow tight, winding, sometimes rocky singletrack past the reservoir (down to the left).

7.5 The trail forks. Go left and head down to Broad Run. This is a great place to hangout and take a break. Cross the stream and then climb up tight, rocky trail to a junction.

7.6 Go right and climb up a wide trail to a road.

8.0 Go right and head down the gravel road.

8.8 A spur road goes right; continue straight.

9.2 Continue straight past the parking area.

9.3 Go left onto a tight, rocky singletrack trail.

9.4 Go right on twisting, tight, rocky tread.

10.0 Cross a doubletrack trail. Continue on rocky singletrack past several technical sections.

10.9 Cross a doubletrack trail. If you think the trail can't get any rockier, it does! Continue straight, past several tight, rocky sections to calmer waters.

11.1 Go right on rocky tread and follow the white blazes.

11.4 Go right for more tight, rocky, technical riding.

12.0 Come to a dirt road. Thank Heaven for some smooth tread. Go right. Head down PA 93 and back to the parking area.

13.0 Cruise into the parking area.

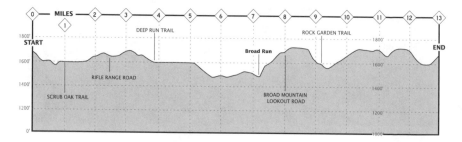

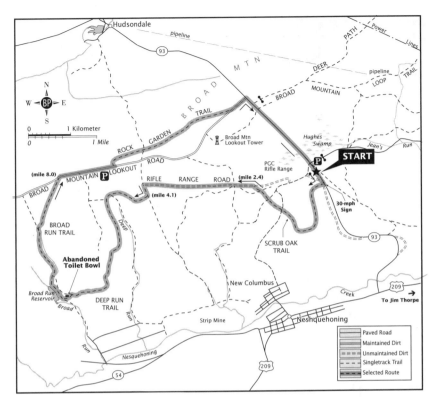

Ride Information

📞 Trail Contacts:
Northeast Pennsylvania Game Commission, Dallas, PA; (570) 675-1143 or *www.pgc.state.pa.us* • **Blue Mountain Sports,** 34 Susquehanna St., Jim Thorpe, PA; (570) 325-4421 or *www.bikejimthorpe.com – they offer local group rides and tours*

❓ Local Information:
[see Ride 28: Lehigh River]

💡 Local Events/Attractions:
[see Ride 28: Lehigh River]

🛏 Accommodations:
[see Ride 28: Lehigh River]

🍴 Restaurants:
[see Ride 28: Lehigh River]

🆖 Maps:
USGS maps: Carbon County, PA • **Pennsylvania State Game Lands** No. 141 map – *available from the park office at (570) 675-1143*

Flagstaff Mountain

Ride Specs

Start: From the Jersey Central Railroad Station in downtown Jim Thorpe
Length: 9 miles
Approximate Riding Time: 1½–2½ hours
Difficulty Rating: Moderate, with a long, steep climb up to Flagstaff Park
Terrain: Singletrack, doubletrack, dirt and paved roads
Elevation Gain: 1,377 feet
Land Status: Carbon County Park
Nearest Town: Jim Thorpe, PA
Other Trail Users: Hikers and motorists

Getting There

From King of Prussia, PA: Travel north on the I-476 (PA Turnpike, Northeast Extension) to the Mahoning Valley exit. Follow PA 209 north for 5.5 miles to downtown Jim Thorpe and the Jersey Central Railroad Station. The mileage starts at the Jersey Central Railroad Station. *DeLorme: Pennsylvania Atlas & Gazetteer:* Page 67 A-5

Mauch Chunk Lake Park, located on the Lentz Trail Highway (SR 3012) between Summit Hill and Jim Thorpe, offers 2,300 acres of fun-filled recreation for visitors to the Jim Thorpe area. At the heart of the park is the beautiful creek-fed Mauch Chunk Lake. The park has 85 camping sites, plus two large group sites. A boat launch and three large picnic pavilions are also located within the park, as well. A beach and a guarded swimming area are located close to the boat launch. Each June the park is host to the Jim Thorpe Mountain Bike Festival. For more information on events and camping in the park, call the park office.

The park has a number of well-maintained trails worth exploring. The famous Switchback Trail cuts through the eastern portion of the park, on its way to Summit Hill. The Shoreline Trail hugs the shoreline of the lake and wanders through deciduous forest, hemlock stands, and rhododendron and laurel thickets. The Shoreline Trail is the main nature trail in the park and has over 30 points of interest along its one-and-a-half-mile length. Insightful brochures, available at no cost from the park office, tell you all that you would ever want to know about the trail. The Woods Trail is located in the western end of the park, an area that supports a wide variety of plant and animal life.

Housed in a converted barn is the park's Carbon County Environmental Education Center. The center's motto is "conservation through education," and it offers an array of environmental programs which are open to the public. The center offers children's programs, scout requirement classes, hunter/trapper education

classes, wildlife research, wildlife rehabilitation, and environmental education classes. Wildlife rehabilitation is one of the main focuses of the center. In the program injured animals are nursed back to health and eventually released back into the wild.

Your ride into the Mauch Chunk Lake Park starts at the Jersey Central Railroad Station in downtown Jim Thorpe and follows the Switchback Trail up to SR 3012 and Flagstaff Road. From SR 3012 the ride rambles up Flagstaff Road on a steep paved road. The hill climb up to Flagstaff Mountain will challenge most beginners and intermediate riders. At the top of Flagstaff Mountain, take a minute to enjoy the views of Jim Thorpe and the surrounding mountains. Once on top you can't help but notice the old Flagstaff Inn. Some of the country's top swing bands, including the Glen Miller and Tommy Dorsey bands, played at the now defunct inn. Take a well-deserved rest and then retrace your route back to downtown Jim Thorpe.

MilesDirections

0.0 START by pedaling west on Broadway.

0.2 Go right at the Opera House onto Hill Road.

0.6 Go left onto a trail just before the top of the hill. Cross the paved road and continue straight on singletrack and pass a water treatment plant and a bridge. Come to SR 3012 (Lentz Trail Highway).

1.9 Go right on SR 3012 and pedal a short distance to Flagstaff Road.

2.0 Go left on Flagstaff Road and begin an extended climb up to the top of the hill to Flagstaff Mountain Park.

3.6 The Mauch Chunk Ridge Trail turns right. Continue straight to Flagstaff Mountain Park.

4.5 Reach Flagstaff Mountain Park. Catch some air (for your lungs) and enjoy the view. Then, retrace your route back to Jim Thorpe.

9.0 Cruise into the Jersey Central Railroad Station.

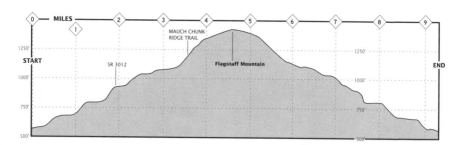

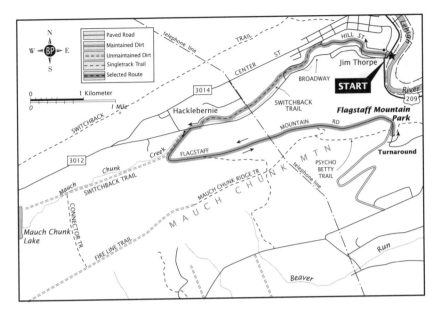

Ride Information

🔵 Trail Contacts:

Mauch Chunk Lake Park, 625 Lentz Trail Highway, Jim Thorpe, PA; (570) 325-3669 • **Blue Mountain Sports,** 34 Susquehanna St., Jim Thorpe, PA; (570) 325-4421 or *www.bikejimthorpe.com – they offer local group rides and tours*

❓ Local Information:

[see Ride 28: Lehigh River]

💡 Local Events/Attractions:

Carbon County Environmental Education Center, 151 E. White Bear Dr., Summit Hill, PA; (570) 645-8597 • **Jim Thorpe Mountain Bike Festival,**

held in June, Jim Thorpe, PA – *send pre-registration (SASE) to:* MBW '99, c/o Dave Boucher, 634 South Spruce St., Lititz, PA 17543 • *[see Ride 28: Lehigh River]*

🛏 Accommodations:

[see Ride 28: Lehigh River]

🍽 Restaurants:

[see Ride 28: Lehigh River]

Ⓝ Maps:

USGS maps: Carbon County, PA • **Mauch Chunk Lake Park map** – *available from the park office*

37

Switchback Trail

Ride Specs

Start: From the Jersey Central Railroad Station in downtown Jim Thorpe
Length: 17.2 out-and-back
Approximate Riding Time: 1½–2½ hours
Difficulty Rating: Easy, with a few moderate sections
Terrain: Singletrack, doubletrack, paved and gravel roads. Most of the riding is on a flat recreational trail.
Elevation Gain: 1,104 feet
Land Status: Private, state, and county land
Nearest Town: Jim Thorpe, PA
Other Trail Users: Hikers, joggers, and vehicular traffic

Getting There

From King of Prussia, PA: Travel north on the I-476 (PA Turnpike, Northeast Extension) to the Mahoning Valley exit. Follow PA 209 north for 5.5 miles to downtown Jim Thorpe and the Jersey Central Railroad Station. The mileage starts at the Jersey Central Railroad Station. *DeLorme: Pennsylvania Atlas & Gazetteer:* Page 67 A-5

C oal production was the number one industry in Carbon County in the early 1800s. In 1827 Josiah White developed the Switchback Gravity Railroad, which solved the problem of transporting the coal from the mines in Summit Hill down to the town of Mauch Chunk (known today as Jim Thorpe) and the Lehigh River. Railcars full of coal descended from the mines atop Summit Hill on wooden tracks by means of gravity. Mules were used to pull the empty cars back up to Summit Hill from Mauch Chunk. The gravity system was replaced by more efficient steam engines in the 1870s. The Gravity Railroad continued to operate as a scenic rail for tourists until 1933.

Josiah White was quite the inventor. A man of remarkable intelligence, White was largely responsible for the industrial revolution in Carbon County. His most famous invention was the bear trap lock, a system of dams and locks which allowed large ships to navigate shallow rivers. The Lehigh was the first river in the United States to use this system.

The Switchback Trail follows the old Switchback Gravity Railroad line from Summit Hill to the Lehigh River Canal. Carbon County and the Federal Heritage Conservation and Recreation Service developed the Switchback Trail to link all of the wonderful recreational actives in the Jim Thorpe area. Your ride starts in downtown Jim Thorpe and follows the Switchback Trail up to Mauch Chunk Lake Park. From the lake, the trail crosses the Lentz Trail Highway (SR

3012) and leads up to Summit Hill. This section of the trail is especially beautiful. You pedal through a dense forest of oak trees, rhododendrons, and mountain laurels. At Summit Hill you turn around and retrace your route back to Jim Thorpe. Along the trail are many places to stop and enjoy the natural scenic beauty of the area, so take your time and enjoy all the things that this beautiful recreational trail has to offer.

MilesDirections

0.0 START by pedaling west on Broadway.

0.2 Go right, at the Opera House onto Hill Road. Pedal up a steep grade to a trail on the left, at the hairpin turn just before top of hill.

0.6 Go left onto a singletrack trail. Cross a paved road and continue straight on singletrack, past stands of mountain laurel, to the water treatment plant and a bridge. Come to SR 3012 (the Lentz Trail Highway).

1.8 Go right on SR 3012. Pedal a short distance to Flagstaff Road.

1.9 Go left on the trail along the beautiful Mauch Chunk Creek.

3.0 Cross a bridge. A picnic table is on the left.

3.5 Turn right, bypassing the breast of the dam.

3.6 Reach a trail junction. Go left and head down past the park garage.

3.8 Go right onto a wide doubletrack trail and head up to the park's main entrance and SR 3012.

4.2 Use caution. Cross SR 3012 to the Switchback Trail and cruise along wonderful tread, passing private residences.

5.1 Pisgah Mountain Trail goes right. Continue straight.

6.6 A spur trail goes right at the power lines. Continue straight.

8.6 Reach Summit Hill and the end of the Switchback Trail. Take a break and then retrace your route back to Jim Thorpe.

17.2 Arrive back at the Jersey Central Railroad Station.

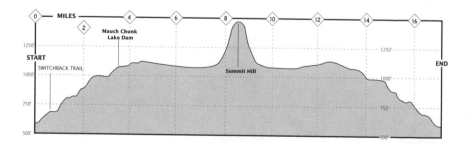

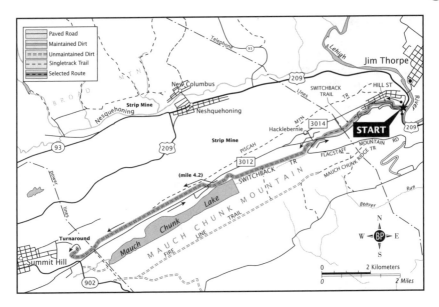

Ride Information

📞 Trail Contacts:

Mauch Chunk Lake Park, 625 Lentz Trail Highway, Jim Thorpe, PA; (570) 325-3669 • **Blue Mountain Sports,** 34 Susquehanna St., Jim Thorpe, PA; (570) 325-4421 or *www.bikejimthorpe.com – they offer local group rides and tours*

❓ Local Information:

[see Ride 28: Lehigh River]

💡 Local Events/Attractions:

[see Ride 28: Lehigh River]

🛏 Accommodations:

[see Ride 28: Lehigh River]

🍴 Restaurants:

[see Ride 28: Lehigh River]

🅽 Maps:

USGS maps: Carbon County, PA • **Mauch Chunk Lake Park map** – *available from the park office*

38

Twin Peaks

Ride Specs

Start: From the Jersey Central Railroad Station in downtown Jim Thorpe

Length: 20.3-mile loop

Approximate Riding Time: 1½–2½ hours

Difficulty Rating: Moderate, due to its length and a few strenuous sections

Terrain: Rocky singletrack and double-track, paved and gravel roads

Elevation Gain: 1,749 feet

Land Status: Private, state, and county land

Nearest Town: Jim Thorpe, PA

Other Trail Users: Hikers, joggers, and vehicular traffic

Getting There

From King of Prussia, PA: Travel north on the I-476 (PA Turnpike, Northeast Extension) to the Mahoning Valley exit. Follow PA 209 north for 5.5 miles to downtown Jim Thorpe and the Jersey Central Railroad Station. The mileage starts at the Jersey Central Railroad Station. *DeLorme: Pennsylvania Atlas & Gazetteer:* Page 67 A-5

This ride is named after the two peaks it ascends, Flagstaff Mountain and Mount Pisgah. The ride starts in downtown Jim Thorpe and takes the first two miles of the Switchback Trail up to Flagstaff Road. You'll gain some altitude as you climb a steep grade up the gravel/paved road. The ride goes right, through a gate at the 3.5-mile mark, and then climbs left up some sweet, tight singletrack. Here you gain the Mauch Chunk Ridge, with beautiful views to the south and west. Follow the cues closely to connect with the Fire Line Trail.

The Fire Line Trail is a wonderful 3.5-mile stretch of great singletrack and doubletrack riding. At the end of the trail, go right and head down County Road 642 to the power lines. Here the ride drops down some serious rocky tread and then goes left out to the highway. Go right on Pennsylvania 902 and ride to the Lentz Trail Highway (SR 3012). Turn right on SR 3012 and head to the entrance of Mauch Chunk Lake Park. At the park entrance, go left onto the Switchback Trail. You'll pass several private homes along the trail as you cruise up to a trail junction. At an old stone trestle, go right and head up a great singletrack trail to Mount Pisgah. A spur trail on the left at the 18.9-mile mark offers outstanding views of the Lehigh River, Jim Thorpe, and the surrounding mountains. A steep drop down the Wagon Road leads you back to town. From here cruise on paved roads back to the Jersey Central Railroad Station. This is a long ride, so pack plenty of liquids and snacks.

Fall colors on Mauch Chunk Ridge.

Ride Information

🚲 Trail Contacts:
Mauch Chunk Lake Park, 625 Lentz Trail Highway, Jim Thorpe, PA; (570) 325-3669 • **Blue Mountain Sports,** 34 Susquehanna St., Jim Thorpe, PA; (570) 325-4421 or *www.bikejimthorpe.com – they offer local group rides and tours*

❓ Local Information:
[see Ride 28: Lehigh River]

💡 Local Events/Attractions:
[see Ride 28: Lehigh River]

🛏 Accommodations:
[see Ride 28: Lehigh River]

🍴 Restaurants:
[see Ride 28: Lehigh River]

Ⓜ Maps:
USGS maps: Carbon County, PA • **Mauch Chunk Lake Park map –** *available from the park office*

MilesDirections

0.0 START by pedaling west on Broadway.

0.2 Go right at the Opera House on Hill Road. Pedal up a steep grade to a trail on left, at a bend in the road, just before the top of hill.

0.6 Go left onto the singletrack trail. Cross a paved road and continue straight on the singletrack, past stands of beautiful mountain laurels, a water treatment plant, and a bridge. Come to SR 3012 (the Lentz Trail Highway).

1.9 Go right on SR 3012. Pedal a short distance to Flagstaff Road.

2.0 Go left on Flagstaff Road. Begin an extended climb up to the top of the hill and to a dirt road on the right at a gate.

3.5 Go right on wide tread just after the gate and ride to a singletrack trail on the left.

3.6 Crank left up tight, rocky singletrack and pass a spur trail on the left. Continue straight to a trail junction.

4.0 Go left on the wide, rocky trail. Drop down a short, steep, rocky hill to an intersection.

4.2 Go left on rocky tread and head to a trail junction.

4.4 Turn right on rocky tread and head to a spur trail on the left.

4.5 Pedal on smoother tread to an intersection. Continue straight to a trail junction.

4.7 Go left on a tight singletrack trail. The trail climbs past a pit on rocky tread. Continue straight on rocky single-track to a trail junction.

5.7 Continue straight to the Fire Line Trail.

5.8 Go right onto the smooth Fire Line Trail.

6.3 A spur trail goes right. Continue straight on the Fire Line Trail.

8.4 Climb a short hill. Continue straight to a gate and a dirt road.

9.3 The Fire Line Trail ends. Go right and head down a dirt road to a spur trail at some power lines.

9.5 Go right and head down steep, loose, rocky tread to a spur trail on the left.

9.9 Go left onto a wide doubletrack trail. Pedal through dense forest to PA 902.

10.4 Roll right on PA 902 to an inter-section.

10.9 Turn right on SR 3012 and ride 2.6 miles to the Mauch Chunk Lake Park's main entrance.

13.5 Use caution. Go left, across SR 3012, and head to the Switchback Trail.

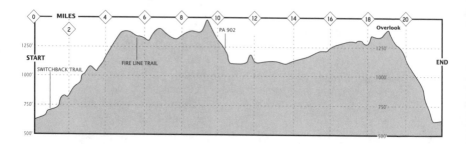

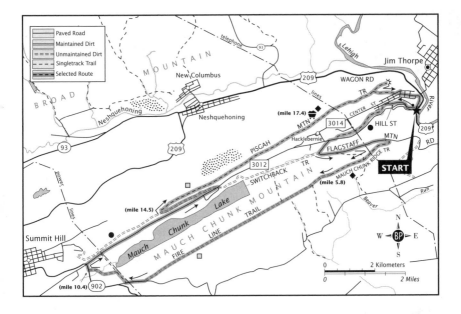

MilesDirections

Pedal up the trail to a junction, just past an old stone trestle.

14.5 Turn right onto Pisgah Mountain Trail. Continue straight on beautiful tread to a trail junction.

17.2 Go right on tight singletrack.

17.4 Reach an old abandoned mine on the left. Continue straight for 50 feet to a spur trail on left. Ride or walk up the steep spur trail to main trail.

18.8 Reach a great overlook of Jim Thorpe. Roll down rocky tread to a spur trail on the left. Continue straight to a second spur trail on the left.

18.9 Walk or ride up the spur trail for great views of the Lehigh River Gorge, Broad Mountain, and the surrounding hills. Go back down to the main trail.

18.9 Continue straight down the "Wagon Road."

19.5 Go left and ride to Pine Street. Go one block to Center Ave. and then turn left.

19.7 Continue straight, past the stop sign. Go down a very steep, fast hill and pass the Asa Packer Mansion.

20.3 Cruise into downtown Jim Thorpe and to the Jersey Central Railroad Station.

Mauch Chunk Ridge

Ride Specs

Start: From the Jersey Central Railroad Station in downtown Jim Thorpe

Length: 10 miles out-and-back

Approximate Riding Time: 1½–2½ hours

Difficulty Rating: Moderate, with a few strenuous sections

Terrain: Rocky singletrack and double-track, paved and gravel roads

Elevation Gain: 1,179 feet

Land Status: Private, state, and county land

Nearest Town: Jim Thorpe, PA

Other Trail Users: Hikers, joggers, and vehicular traffic

Getting There

From King of Prussia, PA: Travel north on the I-476 (PA Turnpike, Northeast Extension) to the Mahoning Valley exit. Follow PA 209 north for 5.5 miles to downtown Jim Thorpe and the Jersey Central Railroad Station. The mileage starts at the Jersey Central Railroad Station. *DeLorme: Pennsylvania Atlas & Gazetteer:* Page 67 A-5

I n the 1860s the mining industry in the town of Mauch Chunk (present-day Jim Thorpe) was at its peak. Many mine owners in the area were becoming millionaires. They were living large in lavish mansions; a lifestyle often bought at the expense of the immigrant coal miner who worked long hours in dangerous conditions for low wages. Many miners found themselves deeply in debt to the company stores, which were also owned by the mine owners. With the oppression at its height, many of the miners unified and decided to strike back with coal strikes, acts of sabotage, and even murder.

The mine owners labeled this group of lawless miners the "Molly Maguires"— referring to the infamous Irish secret society whose defense in the face of British oppression could be quite extreme. In 1875 things turned ugly when the miners formed a workers strike to oppose the intolerable working conditions. The mine owners hired the services of the Pinkerton Agency to infiltrate the ranks of the "Molly Maguires."

The Pinkerton detectives spent over two years gathering testimony against the group's leaders. In a series of sensational trials, 10 of the society's members were convicted and sent to the gallows. Six of the men were taken to Pottsville to be executed. The other four awaited their hanging in the Old Jail in downtown Jim Thorpe. Legend has it that one of the men, before being taken to the gallows, placed his hand on the wall in Cell 17. That handprint is still visible today.

After the trials, the voice "Molly Maguires" was silenced. What was not silenced, however, was the voice of injustice. Exploited mine workers throughout

the country began to speak out against the horrible working conditions within the mines. Workers everywhere should thank the Mollies for their effort and sacrifices in bringing worker rights to the United States.

This ride starts at the Jersey Central Railroad Station in downtown Jim Thorpe and follows the Switchback Trail for two miles up to Flagstaff Road. The ride makes a steep climb up the top of Flagstaff Mountain on a rough paved road. At the top, the ride turns right to Mauch Chunk Ridge. The riding on the ridge is on excellent singletrack through some very rocky terrain. The ride follows the Mauch Chunk Ridge Trail past an old mining pit and up to the Fire Line Trail. Follow the beautiful Fire Line Trail for a short distance to the Mauch Chunk Ridge Connector Trail on the right. The connector trail takes a very steep, technical line down to the Switchback Trail. From here, go right on the Switchback Trail and ride to the Lentz Trail Highway (SR 3012). Retrace your route back into town.

MilesDirections

0.0 START by pedaling west on Broadway.
0.2 Go right at the Opera House onto Hill Road. Pedal up the steep paved road to trail on left, at bend in the road, just before top of hill.
0.6 Go left onto a singletrack trail across a paved road. Continue straight on the Switchback Trail through stands of mountain laurels, past a water treatment plant and a bridge. Come to SR 3012 (Lentz Trail Highway).
1.9 Go right on SR 3012 and ride for a short distance to Flagstaff Road.
2.0 Go left onto Flagstaff Road and begin extended climb to the top of the hill to a dirt road on the right at a gate.
3.5 Go right onto wide tread and head to the singletrack Mauch Chunk Ridge Trail, on the left.
3.6 Go left and crank up the tight, rocky Mauch Chunk Ridge Trail. The Psycho Betty Trail goes left. Continue straight to trail junction.
4.0 Go left onto a wide rocky trail and head down a short, steep, rocky hill to an intersection.

4.2 Go left on rocky tread and ride to a trail junction.
4.4 Turn right on rocky tread and head to a spur trail on the left.
4.5 Pedal on smoother tread to an intersection. Continue straight to trail junction.
4.7 Go left onto the tight Mauch Chunk Ridge Trail. The trail weaves past a pit on rocky tread.
5.7 Crank straight to the Fire Line Trail.
5.8 Go right onto the smooth Fire Line Trail and ride to a spur trail on the right.
6.3 (Careful! Look hard for this trail.) Go right onto the Mauch Chunk Ridge Connector Trail and head down a steep, rocky hill to the Switchback Trail. What a downhill!
7.0 Pedal right onto the wide, hard-packed Switchback Trail and head to SR 3012.
8.0 Does this place look familiar? Go right onto SR 3012 and retrace your route back to Jim Thorpe.
10.0 Cruise into downtown Jim Thorpe.

Ride Information

🌢 Trail Contacts:
Mauch Chunk Lake Park, 625 Lentz Trail Highway, Jim Thorpe, PA; (570) 325-3669 • **Blue Mountain Sports**, 34 Susquehanna St., Jim Thorpe, PA; (570) 325-4421 or *www.bikejimthorpe.com – they offer local group rides and tours*

❷ Local Information:
[see Ride 28: Lehigh River]

❾ Local Events/Attractions:
The Old Jail Museum, 128 W.

Broadway, Jim Thorpe, PA; (570) 325-5259 – *seasonal* • *[see Ride 28: Lehigh River]*

🗕 Accommodations:
[see Ride 28: Lehigh River]

🎟 Restaurants:
[see Ride 28: Lehigh River]

🅝 Maps:
USGS maps: Carbon County, PA • **Mauch Chunk Lake Park map** – *available from the park office*

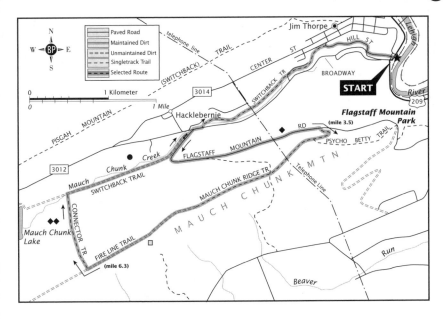

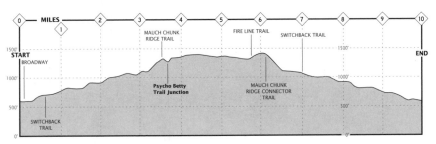

Northern

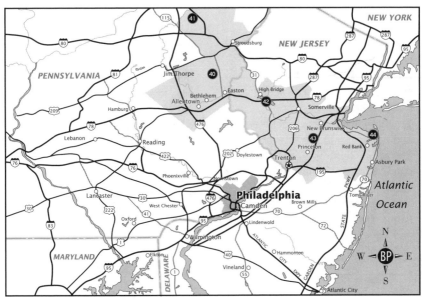

Philadelphia

Jacobsburg State Park

Ride Specs

Start: From the parking area on Belfast Road
Length: 8.4 miles
Approximate Riding Time: 1-1½ hours
Difficulty Rating: Moderate, with some short, technical sections on rocky tread
Terrain: Singletrack, doubletrack, and hard-packed gravel trails
Elevation Gain: 543 feet
Land Status: Pennsylvania State Parks
Nearest Town: Wind Gap, PA
Other Trail Users: Hikers, joggers, and equestrians

Getting There

From Allentown, PA: Follow U.S. 22 east to PA 33. Go north on PA 33 to the Belfast exit. Go left on Henry Road 1.1 miles to Jacobsburg Road. Go right on Jacobsburg for 1.2 miles to Belfast Road. Go left on Belfast Road for 0.7 miles to a parking area on the right. The ride starts here. *DeLorme: Pennsylvania Atlas & Gazetteer:* Pages 68 B-1

Situated on 1,168 acres at the eastern fringes of the Lehigh Valley is Jacobsburg State Park. Within the boundaries of the park is the Jacobsburg Environmental Education Center, one of four centers operated by the Pennsylvania Department of Conservation and Natural Resources/Bureau of State Parks. The center offers a variety of environmental education programs for students and adults interested in the Lehigh Valley. The department's goal is to develop public awareness of environmental issues. It's their belief that an educated public can not only solve present environmental problems, but it can also predict and avoid future ones.

Also of special interest to the visitor is the Jacobsburg National Historical District, located within the boundary of the park. The history of the town of Jacobsburg is, in many ways, the history of the Henry family and their small armory. Weapons produced by the Henry's factory were used in every American conflict between and including the Revolutionary War and the Civil War. The craftsmanship of the Henry family's firearms made them the weapon of choice among the settlers of the western frontier.

The Jacobsburg National Historical District offers a number of interesting programs throughout the year free to the public. The Henry's Woods Trail, located near the historical district, is a 1.9-mile loop around beautiful Bushkill Creek. The trail takes in some of the more dramatic scenery in Jacobsburg State Park and is worth a side trip when visiting the park. A section of the Henry's Woods Trail follows a ridgeline with precipitous drop-offs to the Bushkill Creek, some 200 feet below. Leave your bike in the car as the Henry's Woods Trail is for hikers only.

Ride Information

🛈 Trail Contacts:
Jacobsburg State Park Office, Nazareth, PA; (610) 759-7616

🕐 Schedule:
Sunrise to sunset

❓ Local Information:
The Lehigh Valley Convention and Visitors Bureau, 2200 Ave. A, Bethlehem, PA; 1-800-747-0561 or (610) 882-9200 or *www.lehighvalley-pa.org*

📍 Local Events/Attractions:
Jacobsburg Environmental Education Center, 835 Jacobsburg Road, Wind Gap, PA; (610) 746-2801 or *www.dcnr.state.pa.us* • Dorney Park and Wildwater Kingdom, 3830 Dorney Park Rd., Allentown, PA; (610) 398-7955 • Allentown Art Museum, 5th and Court Streets, Allentown, PA; (610) 432-4333 • Canal Museum, 200 S. Delaware Dr., Easton, PA; (610) 250-6700 • Crayola Factory and Museum, 30 Centre Square, Easton, PA; (610) 515-8000 or *www.crayola.com* • Martin Guitar Company, 510 Sycamore St., Nazareth, PA; 1-800-633-2060 or (610) 759-2837 or *www.mguitar.com* – tours available • Lost River Caverns, 726 Durham, Hellertown, PA; (610) 838-8767 or *www.lost-cave.com* • Lehigh County Velodrome, PA 100 and U.S. 222, Trexlertown, PA; (610) 967-7587 or *www.lvvelo.org – world-class professional and amateur bicycle racing*

🛏 Accommodations:
The Lafayette Inn, 525 W. Monroe St., Easton, PA; (610) 253-4500 or *www.lafayetteinn.com*

🍴 Restaurants:
Angie's Kitchen, 100 East Broad Street, Bethlehem, PA; (610) 866-3556 – *great American deli food at reasonable prices*

🅝 Maps:
Jacobsburg State Park map- *available from the park office*

Your ride starts from the Belfast Road parking area. The ride takes in a number of well-marked singletrack and doubletrack trails throughout the park. The trails are well maintained and offer only minimal difficulties throughout the 8.4-mile course. There are a couple of stream crossings and a few rocky sections, but they are modest and should not deter even the novice rider. It's hard to get lost in the area, so once you've completed the loop, you should feel confident exploring the other trails in the park. For the rider looking for a harder workout, the 18 miles of trails in the park should be enough to keep you busy for the better part of an afternoon.

The folks at the park office are some of the nicest people you'll ever meet. These are the folks you want running all public lands. They don't just understand the concept of multi-use trails; they encourage it. Hats off to these folks and all the volunteers who help keep this trail system open to everyone.

MilesDirections

0.0 START from the parking lot. Pedal past the gate, following the wide green-blazed trail.

0.2 A spur trail goes right; continue straight.

0.5 A spur trail goes left; continue straight.

0.7 A spur trail goes right; continue straight.

1.0 Come to a four-way trail junction. Go straight on tight singletrack.

1.1 Go left and follow the well-marked red/green blazed trail. Beautiful singletrack cuts along the creek.

1.4 The tight singletrack riding along Sober's Run leads to a trail junction.

2.0 Go right and cross a stream, following the yellow/green blazes.

2.3 Cross Belfast Road.

2.6 Cross Jacobsburg Road.

2.9 Cross State Park Road, still following the yellow/green blazes

3 0 Go right and head down rocky tread.

3.2 Go left at a 4-way junction. Cross a small bridge and then go left—following the red blazes.

3.5 The trail crosses under some power lines.

3.8 The trail parallels PA 33.

4.1 Go right.

4.5 Go left.

4.6 Go left at a familiar junction and follow the yellow/green blazes back to the creek.

5.9 Cross the creek and then go right, heading up to Sober's Run Trail.

6.0 Go right on Sober's Run Trail.

6.3 Go left and follow the trail along the power lines.

6.9 Go left on the red/green blazes trail. Make a great downhill run back to Sober's Run Trail.

7.7 Go left and head back to the parking area.

8.4 Reach the parking area and your vehicle.

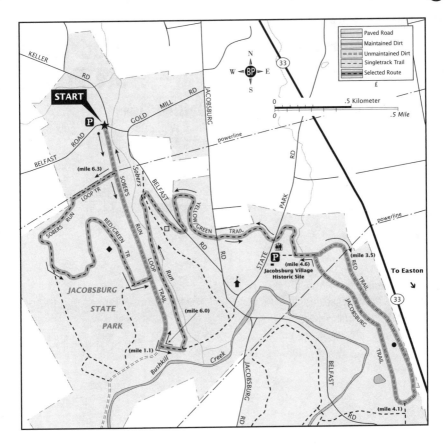

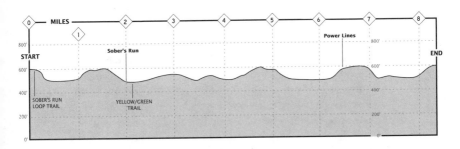

41

Pohopoco Tract
Delaware State Forest

Ride Specs

Start: From the Delaware State Forest/ Pohopoco Tract parking area off of PA 115
Length: 5.8-mile loop
Approximate Riding Time: 1–1½ hours
Difficulty Rating: Easy, with a few moderate sections
Terrain: Singletrack, doubletrack, and gravel roads
Elevation Gain: 694 feet
Land Status: Pennsylvania State Forest
Nearest Town: Blakeslee, PA
Other Trail Users: Hikers, ATVers, and hunters (in season)

Getting There

From White Haven, PA: Go east on I-80 to PA 115. Go south on PA 115 for 5.8 miles to the Delaware State Forest/Pohopoco Tract parking area on the right. *DeLorme: Pennsylvania Atlas & Gazetteer:* Page 53 D-7

T his ride takes you along ATV trails around the perimeter of the Delaware State Forest. There are a number of other trails that go into Pennsylvania State Game Lands No. 129. Feel free to hook up with them to make your ride longer and more demanding. You can spend the better part of a day exploring the trails in this park. Pack a lunch, bring some friends along, and have a great time riding in this unique area.

Of special interest in the area is the Long Pond Nature Preserve—sorry, no mountain bikes allowed. The preserve is located just west of SR 4002, near the small village of Long Pond. The Long Pond Nature Preserve is an area with incredible diversity: swamps, moors, heaths, oak and pine groves, and barrens. All of these features run along the Tunkhannock Creek. The preserve protects Pennsylvania's largest concentration of imperiled plant and animal species—32 in all—seven of which are globally endangered. The Pennsylvania Chapter of the Nature Conservancy purchased the 367-acre preserve in 1992. In cooperation with the University of Pennsylvania, it obtained a grant to study the barrens and find the best ways in which to preserve this unique ecosystem. Animal inhabitants include coyotes, short-tailed weasels, cottontail rabbits, black bear, beavers, deer,

and the scarce river otter. The best way to enjoy Long Pond, if you have the resources, is by canoe along the Tunkhannock Creek. For more information on Long Pond Nature Preserve, call the Nature Conservancy, Pocono Mountains Office.

Also in the Long Pond area is the world famous Pocono International Raceway. The raceway sponsors a variety of stock and Indy-style car events. The anticipated event of the year is the world-class Pocono 500. This premier race is held every year in July and attracts racecar drivers from around the world.

Ride Information

◐ Trail Contacts:
Delaware State Forest, Rt. 611, Swiftwater, PA; (570) 895-4000 • **Peterson's Ski & Cycle,** PA 115 and PA 940, Blakeslee, PA; 1-888-223-7449 or (570) 646-9223

◔ Schedule:
8:00 A.M. to sunset

❷ Local Information:
Pocono Mountains Vacation Bureau, 1004 Main St., Stroudsburg, PA; 1-800-762-6667 or *www.poconos.org*

♥ Local Events/Attractions:
Nature Conservancy, Pocono Mountains Office, Long Pond Road, Long Pond, PA; (570) 643-7922 or *www.tnc.org/pennsylvania* – *for info on the Long Pond Nature Preserve* • **Ski condition hotline:** (570) 421-5565 – *for up to date reports on any resort in the Poconos* • **Jim Thorpe River Adventures,** 1 Adventure Ln., Jim Thorpe, PA; 1-800-424-RAFT or

(570) 325-4960 or *www.jtraft.com* • **Pocono International Raceway,** Long Pond Rd. PA 115, Long Pond, PA; 800 raceway (570) 646-2300 or *www.na-motorsports.com/Tracks/Pocono.html* or *www.poconoraceway.com* • **Monroe County Environmental Education Center,** 8050 Running Valley Rd., Stroudsburg, PA; (570) 629-3061 – **Cranberry Bog Nature Preserve and Kettle Creek Wildlife Sanctuary** *guided tours; also offer exhibits, educational programs, and hiking trails* • **Lacawac Sanctuary,** Ledgedale, PA; (570) 689-9494 – *1 mile long self-guided hiking trail*

➖ Accommodations:
The Pocono Mountains Hostel, LaAnna Rd., Cresco, PA; (570) 676-9076

➊ Maps:
USGS, Monroe County, PA • **Pohopoco Recreation Area map** – *available from the park office*

MilesDirections

0.0 START from the parking area. Head east on the ATV road (Sutter Road Trail). Climb up a short, rocky hill and then float down to a trail junction.

0.4 A marked hiking trail goes right. Continue straight down very rocky tread to a four-way junction at a gate.

0.8 Continue straight on smoother tread. Float down a nice hill to a trail junction.

1.4 Continue straight and then make a quick right onto a great trail.

2.0 Go right.

2.2 A spur trail shoots off to the right. Continue straight on rocky tread.

2.7 Another spur trail goes right. Continue straight on soft, sandy tread up to a trail junction.

3.1 Reigner Road goes right. Continue straight.

3.5 Jam it up a short, steep, loose, rocky hill.

3.7 The Miller Trail goes right. Continue straight, down to the Little Trail.

4.1 Go right on the Miller Trail. Climb up hill, going through a gate to the Plantation Trail.

4.5 Continue straight, past the Plantation Trail, to a four-way intersection. Continue straight onto Jack's Trail. Here the trail wanders through a beautiful pine forest up to a trail junction.

4.8 Continue straight, climbing up steep terrain to a gate.

5.2 Go left at the gate onto Jack's Trail. Climb up steep terrain for a short distance. The trail takes a steep drop down, under the power lines, and leads back toward the parking area.

5.8 Cruise into the parking area.

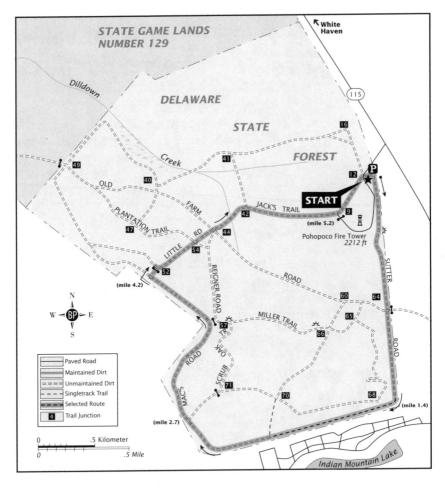

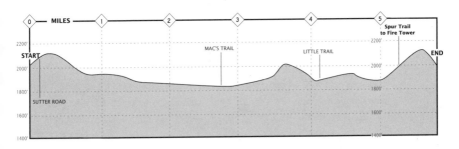

Round Valley Recreation Area

Ride Specs

Start: From the lower parking area below the park office
Length: 10.4 out-and-back
Approximate Riding Time: 1½–3 hours
Difficulty Rating: Very strenuous riding. Expect two long, steep, hill climbs and continuous technical riding.
Terrain: Singletrack, doubletrack, dirt and gravel roads
Elevation Gain: 2,236 feet
Land Status: New Jersey State Parks
Nearest Town: Clinton, NJ
Other Trail Users: Hikers, joggers, and horseback riders

Getting There

From Allentown, PA: Travel east on I-78 to U.S. 22 east (Clinton, NJ, exit). Follow U.S. 22 to Lebanon Stanton Road. Go south for 1.7 miles to the park entrance. Park in the lower parking area below the park office to start the ride.
DeLorme: Pennsylvania Atlas & Gazetteer: Page 69 D-5

W hat a wonderful surprise this ride turned out to be. I heard about Round Valley from a friend, who said it was one of his favorite rides in the Philadelphia area. My son Adam and I decided to make the 60-mile drive from Philadelphia on a beautiful, unusually warm February day to check it out. The park is located just south of Clinton, New Jersey, and is easily accessed from Interstate 78 or U.S. 202. The course's terrain is hilly and technical. This is one of the few rides in book where you'll feel like your riding out west. The climb up to Cushetunk Mountain is long and strenuous, with rocky, technical sections that demand a good effort from the best of riders.

Round Valley is very popular with mountain bikers in northern New Jersey, due to closures at the Watchung and South Mountain reservations. The staff at the park office are extremely pleasant and more than willing to give information on mountain biking in the park. They spent a fair amount of time showing us the trails on the park map and seemed genuinely interested in our having a good time. Still, the trails see a lot traffic from mountain biking, and it's imperative that we, as a group, show respect to other trail users and do whatever it takes to keep this great resource open to mountain biking. The park also sees a lot of traffic from horses and hikers. It's not always easy to balance the needs of everyone, but the staff has done a wonderful job so far. Hopefully the future of mountain biking at

Round Valley is bright. To avoid the crowds and to lesson the strain on the trails, visit Round Valley during the week, if you can. The solitude is just wonderful.

This is not a ride for the unskilled cyclist. There are some demanding sections that are very difficult and could prove agitating to the inexperienced. Experienced cyclists will, more than likely, enjoy the obstacles this ride presents.

The Round Valley Recreation Area offers a variety of outdoor activities, including swimming, hunting, boating, cross-county skiing, wilderness camping, and scuba and skin diving. The Round Valley Reservoir covers over 4,000 acres (of the 5,288 in the park) and is over 180 feet deep—making it the deepest artificial lake (or natural lake, for that matter) in New Jersey. Deer, waterfowl, wild turkeys, and other wildlife can be observed from two viewing areas located within the park boundary. The 1,288-acre recreation area includes a guarded swimming beach, picnic sites, and wilderness campsites.

Ride Information

🕿 Trail Contacts:
Round Valley Recreation Area, 1220 Lebanon Stanton Road, Lebanon, NJ; (908) 236-6355 • **KIMBA (Kittatinny Chapter of the International Mountain Bike Association),** 107 Sidney Road, Annandale, NJ; (908) 735-6244 or *www.gorockclimbing.com* • **Garden State Bikes,** 405 U.S. 22 East, Whitehouse Station, NJ; (908) 534-1088 or *www.gsbike.com*

☉ Schedule:
8:00 A.M. to sunset

💲 Cost:
There's a park entrance fee from Memorial Day to Labor Day. It's $7 on weekends and $5 on weekdays, per car. It's $1 if you enter by bike or on foot.

❓ Local Information:
Flemington Welcome Center, 39

Stangl, Great Freight Station, Flemington, NJ (908) 237-1072 or *www.fbanj.com* •**Hunterdon Area Rural Transit** (908) 788-5553 *www.cohunterdon.nj.us/ depts/hart/hart.htm*

♀ Local Events/Attractions:
Hunterdon Historical Museum, 56 Main St., Clinton, NJ; (908) 735-4101 • **Hunterdon Museum of Art,** 7 Lower Center St., Clinton, NJ; (908) 735-8415 or *www.clintonnj.com/clinton3.htm* or *www.primedirectory.com*

🎪 Organizations:
Flemington-Raritan Greenway, Bicycle and Pedestrian Access – *an advocacy group trying to connect local greenways in the Flemington area. Call Dan Force at (908) 782-5915.*

Ⓝ Maps:
Round Valley Recreation Area map – *available from the park office*

MilesDirections

0.0 START from the parking area. Pick-up the well-marked Cushetunk Trail. Go down tight singletrack, weaving along the Round Valley Reservoir to a trail junction.

0.2 A dirt road goes right up a hill. Go left and begin a climb on doubletrack tread up to a service road.

1.0 Cross the road and continue on singletrack up through a wooded area. The Cushetunk Trail goes down along a fence and over numerous waterbars. Make a sharp left onto smoother tread and fly down to an open area with the dam on the left. Be on the lookout for deer in this area. Continue straight on the Cushetunk Trail to a small bridge.

1.6 Cross over the bridge and crank past several waterbars to a paved path.

2.1 Cross the paved path and crank up a short hill.

2.4 Make a left and then a quick right. Head up to a trail junction.

2.6 Go right and ride to a trail junction.

2.8 Go right and begin an extended climb on rocky tread up Cushetunk Mountain.

3.4 The grade eases.

3.7 Encounter some fun log jumps. Continue straight on winding single-track.

4.0 A spur trail goes right. Continue straight, past rocky tread, to a fun downhill. Watch out for the log jump at the bottom of the hill.

4.7 The tread becomes very rocky. Use those great riding skills to negotiate several technical sections all the way down to the wilderness campsites.

5.2 Arrive at a paved service road where you'll find bathrooms, water, and a phone. Re-group here, and then retrace your route back to the parking area.

10.4 Crank up a short hill to the comfort of your car.

(Want more? You can add 7.6 miles by continuing past the 5.2-mile marker to where the trail terminates.)

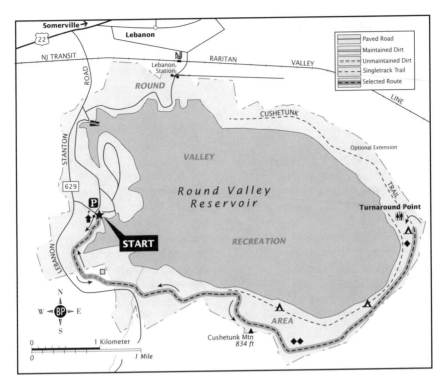

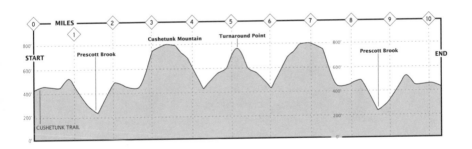

Delaware & Raritan Canal

Ride Specs

Start: From the New Brunswick Train Station

Approximate Riding Time: 4–6 hours

Length: 30-mile point-to-point

Difficulty Rating: Easy to moderate due to the flat nature of the path and the length

Terrain: Dirt canal towpath, paved multi-use trail and on road segments

Elevation Gain: 400 feet

Land Status: State park

Nearest Town: Princeton, NJ

Other Trail Users: Hikers, joggers, and equestrians

Getting There

From Philadelphia: Take I-95 North into New Jersey and take the U.S. 1 North exit to the Alexander Road exit. Turn right (east) on Alexander Road and follow signs for Princeton Junction station. Buy your ticket at the ticket office or from one of the ticket machines. Board the train on the northbound platform (Trains to New York) and get off at New Brunswick Station. If you don't want to take the train, you can shuttle a car to most any road intersection with the Towpath. (See the route map for suggestions.) ***DeLorme: New Jersey Atlas & Gazetteer:*** Pages 42, G-9

By Train: 🚲

From Philadelphia: Take the SEPTA R-7 Trenton line from Market East Station to Trenton Station. Transfer to the NJ TRANSIT Northeast Corridor Line Train and get off at New Brunswick Station.

Transportation from an earlier time is the theme of this ride. NJ TRANSIT's Northeast Corridor Rail Line serves as a shuttle to the start point. In the 1890s combining bicycles and trains was a common form of transportation. Some railroad companies actually hooked up special bike cars on their trains to meet the demand. In recent years bike transportation advocates have been able to regain access on buses and trains. If you want to experience the freedom of intermodal transport then this is the ride to try. You'll be whisked to New Brunswick at 100 mph in about 13 minutes. (To find out about taking your bike on the train, call NJ TRANSIT or visit their website. See Ride Information.)

Long before our dependence on skyways and interstates, canal works aided rivers as thoroughfares for our commerce and travel. This route follows the Delaware & Raritan Canal along an old towpath where for years teams of mules dragged coal barges and passenger vessels to their ports. Built in 1834, the canal formed an important transportation link between New York and Philadelphia until it closed in 1932. Highways have since broken the canal into two sections: the 34-mile main canal, which flowed between New Brunswick and Bordentown; and the 30-mile feeder canal, which supplied water for the canal from the Delaware River. Today the canal is managed as a state park.

Leaving from the train station the ride follows New Jersey 27 across the Raritan River into Highland Park, where a paved bike path leads to the Landing Lane Bridge and the canal trailhead. From there the ride follows the canal all the way to Princeton, passing historic lock houses and bridges. After passing the crews rowing on Lake Carnegie you'll then travel the last two miles on the road to Princeton Junction back to your car or train.

It is smooth and easy riding for much of your trip, however there are sections of the towpath that can get muddy during wet periods, and tree roots might temporarily disturb your bliss. Also look out for heavy pedestrian traffic in the Lake Carnegie section on the ride.

The section of the Delaware & Raritan Canal from South Bound Brook to Trenton is an officially designated section of the East Coast Greenway, which when completed will span from Maine to Florida. To find out more about the East Coast Greenway visit their website at *www.greenway.org*.

Cruising along the D&R Canal towpath.

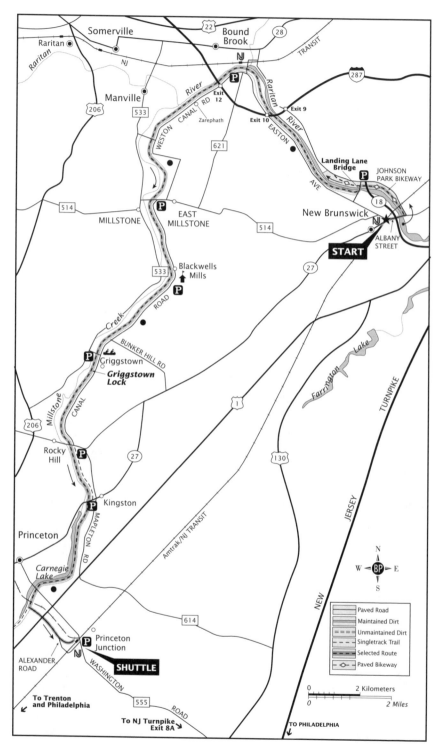

MilesDirections

0.0 START at the New Brunswick Train Station and make a left on Albany Avenue. Cross the bridge into Highland Park.

0.6 Turn left at the first light onto River Road.

0.8 Cross River Road to access the parallel paved path in Johnson Park; follow this path to the Landing Lane Bridge.

2.5 Turn left at the Landing Lane Bridge and cross the Raritan River.

2.8 Right on the D & R Canal Towpath.

8.1 Cross the busy road, which links South Bound Brook and Bound Brook. NJ TRANSIT rail service from Newark and the Bound Brook Diner are across the river. Portable toilets are one-tenth of a mile ahead on the trail at the South Bound Brook Lock.

11.2 Cross a road which leads into the town Zarephath, where you'll find the Alma T. White Bible College and the "Pillar of Fire" church.

13.9 Cross the Millstone Causeway. A right over the long bridge will lead to a convenience store.

16.0 Reach Blackwells Mills. The park office is on to the left on Canal Road.

19.5 Reach the Griggstown Causeway. The Muletenders' Barracks Museum is on the right. Across the causeway is a canoe livery that also sells snacks.

22.6 Use caution when crossing County Road 518 in Rocky Hill.

24.5 Ride through the tunnel to the Kingston Lock. The trail surface improves here and this section can get quite busy.

24.8 Lake Carnegie is now on the right. The Princeton University rowing crews can often be seen training and competing on the lake.

26.7 Cross Harrison Street.

27.3 Cross Washington Road. Princeton University is one mile west of here.

27.7 Go under the Princeton Shuttle railroad viaduct, known locally as "The Dinky." It connects Princeton University with the Northeast Corridor Line.

27.9 Turn left on Alexander Road; you'll cross over U.S. Route 1.

29.7 Turn left at a traffic light onto to the Princeton Junction station access road and through an enormous parking lot.

30.0 Southbound train riders returning to Philadelphia will board on this side of the station. Ticket machines are located near the underpass and accept ATM cards. If you parked on the northbound side of the station use the railroad underpass to get to your car.

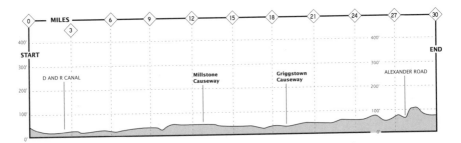

The canal near the Griggstown Causeway.

Ride Information

📞 Trail Contacts:
D & R Canal State Park, 625 Canal Road, Somerset, NJ (908) 873-3050 • **NJ TRANSIT**, Newark, NJ (973) 491-9400 or 1-800-772-3606 or *www.njtransit.state.nj.us/bikeperm.htm*

🕐 Schedule:
Sunrise to sunset

❓ Local Information:
Trenton Convention and Visitors Bureau, Lafayette at Barrack streets, Trenton, NJ (609) 777-1770

💡 Local Events/Attractions:
Bicycling Hall of Fame, 166 West Main St., Somerville (908) 722-3620 – *Hall of Fame induction ceremonies are held during the Tour of Somerville Race in May* •

Drumthwacket, 354 Stockton St., Princeton NJ (609) 683-0057 – *The Historic Governor's Mansion open for tours.* • **Muletenders' Barracks Museum**, Griggstown, NJ (908) 359-5970 – open Sat./Sun. 10 A.M. to 4 P.M.

👥 Organizations:
East Coast Greenway Alliance, 135 Main Street, Wakefield, RI (401) 789-4625 or www.greenway.org – *They sell a detailed map of the Bound Brook to Trenton segment of the park.* • **Bike New Jersey**, Chatham, NJ (973) 635-2211 or *www.bikenewjersey.homestead.com* – *New Jersey's Bicycle Advocacy Group*

🅝 Maps:
Park Map – available at the Blackwells Mills park office

Navesink Highlands

Ride Specs

Start: From the parking area at the Huber Woods Environmental Center
Length: 11.4-mile circuit
Approximate Riding Time: 2-3 hours
Difficulty Rating: Moderate, with some sandy sections and short steep eroded trails
Terrain: Hilly with tight singletrack, double-track, and paved trails-two on road segments
Elevation Gain: 1,697 feet
Land Status: County park
Nearest Town: Highlands, NJ
Other Trail Users: Hikers, trail runners, and equestrians

Getting There

From Philadelphia: Take U.S. 1 North (Roosevelt Boulevard) to the Pennsylvania Turnpike (I-276). Proceed east on Pennsylvania Turnpike to the New Jersey Turnpike North. Take the New Jersey Turnpike to I-195 (Exit 7A). Take I-195 east to the Garden State Parkway North. Take the exit for Red Bank (Exit 109) and head right (east) on Newman Springs Road (CR 520) to NJ 35. Turn left on NJ 35 and cross the Cooper River Bridge and turn right onto Navesink River Road. Follow Navesink River Road for 3.7 miles and turn left onto unpaved Browning Road. Park in the Huber Woods Environmental Center parking lot. *DeLorme: New Jersey Atlas & Gazetteer:* Page 45, B-16

For Philadelphians who have vacationed at the New Jersey Shore for generations, it's doubtful that the phrase "interesting topography" comes to mind. In fact, mention such a phrase and they'll probably laugh in your face. Thanks to the Atlantic City Expressway, and the railroads that came before, our vacation homes tend to be in dead flat southern resort communities such as Margate, Stone Harbor, and Wildwood.

Yet if you were to point your compass northeast toward Sandy Hook, you'd find a range of small hills bordering the lovely Navesink River. Sailboats coexist with motorboats in New Jersey's answer to Long Island's North Shore. Bruce Springsteen and Geraldo Rivera reside on the south bank of the river in Rumson. The nearby towns of Red Bank and Leonardo were settings for the Kevin Smith movies *Chasing Amy* and *Clerks*, respectively.

Fortunately two large former-estates in the Navesink Hills are protected and open to mountain bikes. The ride starts in Huber Woods Park, the smaller and less crowded of the two. Huber Woods contains six miles of mostly easy and intermediate trails. The ride works east through the park and out on the road crossing the tidal Claypit Creek before turning into the larger and hillier Hartshorne (pronounced HARTS-horn) Woods Park. This popular park contains some excellent smooth singletrack and offers great views of the river and the ocean. The eastern end of the ride circles the Rocky Point section of the park. A highlight of this section is the Battery Lewis, a bunker that was part of the World War II coastal defense system.

This can be easily broken up into two rides; park maps are available at each trailhead. Other nearby attractions include the Historic Twin Lights, Sandy Hook Lighthouse, the fishing village of Atlantic Highlands, and the paved nine-mile Henry Hudson Bikeway. Ferry service to Manhattan is available in Highlands.

Views of the Atlantic Ocean from Rocky Point.

Battery Lewis WWII bunker.

Ride Information

Trail Contacts:
Monmouth County Park System, Freehold, NJ; (732) 842-400, ext. 237 or 257, or *www.monmouthcounty-parks.com*

Schedule:
Sunrise to sunset

Local Information:
Monmouth County Economic Development/Tourism, Freehold, NJ (732) 431-7476

Local Events/Attractions:
Gateway National Recreational Area, Sandy Hook Unit; Fort Hancock, NJ (908) 872-0115 – *Sandy Hook Lighthouse, historic Fort Hancock, and six miles of ocean beaches*

Twin Lights Historic Site, Lighthouse Road, Highlands, NJ (908) 872-1814 • **Monmouth Battlefield Park**, 347 Freehold-Englishtown Road, Manalapan, NJ (908) 462 9616 – *Revolutionary War battlefield best known for heroine Molly Pitcher manning the cannon after her husband fell wounded.*

Maps:
USGS maps: Sandy Hook • **Monmouth County Park maps** – *available at the Huber Woods Environmental Center*

MilesDirections

0.0 START on the mowed trail behind the park map and head toward the wood line.

0.1 Turn left on the Fox Hollow Trail.

0.2 Fox Hollow Trail turns right at the marked trail junction with Valley View Trail.

0.5 Turn left at fork onto the Valley View Trail.

0.7 Turn left onto the Claypit Run Trail just before the signpost that reads "Trailhead."

1.2 The trail ends at a wide gravel road. Turn right out to the park exit.

1.3 Turn left on Locust Point Road.

1.4 Turn right onto Locust Avenue over the bridge.

1.7 Turn right at the Stone Church onto Navesink Avenue following the curve.

2.2 Go right at the Buttermilk Valley parking area into Hartshorne Woods.

2.3 Turn left after entering the trail system onto the doubletrack Laurel Ridge Trail.

2.8 The Laurel Ridge Trail goes right at a four-way intersection. Continue straight on to the Cuesta Ridge Trail.

3.8 Turn left on the paved Command Loop.

3.9 Emerge at the Portland Road parking area and turn right toward the bunkers.

4.1 Turn left and follow signs for Lewis Overlook. The trail goes under the Battery Lewis bunker, built in 1942.

4.2 Dismount your bike and place it on the bike rack adjacent to the bunker. Hike up the trail to the top of the bunker for a tremendous view of the town of Sea Bright and the Atlantic Ocean. Return to your bike and continue on the paved road circling Battery Lewis.

4.3 Turn left on the unmarked trail that follows the clearing out to the Rocky Point bunker.

4.7 Turn Right on the Battery Loop Trail.

5.0 Turn left to head toward Blackfish Cove.

5.2 Take the left loop as you enter a small picnic area, and continue down the road to the banks of the Navesink River. Great photo spot! Turn around and climb back up the steep hill.

5.5 Turn left at the top of the hill to resume the Battery Loop. Follow the Battery Loop back out to the Portland Road parking area.

6.3 Turn left and then right back onto the Cuesta Ridge Trail.

7.6 Turn left at four-way junction onto Laurel Ridge Trail.

7.8 At the junction with Grand Tour Trail, turn

Historic Twin Lights.

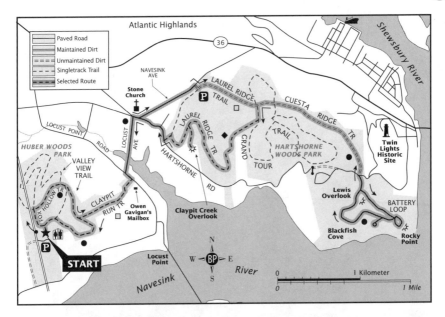

Legend:
- Paved Road
- Maintained Dirt
- Unmaintained Dirt
- Singletrack Trail
- Selected Route

MilesDirections

right to continue on Laurel Ridge. This section offers the most technical challenge of the ride.

8.6 Go left at the fork, toward the Claypit Creek overlook.

8.8 Reach a dead-end. The overlook is mostly overgrown in summer, but you can see the Navesink River if you peer through the trees. Return the way you came.

9.0 Bear left at the fork to continue down the Laurel Ridge Trail. A heavily eroded, extremely steep downhill is followed by moderately eroded, less steep downhills.

9.4 Turn left on the Connector Trail, which is marked by four short wooden posts. Pedal out to Hartshorne Road.

9.5 Turn right on Hartshorne Road and merge with Navesink Avenue at the Stone Church.

9.7 Turn left and retrace the paved route back to Huber Woods, which is next to Owen Gavigan's mailbox.

10.2 Turn left on the Claypit Run Trail.

10.7 Reach the trail junction, and turn left onto the Valley View Trail at the sign marked "Trailhead."

11.4 Arrive at the trailhead, and turn left on the mowed trail that leads to parking are and your car.

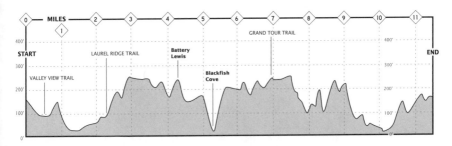

Appendix

Local Clubs

Bicycle Club of Philadelphia
Pete LaVerghetta
P.O. Box 30235, Philadelphia, PA 19103
(215) 735-2453
www.libertynet.org/bikeclub

Brandywine Bicycle Club
Club newsletters available at most Chester County bicycle shops.
P.O. Box 3162
West Chester, PA 19381
www.hometown.aol.com/mantis64ti

C-Quad Cycling
A club in the Philadelphia area. "We are basically a group of recreational cyclist who ride together throughout the year in charity and local cycling club events. Many of our members belong to clubs such as Suburban Cyclist Unlimited, Outdoor Club of South Jersey and Bicycle Club of Philadelphia. In 1997 C-Quad entered into amateur racing."
www.cquad.org

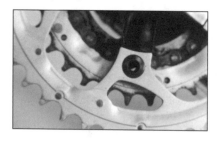

Central Bucks Bicycle Club
Serves Bucks, Montgomery, Philadelphia, Hunterdon, Mercer counties.
P.O. Box 1648
Doylestown, PA 18901
http://cbbc.cycle.org

Cycling Enthusiasts of the Delaware Valley
9325 Marsden Street
Philadelphia, PA 19114
(215) 338-9159

Delaware Trail Spinners 334 Grey Bull Dr.
Bear, DE 19701
(302) 834-1133

Delaware Valley Bicycle Club
The Delaware Valley Bicycle Club (DVBC) is a non-profit organization which serves Delaware County and adjacent areas west of Philadelphia, Pennsylvania.
P.O. Box 156Woodlyn, PA 19094-0156
 (610) 565-4058
www.netreach.net/people/elzchris/dvbc/home-page.htm

Doylestown Wheelmen
Founded in 1956 by the late Herbert "Bert" Smith. The club is a member of the United States Cycling Federation and promotes the Annual PA State Track Cycling Championships at the Lehigh Valley Velodrome. Traditionally a track and road racing club. Membership is open to men, women, and junior racers.
P.O. Box 475
Doylestown, PA 18901
(215) 343-0525

Drexel Fat Tire Club
3210 Chestnut Street
Philadelphia, PA 19104
(215) 895-2534

Future Champions Cycling Club
Lehigh Valley, PA also serving riders from NJ A family-oriented, nonprofit organization dedicated to the development of the young cyclist (age 9-18) in Olympic style road and track racing.
Gary J. Lakatosh (610) 398-7119
P.O. Box 652
Trexlertown, PA 18087

Green Mountain Cycling
120 North 6th Street
Denver, PA 17517
(717) 336-7722

GS Lancaster
2145 West Main Street
Ephrata, PA 17522
(717) 733-4127

Harrisburg Bicycle Club

We schedule over 1000 rides a year at all ability and experience levels, leaving from Hershey to the East, historic Carlisle to the West, and many other sites in between.
1011 Bridge Street
New Cumberland, PA 17070-1631
(717) 975-9879
www.igateway.com/clients/mfm5565/hbc.html

Hill Bicycle Club
2051 Bainbridge Street Apt B
Philadelphia, PA 19146
(215) 735-0533

Jersey Shore Touring Society
The Jersey Shore Touring Society is a recreational bicycle club serving central New Jersey (primarily Monmouth, Ocean and Middlesex Counties). We have road and mountain bike rides for cyclists of all abilities. Newcomers and visitors are welcome!
P.O. Box 8581
Red Bank, NJ 07701
(732) 747-8206
www.erols.com/jsts

KIMBA (Kittatinny Chapter of the International Mountain Bike Association)
107 Sidney Road
Annandale, NJ 08801
(908) 735-6244
www.gorockclimbing.com

Lancaster Bicycle Club
P.O. Box 535
Lancaster, PA 17608
(717) 396 9299
www.cris.com/~Outspokn/lbcmain.html

Lehigh University Cycling
Lehigh University Cycling consists of two clubs, the Road Club/Team and the Mountain Bike Club.
www.lehigh.edu/~incyc/cycling.html

Lehigh Valley Bicycle Riders Alliance
Lehigh Valley (Allentown, Bethlehem, Easton)
PA.Steve Schmitt, (610) 770-0133

Lehigh Valley Road and Trail Cycling Club
7441 Springhouse Road
New Tripoli, PA, (610) 481-3385

Lehigh Wheelmen Association
We are a bicycling club, with approximately 350 members. Our name says "Wheelmen", which is an old name for bicyclists, but we are really "Wheelpeople" - women and men of all ages. Our activities are centered in but not limited to the Lehigh Valley of Eastern Pennsylvania.
P.O.Box 356 Bethlehem, PA 18016
(610) 298-3382, www.enter.net/~lehighwheelmen/

Main Line Cycling Club
1044 Lancaster Avenue
Bryn Mawr, PA 19010, (610) 525-8442

Montgomery County Mountain Biking Association
Jac Frech (Tailwind)
(610) 287-7870

Montgomery County Velo Club
c/o Bikesport
371 Main Street
Harleysville, PA 19438
(215) 256-6613

Out of the Saddle Bike Club
c/o Kim Mazur
1124 Butter Lane
Reading, PA 19606
(610) 779-4233

University of Pennsylvania Cycling Team
Gimbel Gymnasium
3701 Walnut Street
Philadelphia, PA 19104
(215) 898-6103, cycling@dolphin.upenn.edu
http://dolphin.upenn.edu/~cycling

Pennsylvania Bicycle Club

Sponsors races and touring rides in the Philadelphia area, including the Wall Climb, the Lower Providence Criterium, and the world famous John Pixton Poker Ride.
P.O. Box 987
Glenside, PA 19038
(215) 871-1100, (215) 643-2329
pcb@cyclery.com

Pennsylvania Trail Hands (PATH)

Contact Mike Brocious at
24 North Field Drive
Downingtown, PA 19335
(610) 970-0812

Philadelphia Bicycle Society

Contact Kirk Resinger at
Performance Bike Shop
Paoli, PA
(610) 644-8522
kirk.reisinger@bentley.com

Princeton Free Wheelers

P.O. Box 1204
Princeton, NJ 08542-1204
(609) 921-6685
http://members.aol.com/JCPowers2/pfwmain.html

Quaker City Wheelmen

c/o Bike Addicts
5548 Ridge Ave.
Philadelphia PA 19128
(215) 487-3006
www.macp.org/clubs/qcw

Suburban Cyclists Unlimited

P.O. Box 401
Horsham, PA 19044
www.fitforum.com/scu1.htm

Team Results Bicycle Club

P.O. Box 34635
Philadelphia, PA 19101
(215) 224-1490

Tri State Velo

739 South 22nd Street
Philadelphia, PA 19146
(215) 790-0612

White Clay Bicycle Club

3 Yale Rd.
Wilmington, DE 19808
(302) 994-2990
www.delanet.com/~wcbc

National Clubs and Organizations

American Trails

The only national, nonprofit organization working on behalf of ALL trail interests. Members want to create and protect America's network of interconnected trailways.
POB 200787
Denver, CO 80220
(303) 321-6606
www.outdoorlink.com/amtrails

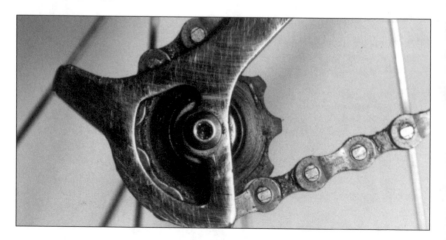

International Mountain Bicycling Association (IMBA)
Works to keep public lands accessible to bikers and provides information of trail design and maintenance.
POB 7578
Boulder, CO 80306
(303) 545-9011
www.greatoutdoors.com/imba

National Off-Road Bicycling Association (NORBA) - National governing body of US mountain bike racing.
One Olympic Plaza
Colorado Springs, CO 80909
(719) 578-4717
www.usacycling.org/mtb

Outdoor Recreation Coalition of America (ORCA) - Oversees and examines issues for outdoor recreation
Boulder, CO
(303) 444-3353
www.orca.org
info@orca.org

Rails-to-Trails Conservancy
Organized to promote conversion of abandoned rail corridors to trails for public use.
1400 16th Street, NW, Suite 300
Washington, D.C. 20036-2222
www.railtrails.org

League of American Wheelmen
190 West Ostend Street #120
Baltimore, MD 21230-3731
(410) 539-3399

United States Cycling Federation
Governing body for amateur cycling.
Colorado Springs, CO
(719) 578-4581
www.usacycling.org

USA Cycling
One Olympic Plaza
Colorado Springs, CO 80909
(719) 578-4581
www.usacycling.org

Dear Reader: It's the very nature of print media that the second the presses run off the last book, all the phone numbers change. If you notice a wrong number or that a club or organization has disappeared or that a new one has put out its shingle, we'd love to know about it. And if you run a club or have a favorite one and we missed it; again, let us know. We plan on doing our part to keep this list up-to-date for future editions, but we could always use the help. You can write us, call us, e-mail us, or heck, just stop by if you're in the neighborhood.

Outside America™
300 West Main Street, Suite A
Charlottesville, Virginia 22903
(804) 245-6800
editorial@outsideamerica.com

Repair and
Mainte

FIXING A FLAT

TOOLS YOU WILL NEED

- Two tire irons
- Pump (either a floor pump or a frame pump)
- No screwdrivers!!! (This can puncture the tube)

REMOVING THE WHEEL

The front wheel is easy. Simply open the quick release mechanism or undo the bolts with the proper sized wrench, then remove the wheel from the bike.

The rear wheel is a little more tricky. Before you loosen the wheel from the frame, shift the chain into the smallest gear on the freewheel (the cluster of gears in the back). Once you've done this, removing and installing the wheel, like the front, is much easier.

REMOVING THE TIRE

Step one: Insert a tire iron under the bead of the tire and pry the tire over the lip of the rim. Be careful not to pinch the tube when you do this.

Step two: Hold the first tire iron in place. With the second tire iron, repeat step one, three or four inches down the rim. Alternate tire irons, pulling the bead of the tire over the rim, section by section, until one side of the tire bead is completely off the rim.

Step three: Remove the rest of the tire and tube from the rim. This can be done by hand. It's easiest to remove the valve stem last. Once the tire is off the rim, pull the tube out of the tire.

CLEAN AND SAFETY CHECK

Step four: Using a rag, wipe the inside of the tire to clean out any dirt, sand, glass, thorns, etc. These may cause the tube to puncture. The inside of a tire should feel smooth. Any pricks or bumps could mean that you have found the culprit responsible for your flat tire.

Step five: Wipe the rim clean, then check the rim strip, making sure it covers the spoke nipples properly on the inside of the rim. If a spoke is poking through the rim strip, it could cause a puncture.

Step six: At this point, you can do one of two things: replace the punctured tube with a new one, or patch the hole. It's easiest to just replace the tube with a new tube when you're out on the trails. Roll up the old tube and take it home to repair later that night in front of the TV. Directions on patching a tube are usually included with the patch kit itself.

INSTALLING THE TIRE AND TUBE
(This can be done entirely by hand)

Step seven: Inflate the new or repaired tube with enough air to give it shape, then tuck it back into the tire.

Step eight: To put the tire and tube back on the rim, begin by putting the valve in the valve hole. The valve must be straight. Then use your hands to push the beaded edge of the tire onto the rim all the way around so that one side of your tire is on the rim.

Step nine: Let most of the air out of the tube to allow room for the rest of the tire.

Step ten: Beginning opposite the valve, use your thumbs to push the other side of the tire onto the rim. Be careful not to pinch the tube in between the tire and the rim. The last few inches may be difficult, and you may need the tire iron to pry the tire onto the rim. If so, just be careful not to puncture the tube.

BEFORE INFLATING COMPLETELY

Step eleven: Check to make sure the tire is seated properly and that the tube is not caught between the tire and the rim. Do this by adding about 5 to 10 pounds of air, and watch closely that the tube does not bulge out of the tire.

Step twelve: Once you're sure the tire and tube are properly seated, put the wheel back on the bike, then fill the tire with air. It's easier squeezing the wheel through the brake shoes if the tire is still flat.

Step thirteen: Now fill the tire with the proper amount of air, and check constantly to make sure the tube doesn't bulge from the rim. If the tube does appear to bulge out, release all the air as quickly as possible, or you could be in for a big bang.

When installing the rear wheel, place the chain back onto the smallest cog (furthest gear on the right), and pull the derailleur out of the way. Your wheel should slide right on.

LUBRICATION PREVENTS DETERIORATION

Lubrication is crucial to maintaining your bike. Dry spots will be eliminated. Creaks, squeaks, grinding, and binding will be gone. The chain will run quietly, and the gears will shift smoothly. The brakes will grip quicker, and your bike may last longer with fewer repairs. Need I say more? Well, yes. Without knowing where to put the lubrication, what good is it?

THINGS YOU WILL NEED
- One can of bicycle lubricant, found at any bike store.
- A clean rag (to wipe excess lubricant away).

WHAT GETS LUBRICATED
- Front derailleur
- Rear derailleur
- Shift levers
- Front brake
- Rear brake

- Both brake levers
- Chain

WHERE TO LUBRICATE

To make it easy, simply spray a little lubricant on all the pivot points of your bike. If you're using a squeeze bottle, use just a drop or two. Put a few drops on each point wherever metal moves against metal, for instance, at the center of the brake calipers. Then let the lube sink in.

Once you have applied the lubricant to the derailleurs, shift the gears a few times, working the derailleurs back and forth. This allows the lubricant to work itself into the tiny cracks and spaces it must occupy to do its job. Work the brakes a few times as well.

LUBING THE CHAIN

Lubricating the chain should be done after the chain has been wiped clean of most road grime. Do this by spinning the pedals counterclockwise while gripping the chain with a clean rag. As you add the lubricant, be sure to get some in between each link. With an aerosol spray, just spray the chain while pedalling backwards (counterclockwise) until the chain is fully lubricated. Let the lubricant soak in for a few seconds before wiping the excess away. Chains will collect dirt much faster if they're loaded with too much lubrication.

Index

Meet the Author

Bob D'Antonio was born and raised in Southwest Philadelphia. His love for the outdoors started at an early age on fishing trips with his father around Eastern, PA trying to find the perfect trout stream. A well-known rock climber with over 700 first ascents throughout the United States and a mountain biker since 1982, Bob divides his time between his two favorite sports and the two places he loves most, Philadelphia, PA and Colorado. Bob is the author of three rock climbing guides and three other mountain bike guides for different areas in Colorado and spends his life living between Philadelphia and Louisville, Colorado, with his wife of 25 years, Laurel, and his three wonderful children, Jeremy, Adam and Rachael.

Author

Euphoria...
in many different states.

The most beautiful, challenging and exhilarating rides are just a day-trip away.

Visit **www.outside-america.com** *to order the latest guides for areas near you—or not so near. Also, get information and updates on future publications and other guidebooks from Outside America™.*

For more information or to place an order, call **1–800–243–0495.**

OUTSIDE AMERICA GUIDE

Mountain Bike
AMERICA™